It *Did* Happen To This Vet

21.10.21

Rod

Best Wishes

Andrew

ANDREW BARTHOLOMEW

First published in the UK by Astoria Publishing Ltd in 2021

7 Arden Court
Arden Road
Alcester
Warwickshire
B49 6HN

astpublishing.org.uk

It Did Happen To This Vet by Andrew Bartholomew
Copyright © Andrew Bartholomew

Every reasonable effort has been made to acknowledge persons or companies
in this book. Any errors or omissions are inadvertent.

ISBN in paperback format: 978-1-8384338-2-6
ISBN in ebook format: 978-1-8384338-3-3

Printed and bound in the UK by 4Edge Ltd, Essex

Astoria Publishing would like to thank Ian at Hutchins Creative
and Alison Huntley for their work on this book.

Author's Biography

As a veterinary surgeon working in general practice, I enjoyed a career spanning forty years. The first five years were spent in three practices in different counties of Southern England.

Subsequently, I joined a practice in Oxford, specifically to build the small-animal interests of this mixed mainly large-animal enterprise. I became a partner in 1983 and sole principal in 1987. The practice is an approved centre for training veterinary nurses and is accredited by the Royal College of Veterinary Surgeons.

My particular interest was in the diagnosis and treatment of injuries to the canine athlete. My caseload in this field included racing and coursing greyhounds, whippets, agility dogs and other working dogs and being consulted on second opinion cases.

I represented the Society of Greyhound Veterinarians on the veterinary and scientific committee, firstly of the National Greyhound Racing Club, and latterly, the Greyhound Board of Great Britain.

I described my view of racing from the perspective of a track vet to the World Greyhound Racing Federation and advised government on the regulation of the sport and the welfare of racing greyhounds.

I have been active in my local community, especially supporting people with impaired mobility and disadvantaged children. As a founder member of a local Rotary Club, I have been part of its international projects in rural Western Uganda, making ten trips to collaborate with subsistence farmers, advising on elementary animal husbandry and since 2007, developing an agricultural microcredit project in various villages in Mubende District.

I retired from practice in 2018. My hobbies include photography, spectating at cricket matches and cruising the waterways in the South of England aboard my narrowboat.

I have been blessed with two daughters, neither of whom showed the slightest interest in following in my footsteps. Three dogs have joined our family, most recently, an opinionated border terrier called Mabel. We have given a home to an assortment of unwanted animals; our current incumbents continue to give us a great deal of amusement and pleasure.

Contents

Times are bad. Children no longer obey their parents
and everyone is writing a book.

Marcus Tullius Cicero

Preface

One Sweet Dream

My desire to write about some experiences and events in my veterinary career has given me the opportunity, in the words of Anais Nin, "to taste life twice, in the moment and in retrospection".

This book is a celebration of a life spent in veterinary practice. As a scientist accustomed to writing concise entries in clinical histories, attempting to produce simple narrative prose, constrained by my limited grasp of the English language and its punctuation, has been a personal battle.

My goal has been to write with candour and compassion, aiming for authenticity rather than aesthetics, whilst avoiding any exaggeration or invention. Inevitably, self-indulgence may have slipped into my scribblings. I did not set out to create a romanticised account of life as a vet nor to invent dialogue when what was said at the time did not lodge in my memory. I readily acknowledge that memory can play the most inconvenient of tricks.

However, unwittingly misremembering something is not the same as deliberate falsification. This account is based on my recollections, supported by references to written records, photographs and discussions with friends and colleagues. The thoughts are mine and the scenes described from my point of view, during a career shaped by my own moral values and intellectual assumptions.

I have recounted some of these anecdotes to clients over the years. Their laughter provided the perfect antidote to some serious but necessary discussions which take place within the confines of the consulting room. Their amusement was tempered when I pointed out that they might find themselves in the book as well.

To those readers who may have dreamt of becoming a vet, I invite you to consider what actions you would have taken when faced with the problems outlined in the following pages. You will find many feelgood stories and some that pack an emotional punch; that is the nature of veterinary practice and these are stories which should be told with honesty and integrity.

Chapter 1

Things I Don't Understand

At 9.30pm, the telephone rang. The insistent jangling of the discordant bell echoed in the downstairs passage. It was a dreadful sound to a nervous new graduate on night duty for his first practice.

The voice at the end of the telephone line said, "Hello, that's Andrew, isn't it? It's Camilla. I'm worried about Flossie, my retriever bitch. She's been acting strangely for several hours and I am not happy with her."

I had met Flossie previously at the surgery when she was brought in with a sore paw. She was four years old and my sort of dog. Her chestnut brown eyes conveyed absolute trust and her long swishing tail, unconditional enthusiasm.

Only after I agreed to see the dog that night did it become clear I would have to visit Flossie at her home. Moreover, it seemed that home was a caravan in a field deep in the Suffolk countryside.

As I negotiated the network of narrow country lanes that winter's night, I was fearful I might not be able to help my patient or I might miss a serious underlying condition. As I settled into my journey, other thoughts came to mind. This job in Halesworth was my first as a qualified vet. It had taken three months to find the position and I was determined to make the most of the opportunity.

The dials on the dashboard glowed brightly in the darkness. Light pollution was minimal in this part of East Anglia; there were no streetlights or illuminated roadsigns beyond the town centre and the rural properties I passed had yet to embrace the use of security lights.

Stopping frequently to decipher the names depicted on the traditional finger-style signposts, these villages did not seem to match those which Camilla had given me. In 1977, there were no mobile phones or satellite navigation systems to guide me, just my ordnance survey map and a sense of direction, engendered during my time as a boy scout. My powerful torch was already proving its worth.

Eventually, trying the last of three options at yet another crossroads, I glimpsed the particular five-bar gate on which I could read 'Hollytrees' and was able to pick out an arrow pointing the way. I collected my thoughts and got out of the car. I remembered my medical case and as my eyes adjusted, I saw a strange sight. From a caravan, tucked away in the corner of this field, suffused a pale pink light creating a peculiar, almost ethereal aura. I picked my way across the tussocks in the meadow to the caravan and tentatively knocked on the door.

Camilla was an attractive woman in her early thirties; tonight she was wearing a short, rather flimsy housecoat. Inside the caravan, the colours of the soft furnishings were accentuated by the pervading pink light, emanating from fashionable table lamps. I thought I detected an expensive fragrance which I had not encountered before. At university, my attendance rate at lectures had been almost one hundred per cent but I felt sure we had not been taught how to deal with situations like this.

One of our last lectures before our final examinations was on the thorny subject of professional conduct. I had been in the veterinary profession for nearly five months and members were expected to observe this code of conduct but who was this code designed to protect? The answer to my dilemma might lie buried somewhere in those lecture notes but they were back at my digs and not here where I needed them.

Fortunately, Flossie appeared to be in perfect health. In an assured and professional manner which masked my nervous tension, I examined her with her owner in close attendance. I couldn't feel anything abnormal in Flossie's abdomen nor could I elicit any pain. In my short career to date, I hadn't auscultated a patient's chest with such diligence as I did that night. Was that my bounding pulse rate I could hear or the dog's? With the ear pieces of the stethoscope firmly inserted in my ears, conversation would normally be impossible, though experience has shown me this is often the moment when even the most reticent client will suddenly remember additional symptoms which must be pointed out immediately.

Tonight, whilst I listened for a moment, I had time to think. Resorting to first principles, I considered possible treatment plans. With the lack of self-confidence experienced by most new graduates, I felt I should do something to justify my visit. I recalled learning about the placebo effect. In clinical trials, forty per cent of clients had reported seeing an improvement in their pet's condition following treatment with an injection of what was, in effect, coloured sterile water.

Bearing this in mind, an injectable solution of vitamin B12 seemed an appropriate option. The drug can stimulate appetite and may give rise to an enhanced feeling of well-being. Moreover, the colour of the solution I drew up in my syringe matched the colours in the caravan. Surely a dose could do no harm and might well do some good in a non-specific sort of way?

Despite the distractions, I administered the injection competently enough and told Camilla she might be worrying unnecessarily. I may have mumbled something about putting up some medicine to be collected from the surgery in the morning. Under the circumstances, I decided against washing my hands. Forgoing attempts to engage in small talk, I made my escape to the sanctuary of my car. Not for the first time, I was glad to have heeded the advice of my mentor in general practice - when visiting a client, always park your car facing the direction in which you intend to leave at the end of your call.

Driving back to my digs, feeling drained and muddle-headed, I asked myself again the trickiest of questions; whatever was it that made me want to become a vet?

Chapter 2

Remember When I Was Young

Why do you want to be a vet?

It's a question I have asked both the pupils from local schools who have come to the practice for work experience and the veterinary students who visited as part of their extramural studies - work experience for the aspirant professional. It is only fair I should try to answer the question for myself. I confess I have found it difficult to express my reasons with originality and honesty.

As a youngster, walking into a room full of adults in which an animal was present, I would naturally go to greet the animal first. I found them more interesting. I preferred to walk my uncle's black labrador, Duke, around the gravel pits near his Uxbridge home than sit with my immediate family hearing about the travails and ailments of relatives who, in most cases, I had not met or could not recall. Duke was traditionally built, a splendidly-phlegmatic character willing to accompany anyone who would take him for a walk. My cousin Mark was only too happy to come with me and escape songs by the Bachelors and another episode of *The Golden Shot*, the bolt being loaded once again by Bernie.

Our first family dog was a golden cocker spaniel. He was eased out when he developed a suspect temperament but I knew very little about that. I came to love our second dog, a black and white cocker spaniel called Dexter, dearly. He had an exquisite dome-shaped crown of his head and a confident, almost swaggering gait. We walked miles together as he listened attentively to my adolescent outpourings and happily fetched the ball as I practised my cricket shots.

Our goldfish, three shubunkins that we won at the local fair, seemed to live happily in a wide-rimmed green enamel bowl with three smooth stones and some weed for stimulation. Unfortunately, one succumbed to a fatal injury when my skyscraper of multi-coloured plastic bricks fell from the window ledge and almost bisected the poor creature. My mother patiently held the edges of the wound together, willing the unfortunate creature to live, but to no avail.

My first 'case' was our blue budgie, an aristocratic cock bird called Twinkle. I remember the shock of returning home one day to find him lying on the floor of his cage. He had lost all strength in his legs and could not grip his perch. I don't think the local vet was involved but many hours of tender loving care, which included feeding him with a dropper, seemed to work a miracle. He recovered and we managed the residual weakness in his legs and feet by providing some new mobility aids - lengths of wooden dowelling, oval in cross section with a wider lateral profile. He could grip these new perches adequately and survived into old age.

My mother had a deep and abiding love for all animals. The birds in the garden were addressed as members of her family and she could not bear any creatures to be harmed or made to suffer. Our various pets lived on an equal footing with us children and woe betide anyone who failed to understand that. Our dog was always fed before she took her meal. Inevitably, some of her empathy has rubbed off on me.

When she was told to expect a blue baby which would not be expected to survive in 1955, my mother was advised to lay on her back for the last six months of her pregnancy. I was brought into the world by Mr Blake, a gynaecologist at the London Hospital, arriving three days late on a cold January morning, snow covering the streets of east London. Born within earshot of St Mary-le-Bow, I can call myself a true cockney. After living for a year in a first-floor maisonette, part of a Victorian terraced house in Bow, we moved to Hutton in Essex, halfway between Liverpool Street and Southend.

Hutton village was centred around Hutton Manor and the nearby fourteenth century parish church of All Saints. It was a small, tight-knit community, surrounded by fields and woodland, with an economy based on agriculture. Developers altered this agrarian landscape during the 1930s and decimated it in the 1950s. The fields between Hutton and Shenfield gradually disappeared, replaced by extensive estates of new houses.

Our home was one of them, costing my parents two thousand five hundred pounds. Initially, they were so financially stretched that upturned orange boxes served as 'easy' chairs on which to lounge in the evenings. Suburbanisation surrounded us; a commuter belt delineated with drives and avenues, crescents and closes, but left with very few lanes. Shenfield Station was just over a mile away, a walk which dad completed twice a day, thereby saving the bus fare.

My sister Hilary was born in March 1957 at the local cottage hospital in Billericay. In time, she would be both a valued companion and a tormentor, often during the same day. She provided me with important insights into how to behave in the company of women, lessons which stood me in good stead later in life when working with female colleagues in the close confines of general practice.

Growing up in this environment in the early Sixties, I passed through the stereotypical phases which many boys do. I was lucky enough to witness the tail end of the era of steam locomotives, entranced by the sight, smell and the reverberant rumblings as they pulled out towards London or the East Coast. Dutifully documenting their numbers in my notebooks, like many a young lad, I dreamed of being an engine driver. In due course, the arrival of the dreaded diesels and the eventual electrification of the line dulled my youthful enthusiasm.

At home, my Triang train set was my consuming pastime. The layout expanded gradually from a simple circular loop of track with a black loco, Princess Elizabeth, and two maroon and cream coaches, to greater sophistication, the track mounted on a wooden board with electrically-operated points and signals, branch lines, sidings, tunnels and stations painted after assembly from Airfix kits. The hours dad and I spent together building and enjoying our creation was irreplaceable quality time.

Back then, three career choices seemed to suggest themselves.

A detective. I was attracted by the deductive and analytical aspects of the job but the policemen in our neighbourhood were not quite the same as George Dixon or Andy Crawford in the TV series *Dixon of Dock Green* which was regular family viewing on Saturday evenings.

A vicar. I had a juvenile crush on a girl at Sunday school. She played her acoustic guitar, offering 'modern' tunes to accompany our hymns. I progressed to serving during the early Communion service at the old parish church and imagined myself leading these services sometime in the future. Eventually, I realised that I simply wasn't good enough. As a young man, I noticed that I prayed more earnestly when I wanted something, which was not a sound basis on which to build a relationship with God.

A vet. By thirteen years of age, there really was nothing else that I aspired to be, or thought I could be, except a vet.

As my career progressed, I developed an impressive portfolio of allergies to all the common animal species that I treated. Could it be the Almighty's way of indicating I had chosen the wrong career? Option two may have been a sensible choice after all.

Primary School

I remember being tearful on the first day my mother left me at All Saints Primary School, just beyond the recreation ground from our family home. Mrs Hillary, my class teacher, did her best to make those early days happy ones. In her mid-thirties, she was kind, understanding and gentle. Multiplication tables were still learnt by the whole class by rote. I enjoyed sums but, as you may have guessed by now, English composition came less easily.

Drawing, painting and craftwork were a challenge. I was quite an active child but physical education, climbing wall bars, benchwork and the like were periods that were simply endured. We were introduced to music and movement classes, which were fun, and country dancing, which was a new experience but judging by the expressions of my partners, I did not excel in this activity either. I looked forward to break time, my small bottle of milk and the playground, when we were allowed to run around and get rid of some pent-up energy. We were read stories last thing before home time, so I left school each day wanting to return for another instalment. I remember with pleasure at the beginning of each term being handed new exercise books, just waiting to be written in!

Having been walked to school every morning by my mother and collected by her at half past three, eventually myself and two friends were allowed to walk home by ourselves. This new-found freedom got us into several scrapes. One afternoon, crossing the sports field after school, I was set upon by the school bullies. The Thomson brothers, neither twins nor musical, were notorious and brutal. The memory of being pinned on the grass, their knees on my shoulders, spittle dribbling from the corners of their snarling mouth, has remained with me. Was this a rite of passage, just part and parcel of growing up?

Later, my sister started at the same primary school. Soon afterwards, I was given the responsibility of escorting her home safely at the end of the school day. She soon found her own friends and I was free, once more, to take part in the impromptu after-school games which flourished on the playing fields nearby.

School holidays were great fun. Cycling around the neighbourhood and later, further afield in the countryside became my favourite way to spend a day. As young boys, my friend David and I were only allowed to venture as far as the First Wash where the River Wid passed under Wash road, about a mile from our home. On such expeditions, I gradually began to notice the changing seasons. I caught sticklebacks, placing them carefully in water-filled jam jars before proudly presenting them to mum.

Later, we were allowed to venture as far as the Second Wash, about three miles from home, where the Wid crossed over a country lane at Buttsbury. It was a constant fascination to watch the plumes of water as another car splashed though the ford. Sometimes, much to our delight, a car came to a halt midstream, to the chagrin of the motorist and their passengers. As I got older, I paid more attention to my surroundings and the natural world. I enjoyed spending time sitting quietly, watching and listening to the creatures scuffling about in the woods and the hedgerows.

We three lads, who walked home together each day from school, were called into the headmaster's office before Christmas in our last year at primary school. Mr Lowdnes informed us we needed 'some practice in taking exams' before our eleven-plus. This 'practice' turned out to be the Common Entrance exam for Brentwood school. In hindsight, I can see this was a brilliant piece of stress management. His prescience and dedication did so much to shape my career.

Having passed this exam, my parents were willing to dig deeply into the family's financial resources to pay the school fees. New school uniforms and the requisite games kit had to be purchased from the school shop rather than on hire purchase from the Freemans catalogue.

Chapter 3

I Know What I Know

Brentwood School

My 'big' school, Brentwood school, was a direct-grant boys' grammar school, inevitably impersonal and highly-structured. In September 1966, I found myself in class 2P with form master Mr Poole, a modern languages teacher; fair-haired, forty-something and always in a black gown. I was suited. Half the boys had been to the school's dedicated preparatory school and knew each other, some of the teaching staff and the ropes. For me, the magnitude of the change was overwhelming.

I was in South house, one of the five houses for day boys. A strong camaraderie quickly developed amongst the boys in the boarding houses. Some toughies in School house, familiar with a system in which knowledge was power, assumed the role of unauthorised enforcers.

No longer would pleasant pieces of classical music precede school assemblies. Mr Rennie, the acerbic senior second master, gave the impression that schoolboys were something of a nuisance in his daily life. The blue-gowned praeposters, distinguished and imposing, their robes trailing in their wake, were nominated to ensure the school rules were obeyed. No talking in assembly or chapel services, no walking on the grass and so on.

Bells rang here and there to signify the end of a teaching period and give us 10 minutes to get to the next high-ceilinged classroom, often in a different and distant building. To this shrinking violet, it seemed a harsh regime, softened slightly by the prospect of hot buttered toast with our milk at morning break. On most mornings, the smell of mince cooking in the school kitchens at the far end of the Chase permeated the academic atmosphere. There was an even chance that roly-poly pudding and lumpy custard would follow.

Despite my sister ensuring I could never be big-headed, I arrived with the notion I might be reasonably bright, having passed the entrance exam, albeit with insufficient marks to get a scholarship. But this idea was quickly dispelled. My name appeared consistently near the bottom of the form when test results were published, basement levels achieved in art and music. For the house choir competition, I was placed on the end of the back row, told to mime the words and smile but on no account to sing.

Many of my contempories could play several musical instruments. I had acquired no such skills. I fumbled with the treble recorder and later the larger tenor recorder but failed to produce much which sounded faintly melodious. My interest switched from playing to listening to music. Dr Brice, director of music, introduced us to the intricacies of classical music. Seated at the harpsichord, an instrument I had never previously seen or heard, he played chamber music by Handel and Bach, patiently revealing elements of structure and texture.

I cycled three miles to school each day. My briefcase became heavy with homework, an increasingly time-consuming nightly exercise. Attendance at school on Saturday morning was compulsory and came as a shock, disrupting our family's weekend routine which until then had been sacrosanct.

A number of different sports were played at various levels of ability on Wednesday and Saturday afternoons. These games quickly became competitive affairs. I played football and rugby at house level but don't recall much in the way of coaching to improve our technical skills. Games were, for the most part, trials of strength or, for the lucky few, speed.

Candidates vying for selection for the school's first XV however were coached by Billy Raybould, a history master and a Welsh rugby international. During his first training session, he lined up the prospects and asked each of them to tackle him. Then he lined them up again and tackled each of them in turn. The impact was so powerful, it knocked them off their feet, leaving them prostrate on the pitch, gasping for breath. Some chose the option of fencing instead.

Cross-country runs were a proven form of exercise to keep boisterous boys in order. Some more enterprising pupils attempted various devious wheezes to minimise the distance they were required to run. Invariably, they were caught and extra suffering ensued. Physical training became increasingly intense: performing sit-ups with a heavy medicine ball behind your head, forward head springs over a pommel horse and during frantic scrabbling up ropes and parallel bars, the master in charge was apt to say, "You will thank me for this when you get older."

Do I? Thus far, an inguinal hernia is one affliction which I have been spared.

I used to play cricket regularly in the park with my father but during the formal cricket nets here, coaches from Essex County Cricket club were on hand to pass on basic skills and advice. The joy of being taught the art of bowling left-arm spin and how to control the flight of a cricket ball was a memorable moment in my education. In the summer term after school, I could walk across Shenfield Road to watch the county XI in action during Brentwood festival week and learn as professional spin bowlers put batsmen under their spell.

Latin entered the syllabus and its logical grammatical basis was instrumental in awakening synapses between my brain cells which had hitherto lain dormant. Was this the proverbial light bulb moment or was this, at the age of thirteen, simply adolescence making itself known? Whatever the case, quite suddenly I had learnt to learn and was now adept at regurgitating facts in a coherent manner for the purpose of passing examinations. Increasingly, my name began to appear near the top of the class results. I was placed in the fast stream, preparing to sit my O level examinations a year early.

The school boasted both army and RAF contingents of the Combined Cadet Force. This was another weekly distraction from lessons, with belts to be blancoed and brass buckles polished before sessions of basic drill that engendered an increased sense of discipline amongst these part-time troops. My father had served with the RAF so I was placed in the blue rather than the khaki corner. I learnt about the principles of flight and navigation.

One summer afternoon, older year groups in the corps were practising in preparation for a visit from senior military bigwigs who visited the school periodically to inspect our efforts at warmongering. Our history lesson was paused whilst our elderly, portly, history master Charles Rance, hearing the sound of bawled instructions below, wandered over to the window of our upstairs classroom. He had experienced the horrors of war and as he gazed down on the proceedings on the parade ground, he muttered, "Little boys playing soldiers."

During physics practicals, we used large, heavy, wooden-framed lead-acid battery cells to provide electrical power for various experiments. One of my classmates, with a lack of common sense often associated with those enjoying double-barrelled surnames, thought it would be easier to carry the battery across the laboratory if he lifted the thing above his head, turning it upside down in the process. We watched in complete fascination as his tweed suit was dissolved by the acid spilling from the battery. His discomfort was temporary and he avoided any serious physical injury. It was the only time we were allowed to dowse a classmate with water without risking detention.

Mr Foreman, a young master with a neatly-trimmed ginger beard and an earnest manner, spent a whole lesson demonstrating how to use a chemical balance. Having emphasised repeatedly how delicate the knife-edge pivot points were to the overall accuracy of the machine, at the end of the lesson, with an overly dramatic sweep of his arm, the sleeve of his jacket caught the balance and knocked the whole assembly from the bench to the floor in a scenario worthy of Monty Python.

After Easter in 1970, as I prepared for my O level exams, the rhythm of family life was disrupted as my mother fell ill and deteriorated steadily. Previously cheerful, active and confident in her Christianity, she was reduced to a morose figure, sitting slumped in a chair, vomiting frequently. I sat these key stage exams with questions about my mother's health swirling in my head. Would I still have a mother?

The diligence of our family GP Pamela Butcher in keeping her knowledge up to date led by chance to a referral. Diagnosed with a brain tumour by Lyndsay Simons, a specialist in nervous diseases in London, our annual summer holiday was promptly cancelled. She was operated on immediately at the National Hospital in Russell Square in London.

Following surgery, we sat with her, though she remained unresponsive for several days.

Gradually, the number of tubes and pipes taking fluids to and from her were removed and she went to Maida Vale for specialist rehabilitation. Left-sided facial paralysis and loss of hearing in that ear, eyelids on the same side no longer capable of blinking, slightly-slurred speech and some disturbance in her balance were the sequelae to her life-saving surgery. She bore these disfigurements and disabilities with great fortitude for the next thirty-five years. She was taught to talk and walk again with the aid of a stick.

Necessity meant my sister and I teamed up and learnt to cook, producing edible evening meals for ourselves and dad when he returned home from work and a hospital visit each evening. Dexter the dog spent much of mum's three-month absence with his forefeet on the radiator in the front room, searching the street outside for signs of her return. He never gave up hope and his patience was rewarded. We were ecstatic to have her back. Christmas 1970 was very special, the best present we could possibly have asked for.

I took a summer job as an assistant in the advertising department of Ford Motor Company in Warley. I was responsible for promoting the launch of a new model of the popular Ford Capri. Provided with my own telephone and desk in a vast open-plan office, the greatest competition in this male-dominated environment consisted of who had the nerve to wear the snazziest shirt or most outrageous tie.

I had to visit several floors of the admin building as part of my duties. Outward and visible signs of climbing the executive ladder were subtle but obvious if you knew the code. After a telephone and a desk, a rubber plant would appear and then a mat in front of the desk. A secretary would materialise who would also acquire these accoutrements in stages. A partitioned and separate office space signified substantive progress as you ascended the managerial ladder towards the higher echelons of the company's hierarchy. It was an enjoyable and invaluable experience for a young man, though it helped me realise I was not cut out for an office-based career.

My O level results were sufficient for me to enter the sixth form to study biology, chemistry and physics-with-maths to A level, only the second time the school had run the latter course. Mr Parker, nicknamed Nosey, inspired us with his teaching of biology, organising weekend field trips to neighbouring woods to listen to the dawn chorus, identify particular birdsong and participate in fungus forays. Nowadays, apps on mobile phones provide electronic assistance in these areas of expertise but the degree of personal attainment is not the same. We learnt where to look and what to look out for whilst enjoying some welcome fresh air.

Increasingly-sophisticated chemistry lessons provided us with notable extracurricular moments. Senior master Mr Nichols, an elderly, grey-haired, florid man, was attempting to distil an organic fluid by heating it and collecting the resultant distillate in a flask as it condensed through an intricate system of glass tubing. Inadvertently, he had failed to open a ground-glass tap which would have allowed the expanding gases to escape. The eventual explosion sent broken glass and retort stands flying across the laboratory and the colourful language of the master added greatly to what could easily have passed for a comedy sketch.

During the Easter holidays in 1971, I went on a residential biology field trip to Flatford Mill in East Suffolk, meeting girls and boys from different schools and backgrounds from all over England. It was excellent preparation for what lay ahead.

Growing up in the Sixties, pop music was an important adjunct to my life. I listened on the radio to the pop charts which were broadcast on Sunday afternoon and I was beginning to acquire a record collection of my own. On Saturday evening in this famous mill, I remember crowding round a transistor radio to listen to Radio 1's In Concert featuring Led Zeppelin playing tracks from their forthcoming Symbols album (Led Zeppelin IV). It was great music, enjoyed with a group of motivated youngsters of my own age and felt very much 'in the moment' and part of the rock music phenomenon which typified that era.

I spent a week on work experience at Wickens and Barfoot, our local vets, in Shenfield. The first case on Monday morning was a rabbit with a fractured back leg which was set and a plaster cast applied under anaesthetic. Later, we piled into a car and were off to visit a local boarding kennels. Oh yes, this was definitely better than working in an office.

In the summer holidays, I had a temporary position at Highwood Hospital in Brentwood, cycling to work along a familiar route past my school. On the recommendation of our neighbour, and with no background checks or training, I was put in charge of a machine for scrubbing and polishing floors, complete with an array of rotating circular brushes and pads. The slightest change in the angulation of the operator's wrist sent the machine veering off in a new, sometimes unintended direction. I was left to manage myself and my workload, which was a useful skill to acquire. Nobody was hurt as I met and chatted to interesting patients and dedicated staff during my summer stint. A bonus was being able to follow various televised sporting events, either Test cricket or Open golf, shown on the many TV screens as I worked my way around the wards.

Having acquired some much-needed funds for clothes and records, I entered the upper sixth form in September, full of confidence and enthusiasm yet painfully naive about potential pitfalls which could lay ahead. I filled in my UCCA (Universities Central Council on Admissions) form and was invited to Bristol for a tour of the vet school, no interview required.

The technicians in the anatomy department situated in the Pre-clinical Veterinary School in Park Row tried their best to deflect budding veterinary undergraduates from their chosen careers. Inside the entrance hall, the spectre of rigid limbs and gruesome poses of greyhounds, soaking in pungent baths of formaldehyde, being pickled for future dissection studies, was almost too much for me to stomach. A conditional offer of a place on the course arrived in the post, which spurred me on to knuckle down and achieve the required grades.

During my final school holiday at Easter, we were required to complete a piece of original, investigative work, written up in the style of a research paper, with accurate, tabulated results and a considered conclusion. I cycled to many of my favourite natural habitats in north Essex, collecting soil samples from sites of varying ecology, including woodland, heathland, riverbank, and lastly our garden. I heated soil samples of equal weights in our domestic oven to dry them and carried out measurements documenting acidity, moisture levels and microscopic examination. I wrote up the work and was awarded the school's biology prize for my efforts. My thesis was submitted to the Essex Naturalist Trust, where it was highly commended in my age group.

In my biology A level exam, I could not answer why bees fly in triangles when they are navigating their route back to their hives. Suffering from acute conjunctivitis as a result of severe hayfever, I assume on mature reflection that my descriptions of chemical reactions involving colour changes during my chemistry practical were wholly inaccurate since I took the exam wearing dark glasses.

Having completed my A levels, on my last day at school, my headmaster Richard Sale handed back the file containing my thesis adding, "I'm told this was a very good piece of work. I didn't understand a word of it."

As closing comments go, it was crushing.

My reflections on my time at the school are mixed. I had been taught by some inspirational teachers but also by some who were eccentric. One master, rumoured to be a fetishist, took us for Civics periods and had given his instrument of punishment, a long piece of orange rubber tubing, a name. He called it Percy. I ensured he never had cause to use Percy on me.

A long tradition of learning and the smell of old books pervaded the Bean Library, which was somewhere I found some solace. It was a privilege to be able to work quietly there in my free periods, occasionally pondering who else had escaped there to study and to think. I had been schooled for success and taught to play the game.

I spent the final free summer of my childhood working in a marine parts department with a classmate from school. Alan and I were given free rein to reorganise the department, creating logical order from the chaos which existed when we arrived. I thoroughly enjoyed the challenge as it suited my temperament and desire for order and method. Our legacy was an alphabetical directory in which each part was listed, including its exact location, together with its minimum stock level. We were both rewarded with a monetary bonus for our efforts which was a welcome gesture.

We travelled to Germany to spend five days in Cologne visiting Alan's father. I remember the imposing cathedral as well as my initiation into the delights of German bierkellers.

My A level results exceeded the grades of the conditional offer from the University of Bristol. I was lucky to be among the eight per cent of the population at this time in being given the chance of a university education. More confident after my summer of work and play, I prepared to leave my family home and head westward to vet school.

Chapter 4

Places In My Past

Veterinary science was the only course I wanted to study and I had the good fortune to attend the university of my choice. In October 1972, I arrived at Bristol and was ready to start my adventure.

I had a place in the modern residential block of Wills Hall, across the Clifton Downs from Whiteladies Road. My room was compact; a bed, a desk with a table lamp and upright chair, a more comfortable armchair, a bookshelf and wardrobe. Along the corridor was a small communal kitchen, toilets and bathrooms. During the week, breakfast and supper were cooked meals taken in the refectory. Sunday lunches were more formal affairs, each student required to present themselves suitably attired in a black undergraduate gown. Saturday and Sunday suppers were collected at lunchtime in a paper bag. The contents, typically a filled bread roll wrapped in clingfilm, a bag of crisps and an apple, were generally disappointing.

There were advantages to living some distance from the city centre and being further away from the hustle and bustle, the noise and the diverse distractions. The major disadvantage was walking two miles to the veterinary school building in Park Row, situated above Broadmead and the city centre. However, this was my only exercise for the day and gave me the chance to chat to new friends studying a variety of courses.

The veterinary field station was out at Langford, about twenty miles south-west of the city, where it rained on our first farm walk. By the end of the first week, our year was reduced to thirty-three students when three dropped out, one of them, it was rumoured, because her hairstyle was ruined.

This was less surprising when I realised that I was one of only three students who had seen any veterinary practice before applying for the course. The selection process, including the high A level grade requirements which had seemed so daunting to a uncertain sixteen-year-old schoolboy, now seemed rather inadequate. Historically, a majority of students on my course were drawn from an agricultural background but fortunately for me, this emphasis was changing. It did mean that I had a great deal to learn, and very quickly, about farm animal management and husbandry.

Freshers' week presented an opportunity for new students to find out about, and perhaps join, a bewildering number of clubs and societies. Remembering my headmaster's comments about my perceived lack of participation in after-school activities, I was keen to take part in some of the sporting and leisure activities on offer. Nevertheless, my absolute priority was to complete my course successfully; nothing was going to deflect me from my goal.

I joined the Film Society, which screened feature films at discounted rates, usually on Friday nights, and I also signed up for the Centaur Society, which catered for Bristol's vet students over all five years of the course, offering both social and educational events.

During the frenetic first week, a plethora of plays and concerts were staged in the students' union building and other venues across the city. I formed an early impression that for many second- and third-year students, whatever the topic, they were against it.

Supping beer in the bar on the third floor of the students' union on my first night as a student was a significant and satisfying moment. The constraints of secondary school and living in the family home had been lifted. This next stage of my life presented a fresh and exciting challenge with so many different options. Voting was taking place on whether the students' bar should be re-named the Nelson Mandela bar in support of his activism against apartheid and in protest at his continuing incarceration. My political awareness was being raised already.

Status Quo played at the FAFFY dance (Find A Friendly First Year) on the Saturday night of freshers' week. The band, with their shoulder-length hair and trademark denim, were on energetic form, playing familiar tracks including Paper Plane which was about to be released and headed for the top ten in the singles chart. I enjoyed the loud rock music, more so knowing I could return to my room at a time that I chose without disturbing my family.

The difference in the intensity of study required for my course compared with other undergraduate courses quickly became obvious. Vet students undertook more than thirty hours of formal lectures and practical sessions a week whereas my friends studying arts courses often had fewer than ten hours of lectures and tutorials per week and attendance at those was treated by many as optional.

I found the step up from sixth-form pupil to university undergraduate colossal. I could easily have floundered in a morass of indecision but I benefitted greatly from being mentored in those early weeks by John Madeley, a third-year vet student. I am indebted to him for his sensible advice.

As autumn turned to winter and the wetness of the West Country became an increasingly-unpleasant feature, I brought my bicycle down to Bristol. This reduced my daily commute time from forty minutes to ten. Motorbikes were a popular form of wheels for students. Hondas were ubiquitous and there were many mopeds clustered around the bike sheds.

John Pearn's venerable BSA 650 was the granddaddy of the motorcycle cavalcade with the measured beat of its engine and rasping exhaust note. His arrival back in hall from another extended weekend in his beloved Manchester was announced whilst he was still some distance away on the Downs.

A fellow vet student and Wills Hall resident was Neil Burnie. He owned an ageing blue Honda 350 cc on which he travelled to Bristol from his home city of Birmingham. He had shoulder-length fair hair, wore glasses and was cheerfully exuberant, often with mischief in mind. A colourful character, I recall him dressed in wellington boots, shorts and a white lab coat, open and flapping in the breeze, leading a group of us down Whiteladies Road in the manner of the Pied Piper whilst playing his flute, much to the amusement of the passers-by.

Hutton 1965

Vet School Park Row 1973

As I settled into a daily routine, I would like to say that my new-found freedom knew no bounds but that would not be the whole truth. I calculated I could live on five pounds per week. This, coupled with the high cost of veterinary textbooks, meant that the opportunities to let my hair down were limited. I was finding it difficult to listen to the lecturer and write comprehensive notes at the same time. I could listen or I could write but seemed incapable of managing both at the same time in those first few weeks. Consequently, it took time each evening to re-read and expand my inadequate jottings, which sometimes amounted to barely half a page.

Each week, I took my place in the queue for the pay phone in the draughty entrance to the quadrangle opposite the porter's lodge. Each week I told my parents I couldn't keep up with my workload and gloomily admitted I was falling further and further behind with my studies. Would I be thrown out before the end of my first term? Many of my new associates gave the outward impression of having a carefree, happy-go-lucky attitude to student life but some admitted privately they were struggling too.

I did find time to explore this beautiful and fascinating city, mostly on foot, discovering the delights of Carwardine's coffee emporium, George's bookshop and the Arnolfini gallery down by the docks. The city embraced its student population, absorbing them readily into its own. There were no barriers, real or imagined, between town and gown. Bristol has many fine buildings and plenty of green spaces and in the 1970s, a relaxed tempo to the rhythm of daily life. I thoroughly enjoyed spending time there.

As vet students, in the first year of our course, we studied biochemistry, physiology, anatomy and animal management. We joined the medical students for generic lectures on the first two subjects, held in the medical school, part of the university's new precinct and striking in its multi-storeyed modern design.

Our veterinary anatomy and histology lectures were held in the shabby pre-clinical prefabricated two-storey building in Park Row. It was a purely functional building, skulking in the shadow of its neighbour, the vast neo-gothic Wills Memorial Building and noted city landmark. The medics were fortunate in only having one anatomical model to learn. We had six - canine, feline, bovine, equine, porcine and avian - each differing from the other and each guaranteed to maximise the confusion of this callow youth. We were presented with a pickled greyhound to dissect, one dog shared between four students. As we delved deeper into this creature's cadaver, the features we identified had to be drawn, labelled and learned.

Having chosen to go out socialising the night before the end-of-term animal management exam, I was awarded a mark of ten per cent for my pains. This came as a massive jolt. Fear of failure began to feature in my thoughts; a persistent shadow which I was never quite able to throw off during my undergraduate years. Chastened, I said good bye to my new friends and returned home for a quiet Christmas break with my family. I needed to spend time re-evaluating my priorities and assessing how I was going to achieve my objectives.

The following term, the content and quality of my lecture notes improved. Rag week, with its magazine full of jokes in seriously bad taste, reared its head. I came to breakfast one morning and found the quadrangle, which had no vehicular access, full of students' cars. These must have been manhandled through the single narrow entrance with its heavy wooden doors, which were normally locked, and past the porter's lodge, a feat involving many students, physical strength and manual dexterity. I had heard nothing about it beforehand.

During that week, I was offered a lift in Mike King's Austin Mini. We got in to find his cherished racing steering wheel had been removed. Oh how we laughed. What concerned us both is the length of time it took to realise it had gone. The pedal car race was another highlight and a further example of the ingenuity and innovation of students. Twenty-four hours of madness and mayhem as a collection of improbable wheeled contraptions of doubtful engineering pedigree or safety, completed circuit after circuit around a disused aerodrome at Whitchurch, chasing sponsorship monies in the name of charity.

As spring turned to summer, with the prospect of some serious exams at the end of our first year, we discovered that our vacations were to be spent working without pay on different types of approved farms. A fortnight would have to be spent on each of a dairy, beef and sheep farms, pig, poultry and equine units; a total of twelve weeks to be completed before commencing our third year of study. My hopes of earning some much-needed cash during the summer holidays were dashed.

Despite my misgivings, I exceeded the requisite pass mark in biochemistry and set off to gain some farming experience during the holidays. I spent the evenings at my beef farm, near Dedham in Suffolk, ensconced in the farmer's study being coached in the complexities of jazz music. I was an eager pupil.

My dairy farm was part of the Duke of Wellington's Stratfield Saye estate in Hampshire. I was deputed to take the milk up to the big house each morning and to tend the calves.

Eventually I got to grips with the vagaries of the milking machine and was allowed to milk the herd without supervision. I was told that the duchess, having expressed a desire to acquire a dairy herd, returned from a holiday and disliked both the new barbed-wire fences and the black and white Friesian cows which, in her view, clashed with the landscaped park. The fencing magically morphed into the traditional wooden post-and-rail type whilst the Friesian cows were sold, replaced by the smaller Guernsey breed with their softer brown colouration.

From time to time in the distance, a motorcade made its way up the main drive as Prince Charles paid another visit to court Lady Jane Wellesley. This scruffy vet student sensibly stayed well out of the way.

In the autumn, I returned to Wills Hall and to a more spacious room in the old building bordering the quadrangle. A gas fire and wash basin *en suite* added to my creature comforts. So did my new hi-fi system, being the first thing to be unpacked and set up when moving into new digs. At that time, it was one of my few possessions of any consequence.

My friend and fellow vet student Neil Craven lived across the landing. Tall, slim, ginger-haired and uber-intelligent, he introduced me to the music of Fairport Convention, Pentangle and Steeleye Span. Over the summer, he had purchased a motobike and I took up his generous offers of lifts into town, riding pillion, a journey requiring much less effort than pedalling on my part. I borrowed his lecture notes to plug the gaps in mine but his writing was atrocious, bordering on illegible.

I had been warned that the second year of my course was a tough year and so it was. From my window, the view of manicured grass banks and much less disturbance from fellow student inmates with their antisocial activities made it a conducive atmosphere in which to study. I knew what was required and I meant to give it my best shot. Neil and I played contract bridge at the weekends, which was mentally stimulating and a refreshing change from textbooks and lecture notes. With music to enjoy and tricks to take, life seemed much less stressful than the previous year.

A friend from school, Steve Brown, resided in the same quad. He was studying botany and provided a different perspective on university life outside my veterinary bubble. Despite approaching his final examinations, he retained an offhand approach to academic work. On the eve of his finals, we visited a number of pubs near the Cheddar Gorge. Steve smoked a large cigar, inhaling deeply whilst pontificating on the meaning of life.

During the Easter vacation, working on a sheep farm near Dunstable gave me a great deal of pleasure. I shared the responsibility of supervising the flock as they lambed down, being allocated the evening shift until midnight. At night, the barns were quiet and peaceful; the nuanced grunts and groans from the ewes was a novel language which I found comforting and advantageous for thought and reflection. It was such a privilege to be allowed to assist in protracted births. The vulnerability of the lambs was striking as they wobbled unsteadily to their feet on the straw. In no time, they gained strength, leaping upwards with unbridled energy and joy, one of the great sights I have enjoyed in my life.

A sustained programme of revision successfully slayed the beast that was the anatomy exam. I managed to pass physiology as well.

My summer was spent at a large riding stables near Hereford and later, a poultry enterprise near Oswestry. On hot summer days, I spent much of my time shifting shit with a shovel, learning little except there is nothing that smells quite so offensive on this earth.

In October 1974, I returned to Bristol to commence my third year, the last of my pre-clinical course, and experienced my lowest point thus far. Leaning over the balustrade in the students' union to look down to the lower floors at the rush of youthful, high-spirited humanity, I felt I could not carry on. The buzz I had found so exciting two years previously had dissipated. I had put so much effort into the successful completion of my second year that I felt a spent force. The medical and surgical lectures and practicals for which I yearned were still another year away. It was only cowardice and the shame of telling my parents I wanted to give up that stopped me doing just that.

Fate is a funny thing. Two days later, on Saturday night, I was dragged out by Neil and Howard to that year's FAFFY dance. I really didn't want to go. I wasn't in the mood. Shakin' Stevens was the headline act and unlikely to be in the same class as Status Quo. I was peeled from my patch at the bar and guided onto the dance floor by Howard. He asked to dance with a tall, slim, dark-haired girl called Julie and happily, her friend agreed to dance with me. Eveleen was shorter, with long wavy fair hair and a willing pleasant smile.

Later, we trekked across the city to the Granary, a club where live bands played until the early hours. She had just come down from Dumfries to study history of art and history. I walked with her back to Manor Hall, whose rooms were solely for girls, and we arranged to meet the following evening at eight o'clock.

By now, I had the use of my mother's car, a grey Vauxhall Victor. Not exactly a 'chick wagon' but a safe set of wheels nonetheless. I arrived in good time and waited and waited and waited. If she didn't appear by half past eight, I would accept defeat and be off. She put in an appearance in the nick of time and we went back to my room at Wills Hall. My vinyl LPs were stored alphabetically according to featured artists in three separate record cases. With carefree abandon, Eveleen scattered them about on the floor.

"We could listen to a bit of this then a bit of that."

As with the length of one's hair, the LPs you purchased helped to define who you were. Playing her choice of my music, was Ev wooing me or was I wooing her? I gathered Gold Blend coffee was a requirement; no other brand would do.

As a teenager cycling in the Essex countryside, I considered where I might meet the love of my life. My sister never missed the chance to taunt me saying I wouldn't find anyone anyway. Events as frivolous as a dance, a party or a discotheque seemed unlikely places to meet someone who would share my interests and perhaps my future.

Now I had a reason to stay at Bristol and the dreadful feelings of hopelessness slipped away. One insoluble problem remained. I had one ticket to see Pink Floyd, who were on tour showcasing their new album *Dark Side of The Moon*. The concert was sold out. What could a poor boy do? Bristol had a rich culture of music at that time; where else would an artist of Rory Gallagher's calibre be playing on the same night as Pink Floyd? I bought her a ticket to his concert and, for one night only, we went our separate ways.

Bridge at weekends was set aside as Ev and I took long walks together on the Downs in Long Ashton country park and sometimes further afield. Brean Down was a favourite haunt, looking down on the bay at Weston-super-Mare. We were frequent visitors to the Granary for live music on Thursday and Saturday nights. She was perpetually late for our assignations but she probably saved my career and I am grateful to her for that.

With difficulty, I managed to maintain my focus during that third year, keeping up with my studies, which now included bacteriology and pathology. In spite of glandular fever before my end-of-year exams, with a pass mark of fifty per cent, I struggled over the line again, by only two per cent in bacteriology.

I enjoyed a rare summer, free of extramural assignments, and was invited to Dumfries to meet Ev's parents. Why did I not guess that her father Bill would have a superior hi-fi system to mine? The sound from his Cambridge Audio loudspeakers was precise, crisp and with vastly better bass definition than my Wharfedales.

Scotland was a new experience. What was a pint of heavy for goodness sake? We walked in the hills above Southerness, enjoying our free time together and discussing our plans for our future.

Chapter 5

Under Pressure

The Clinical Years

Early autumn 1975 marked the start of the fourth year of my course and the beginning of my clinical studies. A year ago, I felt like a busted flush but now I felt excited and ready for the new challenge.

The pre-clinical years were largely theoretical. At last, I was being given a chance to help some patients who might possibly recover. Travelling to Langford field station felt like starting afresh at a different university. Subjects which were relevant to my future career, including veterinary medicine and surgery, appeared on my curriculum. I could begin to acquire the practical knowledge which I would need when I began to practise in less than two years' time.

Our first medicine lecture involved a tour of the stables with Peter Pinsent. In his sixties, he had a wealth of knowledge to impart and an enviable empathy with horses.

On that first day, I picked up a simple tip, the importance of which I have tried to impress on those vet students who have seen practice with me. Approaching a stable to examine a case, pause to observe your patient closely. Describe the patient to yourself; how are they standing, what are they doing, are they eating or drinking, how do they look and what does their expression and their eyes convey?

This principle can be applied to other farm animals and to pets. It is a natural, typically youthful urge to charge impetuously into the loose box to try to do something. Once you or the owner have entered the stable and begun to interact with the animal, the dynamic has changed and useful information is lost. Taking a few moments to assess your patient represents time well spent and is a good example of the art of veterinary medicine rather than the science.

I really enjoyed this first term; there was nowhere else I wanted to be and nothing I would rather be doing than these clinical studies. Becoming absorbed in the veterinary firmament that was Langford, it was all too easy to remain oblivious of events in the outside world. Trips into Bristol at the weekend to visit Ev provided a welcome break from the quotidian routine at the field station. Sitting in her flat in Chesterfield Road, she read her art textbooks and I read weightier tomes with titles such as *Helminths, Arthropods and Protozoa*. When her attention wandered, I caught her reading my book over my shoulder.

Animal husbandry and obstetrics, together with medicine and surgery, were complex and detailed subjects. I was warned that the fourth year was the hardest year of the course and for me personally, it was about to get a great deal harder.

I began to experience bouts of abdominal pain which culminated in being hospitalised in Weston-Super-Mare General for exploratory surgery in the week before Christmas. They guddled about inside me and removed my appendix whilst they were about it.

Dad took me home on Christmas Eve, a journey of nearly 200 miles which was not the happiest experience of my life. The festivities passed in a blur. I remember the intensity of the flashing blue light reflected on the roof of the ambulance as we sped through the night to Harold Wood hospital. I saw in the new year in another hospital bed with a suture abscess producing astonishing amounts of foul-smelling pus. Better out than in, they said. Back home, I spent my twenty-first birthday feeling particularly sorry for myself.

Returning to Langford later than my colleagues and below par, having lost a lot of weight, the rest of that term proved an immense struggle. How badly did I want this veterinary degree? My strength of character was being tested to its limit.

There was no respite and little time for recuperation during the vacation, as we embarked on a further twenty-six weeks of extramural study, gaining experience at different veterinary practices in various locations. I began with three weeks at my foster practice in Braintree, predominately under the tutelage of Phillip Pocock.

He was adept at playing practical jokes. In 1976, before the advent of mobile phones, this practice had radiotelephones to communicate with vets out on their rounds. The practice secretary Julie had the dubious privilege of having the base station and loudspeaker next to her desk by a window looking out on the car park. Finishing a series of calls, Phillip freewheeled quietly into the car park before blasting "Hello Julie" at full volume from the handheld microphone in his car. It was very funny watching Julie through the window, suddenly sit bolt upright and thoroughly startled.

I had requested a placement with Roger Eddy, who practised in Shepton Mallett. He specialised in production medicine, mostly for dairy farms, which was an area of interest for me. In the hot summer of 1976, I found myself treating a succession of lame cows whose feet required paring; their hooves were hard as flints in the dry weather. I swore quietly under my breath as sweat dripped and pooled in the dished lenses of my spectacles, obscuring my vision. In the evening, Roger went back to his home and his swimming pool. I got fitter, stronger and gained new life experience.

Later in the summer, I was in Potters Bar at Miss Freak's practice. She was coming towards the end of her illustrious career as a specialist in the field of canine reproduction and obstetrics. Her traditional approach to small-animal practice contrasted sharply with the commercialised approach I had experienced elsewhere. I learnt a great deal from her about the art of veterinary medicine and the advantages of a gentle, unhurried and intuitive clinical approach.

Returning to Langford for my final year in October 1976, the end was in sight. We began rotations providing skilled support in the various clinical departments of the vet school. This could involve assisting our lecturers with surgical procedures whilst receiving practical advice in the process. We were developing a basic capability in veterinary surgery.

Evening and late-night visits to the kennels, cattery or stables were delegated to us to monitor the progress of patients. Late one evening, I was called to assist Dr Harold Pearson, an avowed Wagner enthusiast, in performing a caesarean section on a cow. We delivered a schistosome calf alive. This poor animal appeared unzipped along its underbelly, with its body turned inside out, its vital organs outside its body wall. It was impossible for the calf to survive because it couldn't breathe. The sight of this grotesque creature lying on the floor, heart beating ever more slowly as its life ebbed away, was the saddest and most distressing sight of my formative career.

On another occasion, a horse box pulled into the yard. Loud bangs and crashes could be heard from a distance as the irate occupant kicked out at the partitions in the vehicle. After a long drive from Wales, the attendant and driver climbed down from the horsebox looking embarrassed.

Telling us their charge didn't travel well and was upset was a statement of the obvious. I was relieved not to be asked to lead the horse out. George, the senior stable groom in his late fifties, had seen it all before. Wearing his brown lab coat, he walked up the ramp disappearing from our view. Gradually, the kicking subsided. A quarter of an hour later, he calmly led the thoroughbred stallion, now meekly submissive, out of the horsebox and down the ramp using a head collar, held only lightly. Fearlessly, George had demonstrated animal management skills of the very highest order. Empathy with animals is something which only some people have.

It was a hard year but at this late stage, the teaching was more purposeful and focused as we were turned into competent veterinary graduates. Our final examinations would decide whether our proficiency across a wide range of skills and species was sufficient to let us loose on the unsuspecting animal-owning public. Attempts to assimilate further knowledge and information reached unprecedented levels in the final term. Our formal lectures completed, I scurried between different clinical departments trying to gain experience whilst seeing as many cases as possible. Revision involved ploughing through files bursting with lecture notes and consulting my textbooks for more detailed information or clarification.

To relieve the pressure, there were two traditional events. The first was a game called the Ha-Ha! The 'pitch' was a muddy ditch bordered on one side by a stone wall which had encircled the gardens of the country house, on whose parkland the Langford campus was based. Two teams of lads clad only in shorts, their torsos adorned with graffiti, scrabbled about in deep cloying mud to gain possession of a deflated rugby ball. The efforts of the combatants were cheered loudly by the rest of the us; it was a good way of letting off steam and getting rid of repressed frustrations.

The second, slightly more cultured happening was the final year review. Students performed theatrical and satirical sketches, ostensibly for the benefit of the teaching staff. It gave us the chance to poke fun at our elders and betters, the same staff members who were shortly to probe the extent of our knowledge in our final exams. I produced a soundtrack recording for the show which included everyday sounds from around the campus such as the bell of the clock-tower striking the quarter hours to the tune of *All Things Bright and Beautiful*. The rock musical backing track from *Joseph and The Amazing Technicolour Dreamcoat* accompanied Jim Elliott performing 'Hamish the Famous' in honour of our eminent orthopaedic surgeon.

"I'm Hamish the Famous an' I'm pretty an' tall, ah ah hah!"

Hamish Denny, so good he made the most intricate surgery look easy. It was an unforgettable pastiche.

Under such pressure, it was tough to remain focused on my studies. When I felt disillusioned by the volume of information I needed to assimilate, I read passages from James Herriot's books. I took a precious night off when he came to speak to our clinical club about his experiences. I was struck by his modesty; he seemed completely unaffected by his celebrity status.

The night before my final *viva voce* examinations, a small group of us visited the equine inpatients, attempting to steal a march on our colleagues and familiarise ourselves with the cases currently under investigation and treatment. The case notes had been removed but we could pool our knowledge for the common good.

As you might expect, the jungle drums beat loudly in such a close-knit student community. The stables were in the form of a quadrangle, with only one entrance/exit. Each of us in turn brought a haltered horse out of the stables and paraded the animal round on the central lawn whilst the rest of us pretended to be clinicians.

I led out a valuable thoroughbred racehorse on a lead rein and head collar. Highly strung and excitable, the animal immediately stood on its hind legs, prancing about, getting more and more agitated, fighting to get free and waving its forelegs in the general direction of my head. I elected to hang on, partly through fear of injury and partly through fear of being shamed in front of my contemporaries.

After what seemed liked hours but was probably a couple of minutes, the horse grew tired of these antics and stood once again on all fours. Muttering a silent prayer of thanks, I led the creature back into its stable. Following that extremely unnerving episode, I have lost any fear I had of horses.

My finals in June 1977 provided a salutary lesson in keeping going when all seems lost. Harold Pearson tetchily tested my knowledge of difficulties encountered in whelping bitches. I failed to identify a pair of equine hoof testers, having never seen them used at university or in general practice. I managed to convince my external examiner that I was not pulling a fast one and he was happy to demonstrate how and when they should be used.

And then it was over. I was too exhausted to experience any sensation of anti-climax or release from my anxiety. There was nothing to be done now but to try to recuperate both physically and mentally, catch up on some sleep and wait for the results to be published in a few weeks.

The months after Easter had been so stressful. It was the accepted norm at the time. You were expected to cope and to deal with the pressure as best you could. With no formal support network, you relied on your friends and colleagues. Mental health was not the concern it is today; the ordeal was something to be endured, helping to develop your character and your resilience for what was to come in your working life and seen as a test of your mental strength as well as your intellectual ability.

At a final-year party in the home of the professor of medicine, a few of us sat with Charles Grunsell on the floor of his sitting room, listening to Fats Waller and other jazz greats from his extensive record collection, whilst discussing the future of the veterinary profession.

Looking around, I wondered what would become of us all. Five years previously, we had been thrown together, arriving from diverse backgrounds to study intensively. We had lost some along the way. Non-conformists, such as Neil Burnie, finally had a haircut and consented to conform. Everyone's foibles, their strengths, their weaknesses and petty vanities were exposed. I looked on as the brightest girl in the year suffered the most excruciating episode of self-doubt before her viva exams. After graduation, would we gather together again, this year of '77?

The day finally came when our results were to be published. As I walked to the vet school in Bristol, I met other colleagues along the way. The word on the street was that six students from our class had been put back for resits.

I felt an enormous sense of relief when I saw my name on the list of those who had passed. This veterinary degree was something I had been working towards for almost half of my young life. It represented not only a great deal of sustained hard work but also a significant amount of financial constraint on the part of my parents, for which I remain forever in their debt. Never again would the course of my future career depend on the deliberations of peers, some of whom I perceived to be out-of-date old buffers. As I write these scribblings, I admit that I am now viewed by some in a similar light. What goes around, comes around!

My proud parents were in the audience in the Wills Memorial Building for our graduation ceremony. I was suited and wearing a gown suitably trimmed for a graduate about to be awarded a bachelor of veterinary science degree. For many students, this ticketed event was a family affair, recorded for posterity.

In the afternoon, we trooped out with our entourages to Langford for another ceremony in which we were inducted as members of the Royal College of Veterinary Surgeons and were finally allowed to practise professionally in our own right.

I have always hated goodbyes. This formal occasion marked the end of our years at Bristol. As each of us went our separate ways, there were many tears and promises to stay in touch, later mostly forgotten.

A quarter of the students in my final year had found themselves jobs before their final exams. They were leaving to begin their professional working lives. Feeling their actions presumptuous, I had focused my energies on my final examinations and only now, greatly buoyed by graduating, did I feel sufficiently confident to begin scanning the positions advertised in the situations vacant column in the *Veterinary Record*. My early applications fell on stony ground, including an interview at a practice in Abingdon, the town where I now live, at a practice which I walk past on most days.

Even the driving job I had secured for that post-graduation summer was not a success. Asked to drive a van showing signs of having been thrashed, I delivered parts to customers in the Bristol/Somerset area. One day, travelling back from a drop in Bridgewater on the M5, the van gave up the ghost. Naturally, being youngest, temporary and last in the door, I got the blame and was suddenly surplus to requirements. This seemed unreasonably harsh but toughened me up for fights in the future.

Returning with Ev from a few days' holiday in north Devon, I noticed an advertisement for an assistant in a practice in east Suffolk. I had enjoyed several family holidays in the countryside surrounding Southwold and I was drawn back to that familiar corner of East Anglia.

In October 1977, I accepted an offer for my first veterinary position as an assistant in a mixed, mainly large-animal practice in Halesworth.

Chapter 6

Suffolk Punch

Halesworth

My new bosses were George and Kevin. George, the senior partner and formerly a lieutenant in the Royal Army Veterinary Corps, retained a bluff military manner. A tough man and a vastly experienced vet, particularly with horses, he had a short temper and did not suffer fools gladly. Kevin was younger, mild-mannered, a patient mentor in that most difficult year of my career, my first.

The practice, catering mostly for farm animals and horses, was based in a substantial double-fronted detached 1930s house. I was on duty every other night and weekend and had one afternoon off each week.

My practice car, a six-year-old mustard Morris Marina saloon, was past its prime. I stocked the boot with the drugs and equipment I might need and waited for my first case, which turned out to be a lame cow. She had a badly-infected claw, a half section of hoof on her hind foot. I carefully pared away the horn on the sole, establishing a channel from which considerable quantities of purulent material drained. I treated her with an injection of antibiotics and left two further treatments for the farmer to give on the following two days. The cow was comfortable now, standing on her foot and the farmer seemed pleased with my efforts. I left the farm feeling quietly satisfied.

You can imagine how my mood changed dramatically when I heard the farmer had called out the senior partner later that day for his opinion. He advised his client to send the animal for slaughter. Disheartened, I reasoned I could not alter the two factors which influenced this outcome - being young and a new arrival at the practice. I had to get over it and move on.

The partners introduced a new venture - routine evening consultations for pets on weekdays. Naturally, I was keen to be part of this initiative. My first consultation was a cat brought in by an elderly, dignified lady who came in wearing a cream coat and green hat, held in place with a decorative hat pin.

Her cat had a sore ear. On inspection, I could see a number of ear mites, pale minute mobile dots whose curious natural habitats are specifically the ear canals of dogs and cats. Their presence can cause severe localised irritation. I prescribed some ear drops containing a drug to kill the mites. *Auroid* was a viscous straw-coloured lotion packaged in small flexible plastic bottles with a green, domed screw cap. I was quite confident my treatment would cure this simple problem. I was wrong.

My client returned a week later, wearing the same hat and coat. Raising her chin slightly with a note of defiance in her voice, she said, "Your drops haven't worked young man!"

During my examination of the cat's ears under the bright light and magnifying lens of my auroscope, I could see the mites still present in similar numbers, along with plenty of powdery ear wax resembling aged brown boot polish in appearance. I noticed the skin lining each ear canal and the wax deposits appeared to be completely dry. The owner had brought the drops with her, perhaps with the expectation of exchanging them for something more effective. I checked her bottle of ear drops which appeared full and apparently unopened. I paused for a moment.

"Could you show me how you put the drops in your cat's ear?"

Unable to hide her annoyance, she turned the bottle upside down and tried to squeeze the drops into the cat's ear with the cap still firmly in place. Gently, I explained that the cap should be removed and demonstrated how some drops should be put in each ear and the ears then massaged for as long as the cat would keep still. It amuses me now to recall this incident but it helped me refine my approach in subsequent cases. Invariably, I offered to instil the first treatment of drops in the pet's ears in front of the client.

These evening small-animal consultations proved more challenging when the industrial discontent spreading through Britain led to power cuts. Vet school had omitted a number of potential scenarios in our course, including consulting by candlelight. The soft light and the smell of burning candle wax imbued the most mundane clinical tasks with a romantic, even a religious air. I thought consultations should continue, although supplies of torch batteries and hurricane lamps ran low in the small market town of Halesworth.

Routine procedures became more difficult in the absence of available light. Either my torch batteries expired or the patient could not be moved. With recumbent cows in distant fields in the middle of the night, I struggled to deliver calves with only the headlamps of farm vehicles for illumination. Though much of the physical manipulation and effort was expended with my arms deep inside the body of the patient, the task seemed more difficult.

The summons to my first case of milk fever came at midnight. When I answered the phone, despite reassurances from the farmer, I felt fear fluttering in the pit of my stomach. The client assured me of my good fortune. Unhappy with the behaviour of the cow earlier in the evening, he brought her into his brand new barn. Having found the right farm, I was escorted to my patient. She was unable to rise, lying flat out on her side on clean straw in a splendid new barn. In fact, the barn was so new, electricity had yet to be installed. Making the mistake of commenting on its absence, the astonished farmer exclaimed, "Mr Howard don't need no electric lights to give 'em un."

The farm vehicle had no serviceable headlights and my car was back at the farmhouse. I was reliant on my hand-held torch. Would the batteries hold out? Cases of milk fever need the remedial solution containing calcium to be administered directly into their bloodstream and quickly. Long, large-diameter needles must be accurately placed in the jugular vein which runs along the underside of the cow's neck.

Tonight, this region of her neck was an inaccessible area of long black hair, lightly smeared with cow muck, adorned with stray stalks of straw and dancing shadows created by the torchlight. I have noticed over the years that the beam from a torch being held by a farmer seems to wander from the actual area requiring illumination in direct proportion to their excitment at telling me about their latest acquisition, usually a bull, which is going to lift their herd to unimaginable heights of productivity with its progeny.

As I placed my needle using all the skill and confidence I could muster, I was mindful of the other important structures adjacent to this huge vein, including major nerves and the prominent pulsing artery supplying blood to the the cow's head. Thankfully, my flutter valve functioned properly that night, the soft rhythmic sound of air bubbles a sweet soundtrack as the revitalising fluid flowed freely, bringing renewed strength to my patient's muscles. Happily, the cow staggered to her feet shortly after I completed my ministrations and looked around in confusion for her calf.

As my career progressed, I had to give such intravenous injections in all manner of awkward situations that presented their own particular challenges.

An old cow with a fine set of horns, resting on some low-lying water meadows, discovered she couldn't get up and in her panic, slithered sideways, spine first, into a steep-sided drainage ditch full of foul-smelling water. I could just see her hooves above the bank as I walked towards her in the evening sunlight.

Left in this inverted position, her rumen (the largest stomach compartment) would fill with the gas produced during the normal digestive processes and this accumulating pressure would eventually suffocate her.

I managed to find her jugular vein and as the restorative solution began to revive her, she became increasingly aware of her precarious position and began to struggle. Her head was secured with a halter to avoid her helpers being injured by her horns and with great difficulty and considerable risk, we were able to place straps around her body in the lulls between her thrashing. These were attached to a tractor and she was hauled back up the bank to relative safety.

My aim was to work in as safe a manner as possible. Nowadays, health and safety advisors would have a jolly time producing risk assessments for such procedures but as with so many situations on farm visits, the needs of the animal ultimately dictated the degree of risk you were required and prepared to take to help them.

My first job had several advantages over subsequent positions I held. From the list of visits in the daybook, I was allocated three or four farm calls to make during the morning, usually having a single patient to attend at each call. The farms were often several miles apart, which created opportunities to stop for a flask of coffee for my elevenses. I had my favourite spots for these brief interludes, most with beautiful views over Suffolk countryside. With luck, I might catch sight of the sun glinting on the sea in the distance.

I had searched for a job with a less pressurised lifestyle after the rigours of university. At the end of the morning round, I had the luxury of enjoying a cooked lunch, a rarity in later practice life. There was a restaurant on the high street offering a simple menu, the food prepared and cooked on the premises. Filling but tasty traditional fare of roast meat or pie and two vegetables and a pudding. The waitresses looked after their regulars well and amongst the worn and faded decor, I didn't feel self-conscious eating my meal whilst smelling faintly of farmyards. The patrons were mostly locals, many of whom I knew and we discussed the issues of the day. The meals were reasonably priced so I could enjoy them on a regular basis without placing undue strain on my parlous bank account.

The subject of food reminds me of my first digs in Halesworth, living with the Hemplemans on their mixed farm with a variety of livestock based around the pig unit. This billet offered a valuable insight into the complexities of the farming community in east Suffolk in the 1970s. Meals, taken around the large dining table in the spacious farmhouse kitchen, were times for talking which developed, on occasions, to inter-generational arguments. Hitherto, I hadn't given much thought to the fluctuations in the stock price of pigs.

I am grateful to the Hempleman family for taking me into their home and treating me as another son, which was a great privilege. Mrs H had a relaxed approach to life and was a magician in her kitchen, effortlessly conjuring hearty meals that kept out the cold. Her pheasant casserole and venison hotpot, both with characteristically-rich flavours, still live in my memory. Wholesome, tasty uncomplicated food with meat cooked in its natural juices and seasonal homegrown vegetables. What would she have made of the super-sophisticated food on current TV cooking programmes, with its hyperbole and coloured spots of this and that?

At the end of the evening meal, the family adjourned to the sitting room to watch the latest episode of *Coronation Street*. What interest and relevance did the storylines in this programme, set in the heart of a densely-populated northern metropolis, hold for this farming family in rural Suffolk? Nevertheless, it was a show which these devotees dared not miss.

The telephone was in an draughty downstairs hallway. I don't remember sleeping through the ringing of the bell, though it was a worry as my bedroom was on the floor above. It was something of a trek to scuttle down to answer an emergency call during the night. Those nocturnal conversations were kept short and succinct.

After a period of being fed and cosseted, I thought it was time to fend for myself. I found Bramble, a prefabricated farm bungalow at Chediston Green, a few miles outside Halesworth. It was owned by a farming client called Mr Ingram. The property came unfurnished and unheated but with open fireplaces.

That February, I moved into a building which was cold and felt damp. Initially, an electric oil-filled radiator fitted with a time-switch, and later a bottled gas heater, did help to make the place more habitable, along with some basic furniture donated by family and friends. At the weekend, open fires cheered the place up considerably but that involved visits to the wood shed, inhabited by an array of almighty arachnids.

Flossie, who featured in the first chapter, produced a litter of golden retriever pups and an engaging male pup from the litter came to keep me company. As with many youngsters, he was always up to mischief, frequently stealing up the garden with a piece of my clothing or a leather moccasin hanging cheekily from his mouth, his jaunty gait giving a clue to his latest misdemeanour.

Mostyn and I enjoyed many relaxing walks across the neighbouring farmland. On my duty weekends, Ev would come up from Bristol where she was working. If the trains were on time, I could meet her at Darsham station nearby. If she missed her connection, I would have a lengthy drive into Ipswich to collect her.

On nights when I was not on duty, I liked nothing better than to visit the White Hart Inn at Westleton and enjoy a pint of Adnams bitter, a beer brewed locally in Southwold. The pub was run by Morrie and Sheila Eves, who became my friends and confidants. There was always a welcome there. They found time to listen if I had had a tough day and would josh with me mercilessly if I ever took myself too seriously.

Morrie dominated the bar with his flamboyant handlebar moustache and expansive gestures, giving a fair impression of the actor Jimmy Edwards* in his later hirsute phase. As you stepped inside the door, he drew you in and immediately included you in the gathering.

Good publicans have become relative rarities. A clean, well-run pub with enthusiastic staff and with a range of well-kept ales can and should be vibrant centres of the local community. Westleton was a picturesque village with an attractive green, elegant church and a hotel as well as the pub. I was not alone in travelling some distance to enjoy the hospitality on offer. Servicemen and women from the US airforce base at Lakenheath frequently arrived in numbers, chatting easily with the regulars. They added to the general feeling of bonhomie which made this pub such a special and relaxing place to visit.

I was fortunate to be given a guided tour of the Adnams brewery in Southwold by John Adnams himself. Founded in 1872, it was a fascinating place. Part of the brewery was still housed in the original brick buildings close to the Swan Hotel. The art and mystery of brewing beer using traditional methods is one of many crafts which should be cherished and preserved. Visits to Southwold were enhanced by that special aroma that only breweries can produce. Wooden casks were still delivered to local hostelries by horse-drawn dray.

On sunny afternoons when I was free to please myself, I parked my car at Dunwich on the coast and walked for miles. The rhythmic, repetitive sound of the waves, pushing pebbles up the steeply-shelving shingle beach, was soothing and conducive to thought and reflection. As the years have passed, I wish I had recorded these soothing sounds to be played as I tried to drift off to sleep after a disturbed night on call.

It was difficult to reconcile such tranquillity with the ferocity of a sea which had caused such extensive coastal erosion. So many buildings, particularly churches, had disappeared beneath the waves.

Returning to the car park, past the small clinker-built fishing boats drawn up on the beach, I talked to the fishermen and bought some fresh fish from that day's catch to take home to cook for supper.

*Jimmy Edwards (1920 - 1988) comedy writer and actor

Yellow Peril Outside Halesworth Practice 1977

The mutinous Morris had been a poor investment, requiring a series of expensive repairs; a broken roadspring finally sealed its fate. I was allowed to choose my next car but not its colour, a Ford Escort in Regency Red. I was elated, motoring around the countryside for the sheer pleasure of driving. It holds the distinction of being the only new practice car I have driven.

Mum and dad came to see their son in action as he learnt the tricks of his trade. I had a number of cows to examine by rectal palpation to determine if they were in-calf. The animals were tied by yokes around their heads, lined up side-by-side in a byre, backsides facing the drainage channel and passageway. The third animal took exception to the gentle introduction of a lubricated gloved arm into her rectum, planting her hind hoof squarely and forcefully in my solar plexus, sending me flying backwards into the wall of the cowshed behind me. I slid to the floor, laying there gasping and winded for several minutes. A painful and undignified experience at the best of times; to have it happen in front of my parents made the incident even more embarrassing.

In June 1978, I settled down to watch John Conteh fight for the WBC light heavyweight world title. The phone rang. I was on duty and the call was a calving. The news got worse. The farmer had tried pulling the calf out using a tractor but could not shift it. This promised to be more akin to a wrestling match at which I was not just a spectator. I rang Kevin to warn him I may have to call for help and drove out to the farm.

The cow had been calving for while. Two hooves were protruding from her vulva, to which the farmer had attached ropes connected to his tractor. The cow's uterus was contracting down, giving me much less room to manipulate the calf *in situ*. Instead of feeling moist and slimey, her passage remained dry however much lubricant I plastered on my arms. The calf's head was deviated ventrally below the cow's pelvis, so that as the farmer pulled, he succeeded only in burying the head further into the wall of the uterus and risked tearing it.

I attached a calving rope to the calf's head and tried to repel the body of the calf whilst trying to raise the calf's head into the passage.

I was taught that if you made no progress after twenty minutes, you should review your approach. I rang for assistance. The farmer was pleased to see Kevin and to have his experience to hand. He confirmed that the calf was dead and was also unable to lift the calf's head. The only option was to remove the calf's head *in situ* using embryotomy wire.

Having resisted calling us earlier, and having made matters worse with his ill-considered intervention, the farmer was now unwilling to allow us to proceed further with the attendant increase in costs and the cow was put down. Despite realising farming was a commercial enterprise, it was hard to accept decisions about veterinary treatment when they were made purely on economic grounds and to the detriment of the welfare of the animal in question. I returned home feeling disgruntled. There was nobody there to sympathise with my frustration but my young puppy listened dutifully to my soliloquy. Such is the duty of a vet's dog fulfilling the role of a solitary companion.

In contrast to the previous evening, it was a very different scenario next day when I visited the extensive pig unit owned by Mr Huxley. The production system was intensive but the animals were very well cared for and at no stage was I ever told that any suggested treatment plan was too expensive or uneconomic.

John, the farm manager, was always cheerful, efficient, fun to work with and empathetic towards his charges. I think he knew what ailed his pigs before I had worked it out but he was decent enough not to make it too obvious. Often, my patients were expectant or newly-farrowed sows with the complications that went with their condition, namely farrowing fever, mastitis or metritis. John's skill with a board, which he used to trap and restrain recalcitrant porcines against a wall in the corner of a pen, was remarkable.

Sent to disbud some calves at the farm next door to my humble homestead, I was met by an extraordinary sight as I got out of the car. The farm hand was next to his tractor, both knees bent in a semi-crouched position, immobile with head bowed. He was like a statue, lacking only a plinth. Agricultural performance art perhaps?

A few grunted phrases uttered with great effort indicated I had my first medical emergency. They hadn't covered this eventuality at vet school either. Jumping down from his tractor, he had 'put his back out' using his parlance, suffered a prolapsed disc in mine. He literally could not move and was in great pain.

Summoning help, we laid him out gently on a five-bar farm gate laid flat with straw bales on top, an inadequate temporary substitute for an orthopaedic mattress. His employer Mr Ingram called an ambulance. The ambulance driver and his colleague had difficulty suppressing grins at first but their professionalism took over. We watched them depart with my first human patient before we got on with the job of disbudding the calves. Later, a thank-you card arrived at the practice with a cartoon of a nurse swathed in bandages resembling an Egyptian mummy and some kind words of thanks inside.

Small-animal neutering operations were scheduled for Wednesday afternoons and took place in a single-storeyed wooden outbuilding at the top of the garden. The operating facilities were basic with no mains running water. A Baby Burco water heater was filled manually with water brought up from the house but it was no longer capable of heating the water.

Male cats were castrated, tightly wrapped in a bath towel and sometimes inside a wellington boot as well, with their tail facing the surgeon. There were no veterinary nurses to assist with these procedures. One vet, usually me, restrained the animal whilst a bleb of local anaesthetic was injected into each testicle. After making a small nick in the scrotum with a scalpel, each testicle was removed by twisting the spermatic cord and subsequent traction.

This simple surgical procedure was less straightforward with a moving target and one I had not previously encountered being used for pets, although it was a similar technique to that used on farms for the castration of calves, which required no towels and with the wellington boots occupied solely by me. The practice did not have a gas anaesthetic machine so all other operations were undertaken using pentobarbitone, a long-acting intravenous anaesthetic.

One Saturday afternoon, I assisted the senior partner as he performed a caesarean section on his friend's Great Dane bitch. Pentobarbitone crosses the placental barrier so it affects the puppies as well as their mother. The pups, now successfully delivered, were alive but very drowsy. I cleaned away discharges from their eyes, noses, and mouths whilst encouraging them to keep breathing until the effects of the anaesthetic wore off. Eventually, their mother woke up and went home with her delighted owner and her brood. Not surprisingly, the operating room looked like a theatre of war. It was I who did the cleaning up.

The skilled assistance of qualified veterinary nursing colleagues became a priority for me in my future career. Many of the best nurses I have worked with have known intuitively what I needed, be it a drug or an instrument, before I did. As a member of team working together, I knew that a higher level of care could and should be offered to domestic pets.

I was again scanning the adverts in the situations vacant columns of the *Veterinary Record.* I had a better idea now of the type of practice in which I wanted to work - ideally as part of a team of young vets and nurses in a mixed practice committed to raising the standard of veterinary care, especially for small animals. I recognised I still had much to learn and needed to consolidate further the knowledge I had gained at university.

In my early career, I had been fortunate to be given support and guidance by Kevin. I heard that several of my classmates had not been so lucky. Their confidence had been quickly eroded and they left under a cloud after only a few months at the coalface.

I suspect that my challenging introduction to general practice in the late Seventies was very different to that experienced by today's veterinary graduate. Since 2007, newly-qualified vets undertake a personal development programme which acknowledges their relative inexperience and need for support from more experienced colleagues. Based on self-assessment, it provides a structure for monitoring their progress and developing their confidence and competence and lasts between eighteen and thirty-six months. Brief records of clinical cases are kept, covering a range of clinical skills and procedures.

On completion of the programme, it is assumed that the graduate will be able to perform a range of common clinical procedures and manage them successfully without supervision.

My disparate thoughts about moving on were crystallised when I heard that the partners had been successful in tendering for meat inspection work at a local poultry packing station. I did not want to be involved in that area of work. I would miss the slower pace of life and the beautiful coastal landscape of east Suffolk. It was tough to leave behind my shiny red car and the White Hart Inn, my second home. Less of a wrench was relinquishing the tenancy of my first home as another winter was imminent.

In October 1978, after detailed discussions with my dog, I said my goodbyes and we headed for East Sussex, feeling apprehensive and excited by the prospect of a new position in a bigger practice.

Chapter 7

Light Sussex

Hailsham

I left Halesworth for Hailsham to join a mixed practice employing five vets, including two partners. There were two other assistants and three qualified veterinary nurses, including Dick, the first male nurse I had come across. A practice manager sorted out the day-to-day niggles that arose in such a sizeable business venture.

This practice provided me with accommodation, a modern brick-built bungalow with central heating in Orchard Close. My car, a white Vauxhall Cavalier, came equipped with radiotelephone, so no more searching for a phone box and for coins to ring the practice at the end of a round of calls. I worked a one-in-three weekday and weekend duty rota, with the partners sharing Tuesday night duties between them. Roughly half the practice income was derived from farm animal and horse work with the remainder from pets.

The pace of life picked up and I was expected to raise my professional game. The youth and camaraderie of my new colleagues, who worked hard and played hard, helped me settle quickly into a new routine. Discussion of cases and new treatment protocols was encouraged and regular evening social events involving both the assistants and nurses helped to strengthen the strong team ethic. We had the pleasant prospect of a purpose-built small-animal hospital block which was about to be built. All rather different from my previous experience in Suffolk.

Our clients included more livestock farms, many employing intensive production methods; most visits involved more animals being presented for veterinary attention. The emphasis was inclined towards production medicine and surgery and away from 'fire brigade' work.

The staff on these farms were highly skilled, which gave the vets the option to offer more technically-sophisticated services. Several farms were using the recent innovation of embryo transfer. Embryos from pedigree continental breeds with superior production potential, including Belgian Blue, Limousin and Simmental, were being surgically implanted into native Hereford-cross females from less genetically-exalted stock.

At calving, a quick vaginal assessment would invariably confirm that the calf was oversized and unable to pass through the birth canal. The calves were of much higher economic worth than the cows which carried them and so were delivered by caesarean section. This surgical procedure became so familiar that, on my arrival, I would find my patient already tethered in a crush with the left flank clipped up, ready for infiltration with local anaesthetic.

Most of these surrogate bovine mothers tolerated this intervention well, with sedation required only on the odd occasion. The quality of the husbandry in these herds contributed to high surgical success rates; all the calves which I delivered were born alive, with the recovery of the dams usually rapid and uneventful. I was not completely comfortable with the ethics but it was proving to be a safe and a profitable venture and I quickly became proficient in carrying out the surgery.

I welcomed the opportunity to be more involved with fertility work in cattle. By rectal palpation of their reproductive organs, I could advise on whether the animal had resumed its oestrus cycle following calving and what stage had been reached in that cycle. With a range of hormone products available for treatment, I could hasten the time when the cows became pregnant again, ensuring they remained productive members of the herd.

Routine veterinary tasks continued to feature in a round of visits. In mid-November, I drove to the South Downs, close to Beachy Head, to castrate about thirty bull calves. I enjoyed many pleasant walks in this area but today, I was there to work and what a picturesque setting to have as a temporary operating theatre.

It was a fine morning with a gentle sea breeze, the sunlight catching the tops of the waves in the English Channel. My helpers were a boisterous band of brothers who arrived on quad bikes, competing to see who could win an unofficial time trial whilst creating the most noise in the process.

The calves were in a pen waiting for me. They were sent along an ever-narrowing funnel made of movable tubular metal fencing panels terminating in a crush. There was a great deal of banter and bravado as one by one, the animals were persuaded to enter the crush.

I injected local anaesthetic into each testicle and cleansed the scrotum with antiseptic. I exposed each testis using 'sharp' surgery, that is by making an incision using a surgical blade mounted securely on a scalpel handle. I passed the scalpel to a helper whose hands had passed my cleanliness inspection. It was to be held away from his body and directed towards the ground out of harm's way. This allowed me to use both hands to separate, twist and remove each testis, working with dexterity beneath the hindquarters of each patient.

The morning's work was going well, accompanied by much testosterone-fuelled comment, not dissimilar to TV motoring programmes and with similar levels of banality. Suddenly, there was silence. Something had happened. Standing up stiffly from my crouched position behind the crush and looking round, I beheld my helper-in-chief, motionless, an expression of pain and fear in his eyes, his complexion matching the famous chalk cliffs.

Somehow, he had managed to stab his thigh with the scalpel, which I could see embedded in his flesh. Another event I don't recall being covered at vet school. And another medical emergency, this time in the middle of nowhere.

Laying my patient down on the grass before he fainted from the sight of his own blood, I removed the scalpel from his leg and wrapped my towel tightly around his wound to act as a temporary tourniquet. One of the brethren left to call an ambulance, whilst another took me, at breakneck speed, back to my car for a selection of bandages and dressings.

I deputed his mates to remove his dirty, blood-stained jeans; I applied dressings and bandages to his wound as tightly as I dared, to stem the flow of blood.

Having alerted the emergency services, the brother returned with a five-bar farm gate and ropes. With my calving gown draped over it, we laid the patient on the gate, no bales of straw being to hand this time. We strapped the gate across the back of two quad bikes. The bikes supporting the improvised stretcher progressed with the precision of a motorcycle display team, across the uneven terrain to a gateway by an access road. By now, my patient had passed the fainting stage and was complaining about the pain in his leg and the tightness of my bandages. I took this to be a good sign. In the valley below, I caught sight of the ambulance threading its way along the lane towards us.

The patient transport returned whence it came and a sense of reality returned to the morning's events. A lively discussion ensued and as the chatter died down, the consensus was that we should complete this batch of castrations. We set about the job in hand with no joshing and a more measured approach.

Driving back to the practice, I reconsidered the protocol I employed to castrate these bovines. I have cringed when I've watched experienced vets, working behind their patient, put the scalpel handle and blade, or sometimes just the blade, in their mouth, gripping it with their teeth whilst manipulating the spermatic cords and testes. In my view, this is a dangerous technique for the vet to adopt, especially considering the risk of getting kicked in the face and possibly wounded by your own instrument. I felt my modus operandi represented the safest option and I had done nothing for which I should reproach myself. I would continue to rely on the ability of my helpers to handle the scalpel with a modicum of common sense. Following treatment, my aide made a full recovery from his self-inflicted surgical intervention.

Two and a half hours into the new year of 1979, I was called to a calving. Happily, it was a straightforward case and having corrected the presentation so that both forelegs of the calf were fully extended and the head positioned correctly in the passage, the farmer and I delivered a healthy live calf. Gratefully, I returned to the warmth of my bed. No sooner had my head hit the pillow than I sat up again. I hadn't checked the cow internally to make sure that she was not carrying twins. Thinking about it, the calf I had delivered was not overly large, considering the size of its mother. The farmer called at the practice a few days later. I strolled over and asked after my patient.

"Marvellous job you did. Tickled her up proper you did. Half an hour after you left, she had another calf, a right bonny thing."

During my undergraduate and extramural training, the mantra, repeated so many times after delivering a calf or lamb, was to feel inside the mother to check for twins or triplets. I developed the practice of inserting antibiotic pessaries after each such procedure so that I *had* to feel inside. Roughly one in a hundred calvings result in the birth of twins and as far as I know, this was the only time I forgot to complete my checks. With those odds, is it any wonder I never buy lottery tickets.

I felt accepted as part of my new practice team as well as part of my local community. Ev successfully applied for a transfer within General Accident from Bristol to their offices in Brighton. She moved to Eastbourne in February to live in a flat above a shop which restored clocks. When I visited, the passage of time was marked by a medley of different chimes from the collection of clocks downstairs. Her flat was heated by a two-bar electric fire and electricity was purchased via a coin-operated meter. Loose change became precious currency, especially during the colder months. On the same floor was an elderly lady who was evidently hard of hearing. In the evening, the TV volume grew loud and later she could be heard reciting her prayers at the top of her voice.

There was a profusion of thoroughbred racehorses and top-class hunters owned by clients of the practice. My equine caseload was increasing as I undertook the detailed examination of horses before purchase and surgical castrations. Initially I was accompanied by another vet but quickly became confident enough to fly solo, supported by a nurse.

At this time, a new disease, contagious equine metritis, appeared to bedevil the world of horse breeding. Mares were required to have clitoral swabs taken to ensure they were free from this infection before mating. Most mares tolerated this procedure without any fuss.

I called at a racing yard to obtain one such routine swab from a thoroughbred mare. Chatting to her groom, it seemed this mare had been ultra-possessive of her foal and would not let anyone near her or her youngster. She had been left largely to her own devices to rear her foal with minimal close supervision. Her foal was now weaned and the groom had advised against breeding from the mare again on safety grounds but had been overruled.

Traditional loose boxes or stables were normally at least sixteen feet square and often twenty feet square. This mare was in a small loose box with low breeze block partitions designed to house small calves or piglets. The groom restrained the mare on a bridle using a twitch but she would not let me anywhere near her hindquarters. I would have preferred to move her outside and administer a short-acting general anaesthetic out in a field, since a larger box wasn't available. However, we were concerned she may break free and escape on to the Downs.

With some misgivings, I gave the anaesthetic injection. She took three steps forward and collapsed onto her side on top of the breeze block wall which crumbled under her weight. This ranked as the worst moment of my veterinary life since the episode with the horse in the stables at Langford, the night before my final viva.

I swabbed her and administered the reviving agent. Staggering to her feet, I was able to assess the damage to this most beautiful of fine-skinned animals. There were many superficial grazes with one small open wound over her shoulder. I quickly inserted two dissolvable sutures to draw the skin edges together before she had fully regained her senses. Discussing the incident with my colleagues, we agreed that in spite of the risk of a disgruntled owner and possibly my boss as well, it was best to walk away from a situation like this if you were not happy with the facilities or the competency of staff available to carry out such an intervention.

One time when both partners were away, a small child's pony turned up in the car park for a booster vaccination. Since it was booked for an afternoon appointment during small-animal consultations, the nurses dared me to take the pony into the consultation room for its inoculation. As if it was the most natural thing in the world, I led the pony carefully up the front steps, through the waiting room, past some startled clients and into the consulting room. The pony behaved impeccably and the event was photographed to confirm our wager. I led the pony out through a side entrance into the garden.

In addition to consultations by appointment in Hailsham, the practice rented a lock-up shop premises in Polegate, about five miles away, which was staffed on weekdays by vets and nurses from the main practice on a rota basis. Most cases requiring surgery came to the main practice, where there were two gaseous anaesthetic machines controlled by the nurses. Patients received a short-acting intravenous injection and were kept asleep using a mix of gases, making it easy to control the depth of anaesthesia.

Surgical procedures were a much safer prospect, with most patients waking up shortly after surgery was completed. I carried out caesarean sections frequently on bitches and queens and the pups and kittens delivered were more alert than the Great Dane pups that were delivered in Suffolk, where only longer-acting intravenous anaesthetic drugs were available.

I was called to the practice one Sunday morning to treat a dog that had been involved in a road traffic accident. As my colleagues enjoyed their Sunday off, I unlocked the building, switched off the burglar alarm, turned on some lights and showed my client into the consulting room.

The dog had sustained several extensive skin wounds which would require cleansing and suturing under anaesthetic. However, the owner, a tall, muscular man in his thirties, was more of a concern than his pet.

He remained in control whilst giving me his personal details, the history of the case and during the examination. When I started to explain that my treatment would involve surgery, the owner's eyes began to roll like the dials of a fruit machine.

To reduce the risk of him fainting and possibly injuring himself, and as he was too heavy for me to lift single-handed, I whisked him outside into the fresh air. Unfortunately, that did not cure the problem completely. Every time I returned to the question of treatment, his expression grew vacant and he literally went weak at the knees.

I was reduced to desperate measures, slapping his cheeks to prevent him collapsing completely. A vet is required to explain treatment options in some detail so that their client can give their informed consent for any surgery.

I sat him in his car and the consent form was signed with a verbal agreement between us that I would do what was necessary and treat his pet as if it were my own. When the nurse on duty arrived, we proceeded to repair the skin wounds and the dog's recovery was uneventful. I called the owner and later, when collecting his dog, he remained in the driver's seat, choosing not to look at my handiwork. I lifted the dog carefully into the back of his car and we agreed he would return in a couple of days for me to check on the dog's progress and to pay the account.

I was beginning to build up a body of clients who were asking specifically to see me; it's a very special feeling indeed. Gradually, I acquired a larger caseload, dealing with more technically-complex cases. Among them were Joy Parrish and her whippets. The dogs ran free on a local landowner's estate. They were fine-skinned dogs and frequently presented with wounds and sprains. Her husband John, a retired fireman, was now a groom on the estate and recounted the story of being called to a blaze at an imposing mansion in the Sussex countryside. When the brigade arrived, the fire was well-established. Someone rushed up to John and said, "The annex, the annex, save the annex at all costs."

In the annex was a state-of-the-art recording studio which contained the master tapes of a new rock album representing many months of work. The annex and the master tapes did survive, these tapes forming part of the triple album *Trilogy*, later released by the supergroup Emerson, Lake and Palmer to worldwide acclaim.

I still owned and drove an ageing Vauxhall Victor, registered in 1962, which I had acquired from my mother. It had been in the family since new and had survived university with me and teacher-training college with my sister. Joy's son Gavin was a motor mechanic who, with his partner Roy, worked their annual magic to keep the car roadworthy. After travelling more than 100,000 miles, corrosion finally won.

With the approach of summer, I was offered the chance to join in pre-season nets with Hailsham cricket club. I had not played since I left school but having overcome the initial stiffness brought on by years of sporting inactivity, I looked forward to playing again. Granted a week of leave during the Hailsham Cricket festival, I played on several village grounds in picturesque surroundings along the south coast as far west as Chichester. I watched Sussex play at the Saffrons in Eastbourne and at Hove and even managed to squeeze in a visit to Gray-Nicholls in Robertsbridge, where their craftsmen fashioned classic cricket bats from rough-cut English willow.

Summer sunshine brought holidaymakers into our patch in ever-greater numbers. One evening after surgery, I was called by a farmer to his bull that had a wound on its head requiring repairs. Earlier that day, I had been chatting to a representative from a company making surgical accessories and he had left some free samples of a new suture material called *Vicryl.* It retained its tensile strength for an extended period but was ultimately resorbed, so sutures did not have to be snipped out. Poking about at the front end of a bull was an overrated pastime and avoiding a second instalment seemed a good idea to me.

Arriving at the coastal farm and gathering up some kit, we set off towards my patient and the distant crush. Trapping his head in the yoke to limit further gestures of intent, I fitted him with two halters, one tied tightly to the left-hand side at the front of the crush and the other to the right.

The bull had a deep wound above his right eye, exposing the bone of his skull. This lesion could not be left. After infiltrating the local area with anaesthetic, I decided to try using some *Vicryl,* already swaged with needle attached, to stitch the wound.

As the number of sutures grew and the length of the wound decreased, I became aware I was being watched. Looking up, I could see a crowd of heads peeping over a stone wall nearby. Apparently, there was a caravan site in the adjoining field and word had spread that some free entertainment was on offer. More heads were appearing by the minute, young children given a birds-eye view on the shoulders of their parents.

I hadn't operated in front of a crowd before. Did I place the sutures with perhaps more of a theatrical flourish than usual? Finishing my work, I tidied up, waved to the onlookers and prepared to leave the stage feeling quite pleased with myself. I even considered passing round my tweed cap for donations.

Being saddled with the cautious characteristics of a Capricorn, I made one final check on the wound before departing. To my horror, as the bull sought relief by rubbing his

---

*   *Vicryl [TM] Absorbable synthetic suture manufactured by Ethicon Inc., a subsidiary of Johnson and Johnson.*

head against the bars of the crush, the sutures were progressively coming untied and the wound was reopening. Having failed my audition, I hurriedly replaced the halters before the anaesthetic wore off and used my trusted nylon suture material to re-stitch the wound, placing more throws on my knots than were strictly necessary.

With as much insouciance as I could muster, I acknowledged the dwindling number of gongoozlers who had stayed for the encore and returned to my car feeling I had fluffed my lines. In about ten days, I would have to return to snip out my handiwork. I phoned the rep the next day to deliver my verdict on his suture material. He admitted that he had forgotten to emphasise that many more throws on the knots were required with *Vicryl* than with traditional suture materials.

When veterinary colleagues were away on holiday, locum vets arrived to take their place. Peter, an Irish locum in his fifties, had a relaxed approach to veterinary work. He was a lovely man and excellent company but true to type, he was a heavy smoker and he liked a drink.

He stayed in a local hotel during the week and at weekends visited a lady-friend in Somerset whom he said "did his washing". His stories indicated he had been around the veterinary block, indeed around the world. He was given the use of the spare practice car, an elderly, battered beige Austin 1100 estate.

One Saturday night, I was on duty when I received a call from a police station in the west country.

"Did I know anyone called Peter? He says he is a vet working in Sussex."

I admitted I did. I sensed a note of deflation at the other end of the line. Peter later told me the whole story over a drink.

"Andy, honest to God, I was driving along, minding my own business when the Virgin Mary told me to get out. I stopped the car on the grass verge, yanked the door open and ran away from the car as fast as I could. Looking back, I saw the car was on fire and then it exploded. Holy Mary Mother of God."

He crossed himself again for good measure. Aside from the theatricals and incantations, my interpretation of events was this. It was true when you got in that car, there was an unmistakable whiff of petrol. I think perhaps Peter dropped a fag end which was still alight on the floor of the car. The rest can be laid at the feet of Providence. I heard later that Peter had accepted a job in charge of his beloved horses in the United Arab Emirates in a country where alcoholic drink was forbidden. Possibly he saw this as an opportunity to cap his consumption.

Warm summer evenings were spent with Ev and Mostyn walking along the seafront at Eastbourne, the shore at Pevensey Bay or rambling over the South Downs. Our relationship had survived for nearly five years and during one of our walks above Beachy Head, I asked Ev to marry me.

The following Saturday, in the Hatton Garden district of London, she was choosing her engagement ring. I do remember alluding to a budget. We visited many of the jewellers in the area but the only ring with that elusive wow factor was twice the budget and a bit more. This proved to be a microcosm of our married life. Before we purchased the ring, we went to Welwyn Garden City so I could ask her father's permission for the hand of his daughter in marriage. Bill and Gill seemed delighted, more so after quaffing some excellent champagne.

My new fiancee had endured a Catholic convent education. I was raised in the Anglican faith. I had an inkling this might prove to be a problem and so it was. I agreed to make monthly trips to Hertfordshire on my weekends off. Father Kelly, Ev's local priest, inculcated me in the theology of the Catholic church. To his great credit, he accepted my assurances that our children would be taught the basic principles of all the major religions of the world so that they could choose to be involved as they wished.

The marriage service was to be held in St. Bonaventure's, her local parish church in Welwyn Garden City, and my priest, the Reverend Eric de Lande Jones, would also be invited to officiate. This concession, much appreciated by both of us, was quite liberal for that period.

Shopping trips to London were arranged for Ev and her mother to select a wedding dress. Material was chosen for the bridesmaids' dresses which would be handmade and homemade. Ev's small flat in the sedate environs of Eastbourne, looked like a set on a TV sewing competition, with material scattered about and pins and parts of patterns everywhere.

Having gained more experience in farm work, by the autumn of 1979, I was dispatched to the Ministry of Agriculture's offices in Lewes to be trained as a local veterinary inspector (LVI). On my precious afternoon off, this involved a wide-ranging discussion covering the protocols for carrying out tuberculin tests in cows, obtaining blood samples from heifers for brucellosis testing and how to spot anthrax organisms in stained blood smears under a microscope.

It was all very civilised, with copious amounts of coffee drunk and plenty of time to chew the veterinary fat. But being allowed to write the letters LVI after my signature placed me in an invidious position.

I would arrive on a client's farm at an agreed time to carry out a tuberculin test. The farm provided animals of the correct age groups, the labour and the facilities required. However, I was working on behalf of the government on these occasions and they paid the practice for my services. In fact, I was acting for two different guvnors. In the case of adverse test results, our clients' farm could effectively be locked down with a consequent loss of income. This was an awkward situation as well as a strange juxtaposition. In most other instances, I was expected to act on behalf of my client, in their best interests rather than in mine or that of the practice. Indeed, this is how I would expect a professional person to behave, within certain legal constraints.

Marius, a partner in the practice, came with me to my first TB test. He observed me clip and inject the first seven animals and then left me to it. In this new capacity as an LVI, I found myself starting at six o' clock some mornings, taking blood samples from calves only a few days old, prior to their export to the continent, presumably to be raised for veal. The paperwork was complex. One tiny mistake in the annotation of an ear mark or date of birth could result in the whole consignment of animals being rejected.

Shortly afterwards, the practice agreed a contract with a local meat-processing plant. Arriving at the plant at an unearthly hour of the morning, in my official capacity as an LVI (red meat), I was empowered to break the seal on the rear doors of a refrigerated wagon and supervise the unloading of forty tons of chilled meat.

Within the plant, the large sections of meat were butchered into smaller cuts, repackaged and exported back to mainland Europe. Vets supervising these activities were expected to ensure that agreed protocols were followed, especially those relating to hygiene.

Absolute accuracy in documentation was again required to ensure that the meat in each consignment could be identified at all stages of the process. These meat inspection duties were not especially rewarding from a professional standpoint. Having left the practice in Suffolk to avoid poultry meat inspection work, I found red meat inspection only marginally more bearable.

It is interesting to note that nowadays, training to achieve and maintain LVI status is more intensive and elaborate, with periodic retraining mandatory under government legislation in 2015. With thirty-five years of experience, I found I was expected to pay to undergo this retraining to retain the privilege of performing veterinary work on behalf of the government. I chose not to do so.

Breaking point came one evening. I was scheduled to be on duty and rostered to consult at the main practice until seven o'clock. In mid-afternoon, a call came in for a horse which had been kicked and was now only able to stand on three legs.

Both partners claimed they were busy. One of my colleagues was away during an afternoon off and the other was consulting at the Polegate clinic. I had to complete my list of consultations before hurrying out to visit the injured animal. The patient could not bear weight on a foreleg, having sustained a grossly-unstable fracture of the cannon bone in its lower limb. I put the animal to sleep and returned home distressed. The horse had been left in great pain for several hours and should have been seen much sooner than I was able to do. One of my red lines had been crossed.

I spent a sleepless night weighing up my options. The new small-animal veterinary hospital in Hailsham was nearing completion but was seriously over budget. I would be sad to leave my colleagues but the team seemed liable to break up because of the strains under which we were trying to work. I would miss the Downs and the proximity to the coast, miss some valued clients I had come to know well and compel Ev to move offices yet again.

I resigned with no definite plans and without having another job lined up. I was due to be married in two months and uncertainty at this juncture was extremely unwelcome.

Hailsham Practice 1979

Leicester Practice 1980

Chapter 8

Foxy Lady

Leicester

I moved to Leicester in August 1980. The rushed transfer had not been planned properly and arrangements for our forthcoming marriage had not been finalised. Time was tight.

The main practice was in a detached house in the south of the city and quite limited for space. Routine consultations and simple surgical procedures were also conducted at a branch of practice in the north-west suburbs. I was the sole assistant in a busy mixed practice run by two partners, one a pugnacious Scot, physically strong, competitive and a mad-keen rugby union nut. His partner, slightly older, seemed wearied by the world and its ways. Mrs Statham, short in stature and sparky, was in her fifties and ruled the practice in the manner of a regimental sergeant major. Andrea and Jane were school-leavers who filled the role of unqualified nursing assistants.

Leicester was a vibrant, multicultural city and comfortable with itself. The university enriched city life without trying to dominate it. Traffic flowed freely through a good road network, facilitating travel to the rest of the country. Living in the flat above the main surgery gave me little privacy when off duty but it was certainly handy for the city centre and the shops. I was spoilt for choice with sporting venues, including Filbert Street, where

Leicester City played football, Welford Road, where Leicester Tigers played Rugby Union and Grace Road, where Leicestershire played first-class cricket, all within easy reach.

In those first few weeks, I was given a stark reminder of the gulf in knowledge and technical prowess between the qualified veterinary nursing colleagues I had left behind in Sussex and my new unqualified counterparts in the Midlands.

Ben, a black labrador, had been crunched by a car and the collision had broken his back leg. X-rays showed that the top and bottom sections of his left femur were intact but the main shaft of the bone consisted of several splintered fragments.

The femur is the main weight-bearing bone at the top of the back leg supporting the hip joint. I laboured for a couple of hours to achieve a stable repair using a large stainless-steel bone plate, secured with screws, and cerclage wire to anchor the smaller segments of bone. Fighting fatigue, I took two further x-ray views to satisfy myself that the alignment of the bone was acceptable, if not perfect.

The x-ray plate was laid on the floor rather than on a specially-designed x-ray table, which we used in Sussex, with the injured leg between the x-ray film and the beam.

After the films were exposed, I asked the nurses to return Ben to his kennel whilst I developed the films. Glancing back, I was horrified to see Ben being hauled across the floor towards his kennel by his hind legs, one of which had been the subject of my attention for much of the afternoon.

I knew perfectly well it wasn't their fault. They had the best of intentions but had received little formal training. I could not expect them to have the competency of qualified nurses. It was a lesson I needed to learn.

Fortunately, my repair passed this applied traction test. I was pleased with the alignment and my patient's leg healed very well over the next six weeks. Soon, Ben had some unexpected competition in the healing stakes. Dan, a black and white farm collie, had been run over by a tractor driven by his owner and had come off second best.

Dan's accident occurred the day after Ben's. Dan suffered simple midshaft fractures of his radius and ulna in his right forelimb and of his tibia in his right hind leg. Both these bones are substantial weight-bearing structures. His fractures were immobilised with plaster casts on each of his injured legs.

He was such a resourceful dog that he soon learnt to hop round the kennel area on his two good legs, listing to his left and balancing his body at an angle to the vertical. Both dogs went home the same day. Dan lost out to Ben in the race to regain full use of their injured legs, Ben the clear winner by several weeks.

Dan's full recovery was essential if he was to earn his keep on his master's farm; his mobility needed to be nigh on perfect to keep the sheep flock under control. Eventually, he battled back to full fitness. When I visited the farm, he was never happier than when racing me in my Renault up the farm drive. However, I am sorry to say that the following year, he had another encounter with the farm tractor and this time the accident proved fatal. I missed his limitless joy in running and his pleasure at winning our races.

A nationwide conglomerate owned about ten large dairy farms dotted about the surrounding countryside. Each would require several visits per week to carry out rectal examinations of ten to fifteen animals aimed at maximising the fertility of the cows on these farms. Efficient milk production was paramount. I enjoyed this work and the challenge of raising my veterinary expertise to match the high standard of care lavished on these cows. Our target was that each cow should produce a calf every year. Since her gestation period was two hundred and eighty-one days, there was little time for each cow to recuperate before being mated and becoming pregnant again.

In Leicestershire, considered by some to be the northern most county of southern England and by others to be part of the East Midlands, there were numerous, more modest, family-run mixed farms. Often with characteristic red brick-built farm buildings and low-pitched slate or tiled roofs, these buildings were functional but often poorly-ventilated, causing frequent outbreaks of pneumonia in the young stock they housed. There were noticeably more and larger flocks of sheep.

Several clients ran riding stables populated predominately with hunters and riding ponies but there weren't any racing yards in the practice. I had a whole new lexicon of terms to learn from this farming community. Bullocks were called stirks, their foot infections 'a touch of foul', and ewes were now 'yows'. In the bakery on Saffron Lane, I was referred to as 'me duck', pronounced 'dook'.

I missed the support and camaraderie of my colleagues in Sussex. The team there had been further depleted as other members moved on. In Leicester, the vets seemed to be rushing elsewhere, whether to the branch surgery or to visit outlying farms. It was only at the end of the working day when we adjourned to a nearby pub for a pint of Everards that we could discuss the day's events at length.

As well as adjusting to my new working life in the Midlands, my input was still required in finalising arrangements for our marriage. This was more difficult with my fiancée still living 200 miles away in Eastbourne. She was granted a further transfer to her employer's offices in Leicester to start in October 1980.

I had written my wedding speech on the back of vaccine reminder postcards and each morning, before work, I practised and refined the wording whilst walking Mostyn in the local park. Ev spent her evenings battling the slippery material which she had chosen for the bridesmaids' dresses. Katy, one of the nursing team in Hailsham, was a regular visitor to the flat above the clock shop, as the sew-ins became more frenetic and the pace of stitching frantic. Fittings and adjustments took over the weekends. On my frequent visits south from Leicester, we held several strategy meetings, usually in the Horse and Groom at Rushlake Green.

Ev decided she did not want a posh car to take her to the church but was somehow persuaded by her father. Our marriage service was scheduled for midday. During the short journey to the church, she found she did like travelling in the white Rolls Royce after all and asked the driver to go round the one-way system in Welwyn Garden City again, arriving at the altar in St Bonaventure's church twenty-seven minutes late. Being late for your first date is one thing but being that late for your wedding quite another.

Father Kelly, who had known Ev since she was a child, nearly referred to the bride by her childhood nickname during the exchange of vows. The Rev Jones, my local rector, brought some welcome familiarity to the ceremony for me and my family. We drove to our reception in my Vauxhall Victor, polished for the occasion and resplendent in white ribbons. One of my fondest memories of that afternoon is of both sets of grandparents seated around a table in a bay window, talking avidly, exchanging family truths and probably some myths as well. Morrie and Sheila Eves from the White Hart at Westleton acted as unofficial MCs and ensured everyone always had a drink.

Driving westward down the M4 through heavy rain, we arrived at the Swan Hotel at Goring for our wedding night, where our room had a balcony with a view of the weir and the lock on the Thames. The following morning, we travelled on to north Devon, to the Doone Valley, to spend our first week as a married couple. We were blessed with glorious weather, walking for miles through unspoilt countryside. Hoping for a quiet time and some refreshments, we walked to Watersmeet, at the confluence of the East Lyn River and Hoar Oak Water, situated in a steeply-wooded gorge. Our intimate interlude was rudely interrupted by the arrival of the Territorial Army by zip wire across the gorge, accompanied by a particularly masculine commentary, predictably delivered at high volume.

We headed north to the Lake District for our second week, where we were cursed with awful weather. I am looking at a photograph of Ev on top of Helvellyn, dressed in a new orange cagoule, snow blowing horizontally across the bleak landscape. Sitting in the residents' lounge in the evening, the receptionist put her head round the door and said there was a phone call for Mrs Bartholomew. Nobody moved.

In the early weeks of our marriage, we lived in my bachelor flat above the surgery. The issue of privacy prompted us to buy our first house, Cardless Cottage, described by the estate agent as "a very attractive, nicely-modernised semi-detached cottage" built at the turn of the century in Ashby Magna.

Moving early in 1981 to a small unspoilt village of three hundred souls about eight miles south of the practice was an enormous change. Surrounded by countryside, mostly agricultural farmland, and with a pub at the end of the street, we settled into our new home quickly and happily.

For Mostyn, with so many walks on his doorstep, the location was ideal. We walked past a field of cattle most mornings and not having seen many of these creatures at such close quarters in his recent past, it was a struggle to prevent him expressing his views at the top of his voice at every opportunity.

Eventually, tired of his disobedience, we held a free and frank exchange of views at eye level in the gateway to the field, after which he was more inclined to keep his thoughts to himself.

Driving to Leicester through the villages of Willoughby Waterleys and Countesthorpe was a thoroughly enjoyable prelude to the day's work. These early months of our married life were full of discoveries, including how little we knew about gardening. We had an extensive rear garden on three levels rising towards meadows. The soil was marvellously light, deep brown in colour and exceedingly fertile. Almost anything we planted grew, together with a lot of vegetation which we hadn't sown. We delighted in the taste of our first home-grown vegetables.

Then a pestilence descended on the canine population of Britain afflicting dogs in my patch. An epidemic of canine parvovirus wreaked havoc. We began to see cases, predominately young dogs and particularly puppies, affected by the most virulent attacks of diarrhoea.

In the early stages, the cause was unknown. We admitted these dogs and gave them supportive treatment of intravenous fluid therapy, pain relief and antibiotics. Some patients recovered but a distressing number succumbed, often within a few hours of first showing symptoms.

The number of cases we were seeing escalated rapidly. I felt a degree of hopelessness in the face of such an onslaught; the kennel area was full of animals on drips, every square foot of floor space occupied. One unforgettable characteristic of the disease was the overpowering and nauseating smell of bloody faeces passed in prodigious quantities. Sometimes, this odour could be detected in patients before other symptoms developed.

No amount of ventilation alleviated the vile stench. It seemed the more aggressive the fluid therapy that was given, the better the chances of recovery in our patients. However, it was tricky getting the balance right between giving enough fluids to counterbalance the excessive losses from diarrhoea and overloading the patient's heart and circulatory system, with fluid seeping out into the patients lungs causing death by iatrogenic 'drowning'.

We were being overwhelmed, struggling to cope with the influx of new patients and the speed with which their clinical condition deteriorated. Having worked hard all day, nights on duty were an additional burden which, at times, seemed too much to bear.

The need to motivate oneself to return to the surgery at frequent intervals during the night to check on the inpatients and replenish their drips whilst being seriously deprived of sleep led to some frayed tempers.

Help arrived in the shape of Trevor Whitbread. Similar in age to myself, unflappable and extremely competent, we quickly developed a system based on coordinated teamwork, operating as efficiently as was humanly possible with the resources at our disposal to deliver care to these sick dogs. We were working flat out with little opportunity for rest and recuperation.

Scientists had identified the infectious agent as a virus, similar in structure to the feline panleucopoenia virus, the cause of fatal disease in cats. There was a vaccine for the feline virus but it was licensed only for use in that species.

Using this vaccine, a crash canine vaccination programme began on an unprecedented scale. The initial challenge was to obtain sufficient quantities of vaccine and to free up staff time to administer doses to susceptible dogs. Mostyn had his dose and I did my best to protect him. Returning from work, before entering our house, I discarded all my work clothes in our front lobby, before going upstairs to shower.

Despite these precautions, one evening I arrived home and smelt the smell. Ev had taken the afternoon off work and come home as Mostyn seemed off colour. And he was. There was simply no room at the practice for him, so I had to treat him at home with Ev acting as nurse. It seemed likely I had inadvertently infected my own dog, since the viral challenge in the countryside of Leicestershire was probably low. He was three years old and I think that gave him some resistance to the worst excesses of the disease.

He responded to our ministrations and slowly regained his strength but it was a close call. For weeks afterwards, the dreadful smell lingered throughout the house, despite restricting the dog to our kitchen and utility room with its tiled floor.

Gradually, the eye of the infectious storm passed and practice life began to return to some semblance of normality. This was my first but unfortunately not my last encounter with virulent contagious disease affecting the animal population of Britain. The personal battles that I had fought, particularly at university, stood me in good stead and gave me the inner strength needed to withstand this intense and prolonged period of pressure at work and at home.

This experience increased my self-reliance in dealing with subsequent unforeseen incidents and reversals throughout my career. My adolescent rose-tinted image of a vet's life had been changed at university and was redefined again now. Working in general practice for a period had altered my approach to professional life, becoming less idealistic and more pragmatic. I had gained a life-long friend in Trevor. Whenever we meet at professional gatherings, we smile wryly at the memory of the cataclysmic catastrophe which brought us together and which we negotiated, rescuing a situation which might easily have descended into complete chaos.

Pressure in one's working life and in one's private life can affect each of us in different ways. Nowadays, professional support is available to vets who have experienced mental anguish caused by stressful situations. In 1981, you had to deal with such events yourself. The alternative was to crumble and possibly walk away from the profession.

I saw the effects that chronic stress can have on a vet and I struggled to decide what I should or should not do. One of the partners had separated from his wife with whom he had a young son. As well as his young family, he had a busy city practice to oversee as senior partner. These demands proved too much to bear and he sought solace with alcohol.

His private life was no concern of mine but his professional standards were being affected and that did concern me. On one occasion, on a night off, Andrea, Jane, Ev and I had been to the gloriously-named Leicester Palais to relax and dance.

I had enjoyed a few drinks and was feeling mellow. We were still living above the practice and at midnight, we found ourselves standing in the lobby, contemplating the advisability of a nightcap.

We heard scratching sounds on the outside of the front door. The senior partner was on duty and had been called in to see a case as an emergency. He was so far under the influence, he could not find the door lock, let alone insert his key. I opened the door and he practically fell inside.

Sobering up momentarily, he queried why were we all at work so early? He was in no fit state to do much except go to bed. We called a taxi to take him home and I dealt with the case. But what if I had not been there? As a youngster at school, it was considered extremely bad form to snitch and report poor behaviour to the authorities. I talked about the incident to his partner and I don't doubt serious conversations took place between the two of them, but outwardly, nothing seemed to change.

I found myself trying surreptitiously to adopt some of his small-animal cases but I was only able to do this in certain instances. At a small-animal veterinary conference, I witnessed one of the most poignant sights in my whole career. I went to the conference to learn about the latest scientific advances and innovations. During the Saturday morning session, I noticed my colleague sitting on a bar stool with his young son nearby. On my way to various lectures, I passed the bar several times throughout the day. By mid-afternoon, he was in such a state, he slipped off the bar stool onto the floor in front of his son. What effect did this behaviour have on his son? It was so sad that an intelligent, professional man could be reduced to such a level and in full view of his peers.

For employees who raise uncomfortable issues with their superiors, reprisals often follow. So it was that I was summoned to the office to be told I was using too much catgut suture material when neutering my bitches. I liked to wrap the suture material around my fingers so that I could maintain a good grip, minimising any chance of slippage when tying the ligatures that prevented internal bleeding after the uterus and ovaries had been sectioned and removed.

Annoyed by such pettiness, I replied, "At least all of my bitch speys walk out of the surgery with their owners at the end of the day, alive and well."

My professional confidence was about to take another blow. I had been called in on night duty to the aid of a whelping dachshund bitch. The owner was only interested in having a caesarean section performed and did not wish me to try to deliver the pups by natural means.

The owner returned home. Administering a general anaesthetic with assistance, I carried out her wishes, delivering six live pups. The bitch recovered well from her ordeal and having checked over the puppies, the dam and her litter were discharged to the owner, who seemed perfectly satisfied.

A month or so later, a letter arrived on Royal College of Veterinary Surgeons headed notepaper, something that caused trepidation in its unfortunate recipient. The owner had complained to the college directly rather than to the partners, claiming I had cut the head of one of her puppies.

Naturally, in the opinion of the owner, this particular puppy would have been a winner in the show ring but was now disfigured for life. Fortunately, the pups had been checked before discharge and no such injury had been noted. I constructed a reply, relating the facts as I knew them and enclosed a supporting letter from my colleague who assisted me during that night.

After more correspondence, I learnt with relief that the case had been closed and I was spared the ignominy of being subjected to a disciplinary hearing by my peers but it was still a long and drawn-out process.

Even after this length of time, I remember clearly how dispiriting such an encounter with our regulator can be to a young veterinary surgeon. At such low points, negative thoughts begin to surface. You begin to think you are the worst surgeon in world, unfit to carry out the simplest of tasks.

The guidance I received from advisors representing the practice's professional indemnity insurance company was invaluable. What would the outcome have been had I not had their advice and support?

Inevitably, one's approach to the more complex clinical cases changes and ones mindset becomes increasingly defensive. I started to use more words to qualify my statements and actions. The words 'might', possibly' and 'maybe' replaced 'will' and 'won't'.

Spurious claims for professional negligence, made in many instances for financial gain, can result in talented young vets leaving the profession to avoid being subjected to further, often unfounded, brickbats. A balance must be struck between protecting the public from negligent or incompetent vets and protecting vets from the unreasonable expectations of some of their clients. After all, someone must take responsibility for conducting a caesarean section and it must be accepted that attendant risks go with every act of veterinary surgery. I'm not sure the public does always get what it wants.

We were settled in Ashby Magna. I attended the Easter service in St Mary's parish church, built in the thirteenth century. It was so cold, the vicar wore fingerless mittens whilst administering the holy sacrament. Accepted as part of the local community, I was asked to judge a novelty class at the local pet show. I expected it to be a bit of fun, a small contribution from me to the village in which I lived.

I was allocated the class entitled 'the pet which looks most like its owner'. Ashby Magna is a small village but dog breeders had travelled from distant Derbyshire with their young dogs, hoping to give these young and boisterous canines experience in the show ring.

I awarded first prize to the vicar's son because he showed good knowledge of the care needed by his pet guinea pig. Derbyshire's dog breeders were incensed. I was subjected to intense animosity and some verbal abuse from owners who felt their worthy entrants had been snubbed. The canine competitors were having a great time and they didn't seem to mind much. As soon as I could, I escaped to the sanctuary of my garden and vowed never to judge a pet show again.

The summer of 1981 was not all sweetness and light in the city of Leicester, which experienced riots protesting against monetarism and rising unemployment. John, our latest amiable but unqualified animal assistant, harboured aspirations to become a vet. He was also a special constable. It became commonplace for him to be called out at short notice to provide the local police force with reinforcements. After a particularly heavy night out, I found him in the operating theatre, breathing deeply via a facemask to clear a sore head, a head which soon felt very light and fluffy from the effects of inhaling pure oxygen. These symptoms quickly resolved when I turned the gas off.

I played cricket for a local side, visiting some pretty grounds in the surrounding villages, enjoying both the local brews and the social side of the game. I was carrying out consultations during the Headingley Test that year when the match situation became extremely tense. I was popping out between appointments to hear the updated score on the radio. Botham scored a memorable 149 not out and the Australians needed 130 for victory. Odds of 500:1 were quoted by bookies for an English victory. The Australians were bowled out for 111, losing by 18 runs, with Bob Willis bowling like a man possessed, taking eight wickets.

On duty again over new year, about two o clock on the first of January, I took a phone call from a man in Braunstone who said his dog was very poorly and wouldn't get up. He insisted he wanted a visit and obeying the maxim that you must attend, I went.

I had great difficulty in rousing anyone. After a good deal of time hammering on the front door, a lady in her fifties grabbed her dressing gown and let me in. She looked the worse for wear, her expression suggesting mounting fury. She said nothing but pointed in the direction of the front room. There I found my client, apparently out for the count, slumped on the settee, fast asleep and snoring.

I examined his dog, the only member of the household who seemed pleased to see me. I felt my patient was probably healthy enough but decided to take the dog back to the surgery to protect him from his household. I wondered if the owner had simply tripped over his own dog on his return from the night's festivities. A couple of days later, the owner came to the surgery, collected his dog and paid his account. There's now't as strange as folk.

On the second of April 1982, I drove down to London to attend my fourth veterinary congress in Hammersmith. As I parked under the famous flyover, I heard on the radio that General Galtieri's Argentina had invaded the Falkland Islands. War involving Britain in my lifetime was something I hadn't thought possible. Thus far, I had been fortunate to be free to make my own life choices and not to have my young life blighted by fighting and conflict, in sharp contrast with the lives of my parents and grandparents. What would happen now?

I was relieved the conflict ended quickly in June without nationwide call-ups or conscription. However, clouds were gathering and obscuring my career path in the city of Leicester.

I had replaced a popular assistant vet called Steven. The impression I gained was that he had been something of a blue-eyed boy in the opinion of the partners and especially Mrs Statham. It was clear I could never live up to expectations as his replacement. Having laboured under this burden during my tenure, I learnt that Steven was returning to the practice and joining the partnership. My only sensible option was to move on, as I had no wish to compete in an exercise I was bound to lose.

My departure was hastened by a phone call from Neil Craven, my friend from university. While I was on holiday in Cornwall, he was working as a locum in Oxford and his practice was looking for a veterinary assistant with a view to partnership.

I called in on our way back to the Midlands on a sunny Sunday afternoon. Mr Sheriffs, in his seventies, was the senior partner. Mr Kyle, in his forties, conducted my interview in a T-shirt, shorts and sandals.

The partners were looking for someone to build up the small-animal side of the practice business. To leave our home in Ashby Magna would be an unwelcome wrench and I would be forcing Ev to move to yet another branch of the firm for which she worked. But the opportunity of working in such an historic city, the possibility of a veterinary partnership and Steven's return to the Leicester practice were all factors which persuaded me to accept the job offer. We were on the move to Oxford.

Chapter 9

Spiralling Dreams

On my father's sixtieth birthday, I left my wife and our home in Leicestershire and travelled south to start work in my fourth veterinary practice. Iffley Road is part of the old Oxford to Henley Road. Number 35 is in an area of varied architectural heritage, south of Magdalen Bridge and the Plain roundabout, where three major roads leading to the city centre, Headington Road, Cowley Road and Iffley Road forming the trivium.

First impressions of working in this late Victorian semi-detached house were stairs, lots of them. The building comprised four floors, though only the basement and the first floor were occupied by the veterinary practice. The upper two floors were separate furnished flats providing accommodation for members of staff. I was allocated the lower and larger of the two flats, which shared the front door and entrance hall with the practice.

Clients climbed seven stone steps to the front door and entrance hall, with two sash windows providing plenty of natural light. To the left was a spacious front room looking out on Iffley Road, with Magdalen School opposite and some woodland scrub separated by the entrance to a university sports ground.

This room served as a waiting room with beige-patterned lino and an assortment of post-war wooden dining chairs whose seats had suffered from the weight of numerous occupants.

Opposite the waiting room was a small reception area with a two-tiered cream-coloured home-made counter on which sat a matching wooden drawer containing small-animal case record cards, A4 diaries served as a visit book and message book. Reception was the domain of the formidable Ann Higgs, surveying visitors over her half-moon, gold-rimmed glasses.

The consulting room was at the far end of the entrance hall with a window facing out onto the back garden. Its position helped me form an initial assessment of my clients. Most parked behind the property, walking up the path towards the side gate leading to the front steps. As they did so, I noted the owner's body language and the natural gait of their canine pets whilst pockets were patted for car keys and latterly, mobile phones. I gained a valuable insight into the mood of my clients before they arrived at reception, let alone entered my 'office'.

The remaining room at the opposite end of the entrance hall also faced the back garden. Serving then as an operating theatre, there were some home-made recovery cages either side of a chimney breast with a boarded-up fireplace.

I noticed a plastic canister, part of the anaesthetic circuit designed as an airtight container for soda lime, was badly split and had been repaired ineffectually with clear adhesive tape.

The anaesthetic gases could escape under pressure through the cracks in the cover into the atmosphere, representing a serious health risk to those in the room. I was amazed the nurses didn't fall asleep during an operation. This had to be replaced as a matter of urgency. Subsequently, I learnt the anaesthetic trolley we used had been dropped by parachute during the war, although exactly which war wasn't entirely clear.

There were two flights of stairs down to the basement and on the right was formerly a dining room, its walls still adorned with a waist-high dark-wood wainscot. Animals ate now in home-made kennels and cat cages, secured with galvanised heavy-duty wire-mesh doors.

A repurposed large kitchen table, covered with grey-flecked linoleum, served as an x-ray table, the legs struggling under the weight of the obligatory lead lining. Across the corridor was an office equipped with army surplus filing cabinets and a small antique writing desk covered with a thin green leather inlaid top, raised on house bricks for the comfort of Phyllis Timbs, our tallish elderly bookkeeper. The other rooms were used for storage of drugs and equipment.

The practice had moved from Cowley Place, a cul-de-sac at the foot of Magdalen Bridge, to Iffley Road in the 1930s. Number 35 had to accommodate a great deal of veterinary paraphernalia and its Victorian heritage was a challenge. Situated in a recently-designated conservation area, the scope for lawful expansion with additional building works had been curtailed.

When I arrived, the practice was a mixed, mainly large–animal practice. The partners, Jimmy Sheriffs and Russell Kyle, did the bulk of the visits. My remit specifically was to expand the small-animal side of the business. An all-rounder with a small-animal bias matched the partners' current requirements. After completing the few consultations and operations required, the rest of my day was filled with a round of visits.

As in Sussex, the vets were assisted by Royal Animal Nursing Auxiliaries (RANAs), Liz and Lorraine. What a delight to have two qualified nurses on hand to tend the in-patients in a professional manner and assist in surgical procedures.

Liz was short in stature but with a dominant personality and a manner reminiscent of a pocket battleship going into action. She knew intuitively what was needed; I noticed when she wasn't there. Lorraine was taller, thinner in the face and with her trademark ponytail and her matter-of-fact approach, they complimented each other perfectly. Things got done in an efficient and timely manner. Both nurses shared a soft spot for Jimmy; for him nothing was too much trouble.

So it was, one gloomy Monday morning in November, I donned a traditional knee-length white clinician's coat, more suited to a medical museum than a modern clinic, and began to consult.

Oxford had a different demographic to Leicester and the demarcation between town and gown remained definite and distinct. As I tried to get to grips with the way things were done here, a young woman in her twenties came into my consulting room. She was wearing a large circular badge bearing the legend 'The Future Is Female'. Deference towards professionals was no longer *de rigueur* in Oxford. Yet the sentiment expressed

Front of 35 Iffley Road. 1989

Rear of Iffley Road 1989

Jimmy Mixing Potions 1984

Consult Room 1984

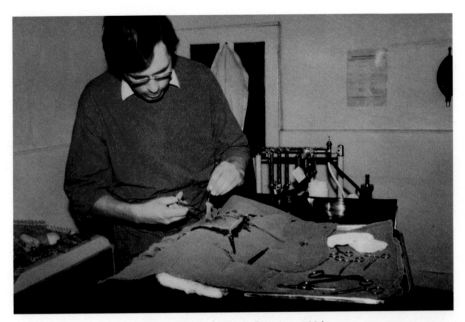

AB. operating theatre in Basement 1984

Cattery Kennels in Basement 1984

by the badge proved prophetic at several levels. In 1982, Britain had a government led by its first female prime minister in Mrs Thatcher and there were increasing numbers of women on the undergraduate veterinary courses. A greater acceptance of women in the profession has been one of the landmark changes I have appreciated during my career.

So-called exotic pets were more in evidence in Oxford, especially rabbits, guinea pigs and other varieties of small furry animals. Lindsay, a glamorous woman in her thirties was another early visitor who came to consult me. With long blonde hair. slim, well-dressed with a dash of French chic, confident and well-spoken, she had brought her hamster for me to examine. The small rodent was nestling in her cleavage, keeping warm. I could distinguish the bulge, formed by the animal under her dress, moving occasionally to a more comfortable position. She had thirteen of these small creatures at her cottage and queried,

"How long do hamsters live for?"

"About twenty-two to twenty-four months," I replied.

Tossing her hair and raising her chin defiantly, she said, "Mine will live much longer than that!"

The case history suggested this animal might be suffering from wet tail, a form of chronic diarrhoea. Having exhausted all other polite avenues of conversation, I was reduced to stating the obvious.

"If you want me to examine your pet, *you* need to retrieve it and hold it for me on the examination table."

I treated the animal with an antibiotic injection but gained the impression I had fallen short of the client's expectations in some way. Regrettably, the passage of time proved my estimate of a hamster's lifespan was accurate as the numbers in her horde dwindled. When visiting her home to tend another ailing member, I found they ranged freely as equals in her household. She extricated that day's patient from between the webbing of the sofa.

Gradually, I became familiar with the local geography and discovered the quickest, if not the shortest, routes to various outlying farms and which roads were impassable in winter and when the numerous local water meadows flooded.

The farmers seemed surprised that the young vet who had joined the practice could calve a cow, disbud a calf, treat a lame horse and neuter the farm cat.

These farmers worshipped Jimmy Sheriffs, who was then seventy-six. I never tired of hearing about his achievements, which became ever more fantastic. He qualified in 1929 in the first cohort of graduates from the Royal Veterinary College. Definitely old school, he was the main reason I came to Oxford.

It was a privilege to work with a man who cared so little about money but so much about the patients under his care. The science of veterinary medicine had made enormous progress since he qualified but this ex-army captain personified the art of veterinary science. I owe him a debt of gratitude for the opportunity to absorb some of this art.

He had come to the practice in 1946 following service in the Royal Army Service Corps during the Second World War. A veteran of D-Day, he had risen to the rank of temporary major but was referred to by his farming fan base as 'captain'.

Silver-haired, softly spoken, quite short in stature but retaining great strength, especially in his forearms, he retained a mischievous glint in his eyes, enhanced by his gold-rimmed spectacles. The ravages of repeated attacks of brucellosis were beginning to take their toll and he was becoming increasingly arthritic, especially his hands.

One afternoon, a call came in to attend an old Charolais cow which had prolapsed her uterus after calving. I was expecting to do the visit. Having collected everything I needed, belatedly I realised that Jimmy had already left for the farm. Such a case, where the sizeable slippery soggy uterus of a mature continental-breed beef cow has been pushed out of her body, represented hard physical labour at the best of times. Most men of Jimmy's age would have delegated the job to the younger man but that was not Jimmy's way.

Having concluded the business of the day, I was not content to leave until I knew he had returned safely. Sitting in the basement office mindlessly doing routine paperwork, eventually I recognised his headlights as he pulled into the back garden. I helped him unload his car; he was exhausted but he had treated the case successfully through a combination of skill, willpower, strength and stubbornness, all estimable qualities.

Perhaps unsurprisingly, the clinical approach of vets and the treatment protocols they apply to their cases largely reflects the era in which they studied as undergraduates. Despite the myriad of CPD courses on offer in today's market, I think this remains the case.

Jimmy would augment his treatment regime for a cow which wasn't eating by encouraging the animal to eat fresh ivy leaves, which he would collect from the hedgerows around the farm. He had a revered recipe book, listing the amounts and constituents of lotions and potions which he concocted downstairs in the dispensary with a mortar and pestle, using ingredients which are now, for the most part, of strictly historical interest.

Watching him exercising these skills is a fond memory of this extraordinary man. Many a farmer would call to collect treatment for their animals and ask for "a bottle of Mr Sheriff's liniment" which they might have used to treat their own aches and pains.

As I settled into the practice routine, I hoped that one day the farmers might be pleased to recount some of my achievements to the younger vets who came to work in the practice. I was also realistic enough to realise the time would come when folk would refer to me and my veterinary methods as old-fashioned and out of date. With luck, I might be able to retire before this came to pass.

Russell Kyle was in his mid-forties and lived in Kidlington which, he liked to remind me, was the largest village in England. He had set up a branch of the practice on part of the ground floor of his home, with a small waiting room and a consultation room which doubled as an operating theatre.

He held small-animal consultations on weekdays and Saturday mornings, with a few simple surgical procedures conducted there on Wednesday mornings as required. Broad-shouldered, thinning dark hair, idiosyncratic, he was apt to carry his various papers and a diary in a wooden seed tray on the upturned palm of his right hand, in the style of a French waiter. He wore glasses whose tinted lens darkened markedly according to the prevailing light, making him even more inscrutable.

He struck me as more suited to a solo modus operandi than being a member of a team. In his house, he had a black and white poster of a rhinoceros charging head-on at the camera with the caption 'I have my faults but being wrong is not one of them'. We were never certain we would see him at Iffley Road on any particular day.

Before I could live in the flat, I had to clear out more than sixty empty bottles, mostly wine and spirits, which had been left by my predecessor. The kitchen worktops were covered with them. I learnt from the nurses that, when operating one warm day, things were going badly in the theatre and in a rage, he hurled a scalpel out of the open window, nearly hitting one of the nurses.

It was an unwelcome change to my lifestyle moving from our home in a quiet village in Leicestershire to living alone again for much of the week above the practice on a busy city thoroughfare. I set to and cleaned the flat thoroughly, re-arranged the furniture and made it as comfortable as possible.

An early patient who shared my bathroom for a while was a young kitten whom the owners had found impossible to train to use the litter tray. Nowadays, younger vets would probably refer the owners to a self-help teaching video on the internet.

Relying solely on some practical common sense and patience, over a period of weeks, I persuaded the kitten to adopt a more socially acceptable pattern of behaviour. In return, I enjoyed some company in the evenings. She eventually returned home to the owner with her problem apparently resolved.

A few weeks later, the owner was in contact again. It was six o'clock on a Sunday evening and the kitten was unwell. In this instance, the cause of her illness was iatrogenic. The kitten had urinated inappropriately in the house again, whereupon the owner, a GP, had tried unsuccessfully to put the kitten to sleep using an overdose of insulin.

Such behaviour was scandalous. The kitten was brought to the surgery and ownership signed over to me on the understanding that she would be rehomed if my treatment proved successful.

The comatose creature was put on an intravenous glucose infusion and I popped down periodically to the cattery over next few hours to check on her progress. Happily, she made a full recovery and was rehomed to a family living in Headington where she would be the only cat in the household. I was sorry not to see the kitten again as a patient. I would have enjoyed watching her develop confidence in her new home.

I deliberated over whether to report this disgraceful conduct and decided against it because, in my view, confidentiality in terms of what transpires in the consulting room remained paramount. If owners cannot trust that confidentiality being preserved, they may not seek treatment and their pet could suffer a lingering death.

Another Saturday evening on duty and my wife had come down from Ashby Magna to see me. I went downstairs to let her in. On the doorstep, we found a tatty cardboard box containing six new-born kittens. They might have remained undiscovered until Monday morning with no bedding, not even some clean newspaper.

Why would anyone behave in this way? Oxford was well served by animal charities, easy to approach and readily accessible. They were willing to accept such kittens with little or no notice and at no charge, their aim being to nurture and ultimately to rehome them. We fed a specialised warm feline milk substitute preparation by dropper bottle to these kittens and put them under a heat lamp in a cage with some suitable bedding. The nurses were always delighted to be given the chance to nurse neonates. The difficulty was saying goodbye when the kittens were passed on to foster carers.

It was an awkward time for Ev and I and of course, for our dog, spending short amounts of time together and then having to go our separate ways on Sunday evenings. I travelled back to Ashby Magna for my free weekends but keeping in touch with friends and family was especially difficult with so little time to call our own.

Spending Saturday back at our house, we set off to visit John and Della. John had run a large commercial pig unit near Halesworth (see chapter 6) before moving up near Market Harborough to run an even larger enterprise. His pigs were fed a variety of foods, including wafers and broken biscuits rejected by a local manufacturer.

We pulled up outside John's cottage alongside a recent delivery, deposited by tipper truck beside the drive. We let Mostyn out of the back of the car and his gaze met the mountain of biscuits. The look on his face was magical. He looked at me, then at the biscuits, then at me, waiting for his instructions. We let him eat a few morsels before calling him off and ringing the doorbell.

After several months of this peripatetic existence, it was time for Ev and I to have a serious chat about our future. We had some difficult decisions to make. Would I stay in Oxford, dubbed the 'home of lost causes' by Matthew Arnold, and if so, would I become a partner in this practice which I thought was slightly shabby but had enormous potential? Should we sell our house in Ashby Magna and cut our ties with lovely Leicestershire?

Chapter 10

Good Times Bad Times

I was pleased to accept the favourable terms which were offered. Jimmy, Russell and I became business partners on the first of August 1983. Sheriffs and Kyle became Sheriffs Kyle and Bartholomew. My parents shared my pleasure in the brass plate with my name on it, mounted on the wall of number 35 beside the front path. From the family's perspective, it had been a long journey beginning in the summer of 1969 with discussions about subjects I might study for O levels.

We finally sold our house in Ashby Magna. Ev and Mostyn moved into my furnished flat above the surgery. As space was limited, most of our possessions were stored in the top flat, which was unoccupied at the time. Mostyn, I hoped, would accompany me on my daily rounds.

Cyril Sellar, in his seventies, worn tweed cap on his head, ran a small dairy farm in the quiet hamlet of Denton, eight miles south of Oxford. He lived in a modern bungalow with an extensive vegetable garden at the back, through which he walked each day passing through a small wicket gate which demarcated his home from his workplace. The farm buildings were of much older vintage than his bungalow. Cyril called his cows in by name to be milked standing abreast in the byre. These family traditions were passed down from generation to generation, both in the human context to his son Graham and through the ancestry of the herd, with Ethel 4 and Daisy 2 carrying the current responsibilities for milk production, a livelihood which was disappearing from this part of Oxfordshire. He telephoned me early one morning.

"Cyril Sellar here. I've a cow calving that needs help. Will you come?"

With minimal time pressure, it seemed an ideal opportunity to take Mostyn with me. On arrival, I gathered my gear together and went off to see my patient, leaving the dog in the car with a window partially open. Mostyn howled, his mournful wail echoing round the hillside enclosing the farm, a lament which should not be heard from a vet's pet. His early morning solo must have been particularly popular with those living in this peaceful setting.

I tied him up outside the car but that was no better; the timbre of the wail simply growing more plaintive. Eventually, I secured him to a red Massey Ferguson tractor, just out of sight of my patient. Working in a loosebox, Mostyn could hear my voice and be reassured I was not far away. The calving required much less effort than the management of my dog, with just the minimum of traction needed to deliver a fine healthy Friesian calf. This visit marked the end of my attempts to mould Mostyn into a suitable companion for a farm vet.

Living together once more as a young married couple, Ev and I were able to enjoy the amenities of the city which were on our doorstep: a variety of musical and theatrical events updated on a weekly and sometimes a daily basis, and shops selling a wide range of goods and services. However, living above the surgery in Iffley Road was not a long-term option. We began house-hunting, discovering that house prices in Oxford were almost double those of similar properties in the East Midlands. Indeed, having recently bought into the practice to become a partner, suitable properties in Oxford were outside our price range.

Meanwhile, my caseload was becoming more varied. In the spring of 1984, a small male tortoise was brought in. Having spent the winter in a cardboard box in a damp shed with only some mouldy straw for bedding, he emerged from hibernation but showed no interest in food. He was weak, underweight at just under five hundred grams and was blowing clear mucus bubbles from each nostril. Reaching a diagnosis of post-hibernation anorexia complicated by respiratory disease was straightforward enough.

The owner wasn't prepared to pay for treatment or the prolonged nursing which would be required so I suggested ownership of the tortoise was signed over to me. Environmental factors play a pivotal part in the health of a cold-blooded animal in a temperate climate. We placed him in a cage under a heat lamp, treated him with antibiotic and vitamin injections and fed him daily meals of liquidised fruit and vegetables by stomach tube. When the sun shone, he soaked up the rays on the back lawn of Iffley Road, confined beneath an upturned wire mesh cage. As his appetite gradually returned, we noticed a particular penchant for strawberries. Reflecting the political times in which we were living, we called him Mr T.

He enjoyed some chelonian company when Alex, a huge tortoise from one of the colleges, was admitted as an inpatient. She also enjoyed sunning herself in the back garden. Whenever given the opportunity, Mr T, now fully recovered, would make a beeline for her, stomping manfully across the grass before attempting to mount her. Mr T's shell measured twelve centimetres in diameter whereas Alex's was thirty times the size. Mr T made several valiant attempts to claim his queen but invariably ended up lying on his back, staring at the sky and contemplating another failure. It was good to know this young male's fancy had lightly turned once more to thoughts of love.

The expansion of the small-animal side of the practice was as rewarding as it was swift. Several factors contributed to this growth, including low prices for consultations and preventative vaccinations, a fresh face with youthful enthusiasm and a practice with renewed purpose.

When I joined, small-animal consultations were carried out on an open first come, first served basis. Four consultations in the morning and six in the evening was a typical weekday workload. By the summer of 1984, during evening surgery, clients were queuing down the front path to get into the waiting room to wait for their turn. Twenty-seven cases were seen during an evening session, scheduled to last an hour and finish at six o'clock.

Mr Sheriffs commandeered the operating theatre to see selected members of his fan club from the queue, which helped to ease client congestion. Nevertheless, some clients were experiencing lengthy delays and I was being swamped. I relished the free-and-easy, come-as-you-please atmosphere of the open surgery system but things were getting out of hand. I floated the idea of an appointment system to my colleagues, a suggestion they were happy to support.

Under the new system, clients who turned up without an appointment were still seen when we could fit them in. However, if clients had an appointment at a fixed time, they *expected* to be seen at that time or soon after, putting extra pressure on the consulting vet. My approach was to allow each client and each case the time which was required.

It happened from time to time that what was scheduled as a routine vaccination turned into a protracted discussion about a serious disease identified during the health check. Most clients were only too happy to accept my verbal apology for keeping them waiting, realising it might be their turn to benefit from such flexibility in future.

Alas, a minority were programmed to complain. When an appointment surgery was flowing smoothly, I expected one or two clients to be waiting their turn. When running behind schedule, I found it stressful to hear the noise levels rise as pets and their owners became fractious in an increasingly-overcrowded waiting room. Empathetic nurses, tuned in to my stress levels, soon realised that a temporary solution to the problem was to bring more tea.

Further changes at Iffley Road involved moving the operating theatre downstairs, with the office moving in the opposite direction. It was so much easier and safer to carry a comatose patient back to their cage across a narrow hallway than down two flights of stairs. Phyllis Timbs retired and Hazel Benson, a close friend of Liz, came to run our accounts department on a part-time basis. Hazel was passionate about everything equine and dealt with our debtors in the same way as breaking in a recalcitrant yearling.

The development of the practice and its improved financial performance afforded the partners a degree of wriggle room. Many of our farming clients lived in the villages surrounding Wheatley, about nine miles east of Oxford. If one of us were not passing their farm on our daily rounds, the farmers had to come into Oxford to collect drugs and sundry items. It seemed sensible to have a branch surgery in Wheatley where consultations could be carried out and drugs collected by farmers who lived locally? Work to extend the M40 motorway from Great Milton to Birmingham was underway and Wheatley seemed likely to expand as a satellite settlement along this commuting corridor.

The three partners met in Wheatley to view a bungalow which was being used as a bathroom sales outlet. Its extensive forecourt would solve any parking problems. It seemed ideally suited for our purpose but we could not reach agreement amongst ourselves so the search for suitable premises continued.

Three months later, we stood in the same bungalow and agreed it fulfilled our requirements perfectly. We purchased the building in the summer of 1984, running it as a lock-up branch surgery premises open for an hour at lunchtime and again in the evening by appointment. Clients living in Wheatley and the surrounding villages embraced the new venture wholeheartedly, delighted to avoid further trips into Oxford.

A broader range of clinical cases inevitably meant I was dealing with new conditions I had not previously encountered. Another of Liz's friends, who bred corgis, arrived one morning at Iffley Road. She was distraught, having found her prized stud dog dead in his kennel. He was a fine example of the breed and appeared to be in excellent health before his untimely demise.

I agreed to carry out a post-mortem examination. I found half a dozen triangular-shaped slivers of a semi-rigid light-coloured material in his stomach and small intestine, one of which had penetrated the wall of his gut causing death from peritonitis.

I telephoned the owner to discuss my findings and described these mystery objects. She told me they were shavings of cow hoof, sold and fed as an oral keratin supplement to improve the health of the dog's nails and coat quality. How ironic that feeding a health supplement should cause the death of such a robust and healthy sire.

Thanks to a local estate agent, Ev found a "large semi-detached house with character, built in 1919 for the managers of the Pavlova leather works in Abingdon and occupying a sunny position". Just outside our price range, it became affordable with a small loan from my parents.

Being a Capricorn and true to my star sign, I was cautious by nature. Before parting with our cash, I drove from this house to the practice. The journey took nine minutes with no sets of traffic lights to hinder progress. The speed humps in Kennington were then only a distant concept in the minds of the planners. I thought that was a reasonable journey time to see out-of-hours emergency cases at Iffley Road.

Using a hired van, we moved on one of the hottest days of the year. Much of our furniture and possessions had to be retrieved from the top flat in Iffley Road, resulting in countless lung-busting trips up and down those blessed flights of stairs.

By the late evening, we were exhausted. Assembling the bed could wait for another day and we slept on a mattress on the floor of our second house. Mostyn tore round the garden, delighted to have found a tennis ball in the hedge, and Mr T had a new selection of weeds and overgrown vegetation to explore and sample.

It was a great comfort to have a place of our own again and importantly, some privacy. We are still in that house, thirty-five years later with no immediate prospect of moving. Nowadays, it's a push to complete the journey into Oxford during rush hour in under forty minutes, negotiating seven separate sets of traffic lights.

Who dreamed up traffic-light controlled roundabouts? I've noticed that traffic moves much more freely around Hinksey Hill roundabout when the traffic lights fail, as they frequently do. At dead of night, I can manage the trip in next to no time. The planners continue to ignore the traffic problems inherent in the area, allowing developers to build yet more houses, without the requisite infrastructure improvements and these officials are not held to account.

"Location, location, location" is a cliché used by estate agents and former prime ministers. Two cases underline the veracity of this statement.

Having recently completed the move to Abingdon, I was phoned at six o'clock in the morning by the same corgi breeder about her bitch, which was in difficulty whelping. Although it was an ungodly hour, fortunately she lived just a short distance from our house in Marcham village.

My patient, a maiden bitch, had given birth to eight live pups, a ninth being stillborn. I was able to remove a placenta from the birth canal but I could still feel a significant swelling in her abdomen. I gave her some *posterior pituitary extract,* a hormone which encourages her uterine muscle to contract more forcefully, helping her expel any remaining pups. I was back home in time for my morning ablutions and breakfast.

I took the opportunity to check on her progress on my way in to work. The bitch had passed another placenta and the abdominal swelling was now much smaller. As she had not produced much milk, I repeated the hormone injection to aid uterine contractions and to help her to release milk for the puppies to suckle.

One month later, returning home from work, I was telephoned by another client whose sheltie bitch Tipsy was in difficulty having her pups. She lived less than five minutes away from the surgery in Oxford where we had been living until very recently. How frustrating was that?

Taking a deep breath and having kissed my long-suffering wife hello and goodbye, I returned to Florence Park. I preferred to examine my canine whelping cases in their own home rather than in the strange environment of the surgery. In most cases, the patients were less anxious and it was more conducive to a successful outcome; surges of adrenalin caused by anxiety or undue excitement antagonise the actions of hormones which regulate the strong, muscular contractions of the uterus and a subsequent successful birth.

I rang the doorbell. This bitch was in no mood to let strangers into her house. She was tearing round frantically, barking furiously, with occasional thumps as she bounced off the front door. Miss Andrews and I had a comical conversation standing either side of it. Eventually, the bitch was placed in a cage and I was admitted to the house in relative safety. Tipsy was also a maiden bitch. She remained agitated and in no state to embark on the productive third stage of her labour. Once again, I injected her with *posterior pituitary extract* and asked for an update by telephone in an hour. Having just swallowed my last mouthful of dinner, the owner rang to tell me that two pups had been born, the bitch had stopped straining and seemed to have finished. I wasn't so sure and returned to the house to check for myself.

This time my patient was caged on my arrival. I thought I could still palpate pups in her uterus. In most cases, I would have stayed with the patient, monitoring her progress myself but this bitch perceived my presence in her house as a threat and her angst was not likely to presage success. Injecting her with more hormone, I left and returned home, requesting another update in two hours.

Two further home visits were required, the last being past one o'clock in the morning before I was satisfied that whelping really had finished. The sight of the healthy yet helpless litter of pups was sufficient recompense for travelling more than sixty miles to bring this case to a satisfactory conclusion.

By the spring of 1985, the practice workload had continued to expand to the extent that as partners, we needed some help. We advertised and received an encouraging number of replies. I was on duty on the Sunday after Easter and had arranged to interview Stephanie, a recent Bristol graduate, at midday. Travelling down to Oxford from Huddersfield, she arrived three hours late.

In the meantime, I had seen another hamster, this patient having a thick purulent yellowish-green discharge from its uterus. I hung on, waiting for the arrival of my interviewee. After making her coffee, I asked her, "What experience have you had with anaesthetics in hamsters?"

We used an inhalation gaseous anaesthetic agent with oxygen as a carrier gas. With the tiny creature asleep, speed was of the essence. I quickly exposed and removed the diseased organ and repaired the abdominal wound using resorbable sutures as fine as a human hair.

Nowadays, there are many presentations and courses offering insights into best interview practice. I would agree that my interview technique on this occasion was disconnected and lacked any flow.

"What are you looking for in your next practice?"

"I ... "

"Turn the anaesthetic down a little. What's its heart rate?"

"Heart rate is fine – breathing fine ... I'm looking for a mixed practice. I'm particularly interested in small animal surgery and horses."

"Just skin stitches to go. Could you put a heat pad in its cage?"

We had a more coherent chat standing around the cage watching the hamster recover.

I admired her calm temperament. She could easily have become flustered on finding herself at an interview in this unusual situation but remained unflappable.

We discussed our plans for the future of the practice. I think Oxford and its central position with good transport links was a more important factor in her decision to join us than my skills as a 'small furries' surgeon.

She started a couple of months later as our first veterinary assistant. Long curly fair hair, an open and cheerful disposition, always smiling and a no-nonsense approach, she was never happier than when she got the chance to go on equine visits. She was a great boon to the practice, bringing a balance of skills to our veterinary team. She inherited my Vauxhall Chevette and I bought a used VW Passat estate, a purchase which was later to prove of vital importance.

Working on Christmas Eve with my nurse Kate, it was dark outside and I was mentally preparing to head homeward. Kate sidled up to me, asking sheepishly, "Andy, do you think *Blu Tack* is poisonous to dogs?"

She had left an unopened packet on the settee upstairs in the flat and now she couldn't find it. Just supposing Blossom, her labrador-cross puppy, had eaten an entire strip of this stuff, including the cellophane and cardboard packaging, what should be done about it? An excellent question to which I did not know the answer.

In the days before the internet and the instant access it affords to vast amounts of information, we had a more limited range of options. Kate hurried up the road to buy another packet but it did not tell us what was in the product. I telephoned the offices of the manufacturer but a recorded message told me that the offices were now closed until after the New Year. Unsurprisingly, *Blu Tack* was not listed in my toxicology textbook. Looking at the patient in front of me, Blossom appeared completely normal, ready for a rough and tumble. What should we do?

Paraphrasing the motto of a vet school, related to me by one of their students, their graduates seek the skill to know with which cases they should interfere and which cases they should leave alone. In this case, we decided masterly inactivity might be the best option. The notion of stomach pumps, enemas and injections to encourage vomiting seemed unattractive alternatives. We agreed that Kate would monitor Blossom's behaviour and ring me if she became concerned.

I got in the car and began my journey back to Abingdon. At the traffic lights on Iffley Road, at its first major road junction, I was stationary behind a car, waiting for the lights to turn green. Moments before the car in front moved off, the passenger rear door opened and a box was flung out, landing on the road in front of me.

I got out to move the box and found it contained five live kittens, probably about three weeks old. I could not believe such callousness. Returning to the practice, Kate and I fed the kittens with feline milk substitute and made them comfortable. They all seemed healthy and I phoned a charity which relied on fosterers to take in homeless cats. They were pleased to help and within an hour, the kittens were relocated to a safe house, spending Christmas in a home in which they would be appreciated, even glorified.

Arriving home, I took a panic call from clients who had become my friends. Five days previously, as a Christmas present to each other, they adopted two young adult Old English sheepdogs, a brother and sister, from a local animal shelter.

They were assured both animals had been neutered but half an hour previously, the 'sister' had given birth to a puppy, with every sign there were more to follow. "What should we do?" they asked.

I said there was nothing to be done but to let nature take its course. In some ways, the birth of puppies was simply the icing on their Christmas cake. What a start to the festive season of goodwill.

In the days that followed, the young kittens thrived and eventually went to permanent new homes. I was relieved that Kate saw no sign of the offending *Blu Tack*, nor did Blossom appear to suffer any ill-effects.

It turned out that my friend's bitch only had one puppy in her litter, a puppy which, when I met him, strongly resembled an Old English sheepdog puppy. The most likely explanation was he owed his existence to a mating involving brother and sister, about nine weeks previously. The puppy was more likely than most to suffer from inherited defects as he grew to adulthood but for now, he suckled his dam greedily whilst my friends could only monitor him for possible problems in the future.

On reflection, a satisfactory outcome to a busy Christmas Eve.

Chapter 11

Go Your Own Way

More vets need more nurses to assist with increasing numbers of surgical procedures and to provide the nursing care those patients require.

I interviewed Abigail Drake in January 1986 for a veterinary nursing position. She was a little older than many of the applicants but had a refreshing, unorthodox take on life. She came for her interview having recently returned from acting as a hostess on a privately-chartered yacht in the Caribbean, bringing with her a passion for the music of Janis Joplin and Ducati motorbikes.

We hit it off straight away. She joined our team in April, moving into the top flat and making it home, according to her own tastes. As she settled into her head nurse role, she developed various strategies to let off steam if the pressure was getting too much. One such release was to ride her motorbike on a journey which would invariably include travelling at speed along the B4027 to Islip, with a series of challenging bends. If I worked late, I would see her return an hour or so later, eyes bright with the adrenalin rush that speed had engendered.

At that time, the practice was forced to mount a determined defence against an enforcement notice served on us by Oxford City Council to ban the use of our back yard for parking. Vehicles had parked behind the property since the 1930s. The facility was essential both for the vets who at certain times needed immediate emergency access to their cars together with the drugs and equipment they carried and for clients bringing all kinds of animals to the surgery for treatment.

Injured animals, non-ambulatory dogs, smaller ponies, calves and sheep arrived in a variety of transport, including estate cars, Land Rovers or in trailers. The matter was so critically important that we employed a planning consultant to plead our case.

Overturning this enforcement notice on appeal was crucial to the subsequent success the practice enjoyed. The heavy-handed approach of the council and the increasingly-stringent parking restrictions which have been applied on Iffley Road and the surrounding side street suggests they would rather have these properties set aside for residential housing and occupied predominately by students rather than business enterprises.

The conflict with the council served to highlight the strains of working in a partnership involving three vets of widely differing ages, capabilities and expectations.

Russell complained that the profitability of the practice was declining despite him working long hours, six days a week. His visits to Iffley Road had become sporadic but he might have noticed that Jimmy and I were working equally long days, each at our own pace. Profits were bound to dip because of the increased costs associated with establishing the Wheatley surgery, a venture which would take time to reach its full potential and profitability.

Matters were brought to a head in December 1986 when Russell presented Jimmy and me with a letter stating his intention to withdraw from the partnership, citing both personal and financial reasons. He emphasised his decision was irrevocable. The proposed date for his withdrawal was the thirtieth of June 1987.

Russell had gone as far as mapping out his terms for this withdrawal. Jimmy and I could continue to run a practice from Iffley Road and Russell's practice would operate from his home base in Kidlington. We would share the use of the Wheatley surgery with Russell consulting there at lunchtimes on weekdays and my practice free to use the facilities there in the evenings and at weekends. The farming and horse clients would be placed in the invidious position of having to choose which practice they wished to use. Russell insisted both the staff and the clients must be kept in the dark about the changes until the following May, only two months before the June deadline.

The splitting of the practice was not in my best interest nor in the interest of our staff or clients. I was unwilling to waste the personal effort and the financial investment I had made to develop the practice. Mr Sheriffs decided the time had come for him to withdraw from the partnership as well. He said he was content to leave 'his' practice in my hands and agreed to support me by seeing clients on a consultancy basis.

The scenario was not one I would have chosen. It was never my intention to become sole principal. I would have preferred to be one of a small group of like-minded ambitious young partners but I remained determined to make a success of this new business venture.

For the first time in my life, I had to have formal discussions with my bank manager. To his great credit, Jock Skinner kept things as simple as possible and did not ask me to present a complex business strategy. We discussed my plans for the future of the practice and he agreed to arrange an overdraft facility with my share in the Wheatley Surgery premises being held by the bank as security on the loan. There were several meetings with accountants and solicitors to be fitted in as well as my normal workload and rota of night duties.

On a very cold Wednesday night in February, I visited the farm of one of our outlying clients much nearer Thame than Oxford. I was trying to deliver some lambs from a young fit ewe for a farmer who had not previously met me. Trying was the operative word because I could not advance my hand very far inside her passage. Suspecting a torsion or twisting of the uterus, I had tried rolling the ewe, but that manoeuvre did not improve matters.

"I think we should do a caesarean on her."

The farmer raised his eyebrows and looked at me quizzically. "Have you done one of these operations before?"

I assured him that I had, many times. After a moment's thought, he decided to follow my advice. "Mr Kyle did the last one on top of the chest freezer."

It was my turn to think for a moment. The barn was only dimly lit and I was already chilled to the marrow.

"That's a good idea. It will be cleaner, warmer for the mother and the lighting's better."

I collected my surgical kit and drugs from the car whilst the farmer went off to find his clippers. I was on trial once more, having something to prove. With a sheet covering the makeshift operating table, we heaved the sheep up and laid her on her side. I clipped and cleansed her flank, injected some local anaesthetic and prepared to start the surgery. Opening her abdomen, I could see immediately that her uterus, which was heavily distended with at least two decent-sized lambs, had become twisted on itself. Reversing the twist was now a straightforward process and opening the uterus, I quickly delivered two healthy lambs, passed to the farmer's wife for a brisk rub down with a towel.

Very soon, both were calling for their mum and her milk. Placed in front of the kitchen range, wrapped in dry towels and confined to a washing basket, they had to wait for me finish. I could see the uterus already shrinking dramatically in size as I sutured the incision and began to close the wound in her side. The farmer, now convinced that I really had done several of these operations before, chatted companionably about his farm, about the practice, especially the achievements of Mr Sheriffs, and about the perceived shortcomings of some of the locum vets visiting the farm in recent years.

By the time I had completed my work and the ewe had been cleaned up and installed in a pen, we had given each other a potted history of our careers. The farmer congratulated me on a professional job and I left him rigging up a heat lamp to keep the lambs warm on such an inhospitable night. The lambs were busy suckling their mother, each showing their extreme pleasure by vigorously wiggling their respective tails.

Being professional in my approach to my patients meant that the health and well-being of the animal in my consulting room or on my operating table was my primary concern. This aspiration was difficult to achieve during this particularly hectic period, my first real encounter with sustained pressure in Oxford. I had no choice but to deal with it myself since there were no veterinary counselling or mental health support services available at the time.

Cathy, our new receptionist, worked wonders trying to keep the daily workload within manageable limits whilst Abigail took responsibility for overseeing the surgical bookings, running the hospital, replenishing our stock and resolving the day-to-day staffing issues with help from Hazel.

Our home life was similarly disjointed. Since our marriage, motherhood was not at the top of my wife's list of priorities. If we were enjoying one of our rare nights out and noisy young children were disrupting our evening, we would get up and leave. However, I noticed a dramatic shift in her attitude as she approached her thirtieth birthday. Almost overnight, she found herself gazing out of the window enviously at mothers wheeling prams. I would not have believed her outlook could change within such a short time. Suddenly, having her own baby could not happen soon enough.

Discovering Ev was pregnant brought both of us great joy and delight. Try as I might, I could not arrange time off to be with her for her first ultrasound scan in February 1987. When I arrived home, her expression and the look in her eyes told me all was not well.

The initial scanned image showed that the baby was alive and developing normally but it also hinted at something untoward. Two floors higher up in the John Radcliffe hospital, a second, more detailed scan revealed the presence of a large abnormal structure, very close to or possibly involving her ovary and the horn of her uterus to which the baby had laid claim. No time could be lost. Exploratory abdominal surgery under general anaesthesia was scheduled for Friday the sixth of March. The anaesthetic drugs themselves represented a significant risk to our baby's health, more so even than to the health of its mother.

It was a normal working day for me, with no night duty and a weekend off. As soon as I finished work, I drove to the hospital. The operation completed, Ev was back on the ward and asleep. It was after eight o'clock when the surgeon came to tell me the position. He had removed a mass of tissue including her ovary on the affected side. He found no other cause for concern and our baby was still alive. It would be about a week before we would know the pathology results. I sat, feeling a sense of relief, tempered by extreme emotional fatigue. I bought her a Winnie the Pooh teddy bear to keep her company in my absence. He must have been watching over her as things could not have gone much better.

Later, driving home, I switched on the car radio and heard that the Herald of Free Enterprise, a roll-on roll-off car ferry, had capsized on its departure from Zeebrugge harbour. Many people had lost their lives. Speculation suggested the bow door may not have been fully closed before the ship sailed. That night, I empathised with those poor families, waiting anxiously for news of their relatives.

The mass of tissue turned out to be cystic rather than something more sinister and no future health implications were expected. In preparation for parenthood, Ev and I had a week's holiday in north Devon. In beautiful May weather, we enjoyed gentle walks by the rivers and streams, avoiding the more demanding high moors. As we travelled towards Minehead on our way home, a car came out of a side road without stopping and collided with us, hitting the passenger door next to Ev, the rear passenger door and finally the back wing.

Although Ev was badly shaken, she was thankfully unhurt. Our Volkswagen Passat had been designed and built with safety in mind and the side-impact bars fulfilled their purpose perfectly. We returned home in the cab of a roadside recovery vehicle, which took our car off for extensive repairs. The other vehicle in the accident was a write off.

As division day for Sheriffs Kyle and Bartholomew approached, I was able to tell the staff of the impending changes and letters were sent out to the clients. I was both delighted and reassured that all the staff working at Iffley Road chose to stay and help me with the next phase in the renaissance of the practice. The stock and equipment had to be valued and allocated to whichever practice claimed it and replacements purchased. I found the process, especially discussions concerning the redistribution of assets, rather depressing. Development of the practice, which had recently become more competitive and contemporary in its outlook, was being hindered at a critical juncture.

But we also had plenty to celebrate and on a summer's evening at the end of June, we threw a party in the back garden of Iffley Road. I had to leave the celebrations to see to Dolly, a red setter who had been clipped by a car. Fortunately, it was nothing serious and I returned to the festivities shortly afterwards. Looking round at the smiling faces of the staff, their families and friends, I felt proud they had chosen to throw in their lot with me but also a responsibility for their future careers and prosperity.

Presented with this opportunity to update the practice ideology, I was answerable only to my own conscience, my wife and my estimable bank manager. There could be no excuses. If I remained true to myself and treated everyone fairly, what could go wrong?

As sole principal, I employed seven people in either full or part-time roles. There was a great deal to learn about employment law, business practice, PAYE and VAT and the burgeoning discipline dubbed 'health and safety'. The rent had to be paid for Iffley Road as well as my share of the mortgage on Wheatley surgery and the mortgage on our house. Simple.

Ev had begun her maternity leave. She spent most days reading or knitting in the shade from a venerable pear tree in our garden. On the twenty-eighth of July, she came with me on a farm visit, a rare event in our relationship. She was acting as my scribe at a tuberculin test on forty-odd cows at Sheepstead Farm in Stadhampton. It saved me a lot of time if I did not have to stop and write down details of each cow as well as testing each animal.

On this pleasant mid-summer's day in an idyllic rural setting, Ev was sitting comfortably on a straw bale in the shade. In the days before mobile phones, as the cows shuffled reluctantly down the creaking wooden race towards the rusting cattle crush, I could hear a telephone ringing in the farmhouse kitchen nearby.

The insistence of its ringing demanded a response. It was the practice trying to get hold of me. Our good friend Gavin in Sussex, who helped keep my elderly Vauxhall Victor on the road, had been killed in a car crash.

After midnight, an articulated lorry attempted a U-turn on the busy A22 near Golden Cross. Gavin's car went sideways under the trailer. He was a motivated young man with a successful business, married to the wonderful Debbie. It took a long time to come to terms with this loss.

In the words of Winston Churchill, I had to "keep buggering on". I had no choice. There were cows to calve, horses to vet, bitches to whelp as well as deals to be done with drug suppliers. Keeping all the balls in the air at work and fulfilling more of the domestic duties at home, including the weekly shop, kept me on my toes. There were not enough hours in the day.

I was there supporting my wife when Anna graced us with her presence at six o'clock on the third of September. The pregnancy had been full of incident and the birth was stressful. I was certain a caesarean section was called for but fortunately, for once, the decision to operate did not rest with me. By the time I got home, telephoned our respective sets of parents, our relatives and friends and had something to eat, I was exhausted but content with the outcome of the day. In the silence of the house and nursing a drink, it hit me that I was a father. Who would have thought it?

The pressure on my time and how I might allocate the hours in my week became even more pressing. Naturally, I wanted to spend time at home supporting my wife and enjoying our new baby but I was having to spend far too much time working.

Mr Sheriffs had supervised greyhound racing at Oxford Stadium since 1946. As he began to pass his remaining workload to me, it was time for me to be instructed in the dark art of these duties.

Every practice needs a base of routine work to keep the financial wheels turning when the amount of clinical work dipped. In Sussex, there had been red meat inspection with early starts in a depressing and chilly packing station.

At Oxford stadium, the weekly greyhound racing programme consisted of eight races on Tuesday and Thursday evenings and ten races on a Saturday evening. Thursday evening racing now fell to me. Jimmy did Tuesday evenings and we shared Saturday evenings and trials on Mondays. As an interested spectator, I attended race meetings at Reading and Swindon racetracks to gain insights into the intricacies of race night. I promised Jimmy I would take responsibility for providing veterinary staff for race meetings at Oxford for a year, with the proviso that the management must be reasonable in their dealings with me.

This responsibility remained with me until the track closed at the end of 2012. I developed an affection and deep respect for these wonderful canine athletes. Such speed yet so graceful in their movement, most were gentle, loving animals and not the least bit aggressive.

The national bookmakers began to stage extra afternoon greyhound racing meetings known as BAGS meetings. The first one at Oxford was held in December 1987. Providing veterinary cover for these extra meetings put an even greater strain on my veterinary colleagues, reducing our collective time off still further.

It was a constant battle trying to balance the need to generate the income necessary for the practice to remain solvent yet to provide each vet with an adequate amount of time off to relax and recharge their batteries.

We required some extra veterinary help. Andrew, a recent graduate from the University of Liverpool, came to our rescue, joining Stephanie, Jimmy and myself. Tall, broad-shouldered, good-humoured, good-looking, with a shock of black hair and a northern lilt to his accent, our female clients admired his physique so much they quickly switched their allegiance to 'that new vet man'.

We held a practice Christmas dinner at Cotswold Lodge, with some outrageous outfits and dancing that didn't always match the rhythm of the music. Was this a reflection of increased collective confidence or simply relief that a momentous year had passed?

I was pleased with the progress made but my resolution for the new year was to try to exert more control over events affecting the practice, whilst recognising it was not always possible.

Chapter 12

Sunday Girls

One Sunday morning during a duty weekend in February 1988, a heavy overnight snowfall, an uncommon occurrence in Oxfordshire, had produced significant drifts. The telephone rang at ten minutes to nine. It was Robert, the herdsman from Hollands Farm near Wheatley. He had a heifer calving and she wasn't making progress.

I was busy sorting out a shovel and some sacking in case I got stranded on the way when the telephone rang again. This time it was Brian, the herdsman from Dovehouse Farm in Cuddesdon. He had a cow which had calved during the night. She had continued to strain and had pushed her womb out. Both cases were genuine emergencies and had to be seen urgently.

I rang Jimmy Sheriffs, my colleague and former partner. Now in his eighties, I wasn't happy about asking for his help in such circumstances; both cases would require physical strength as well as technical expertise, quite apart from negotiating difficult driving conditions. We agreed I would attend the heifer calving and he would set out for the farm closest to him at Cuddesdon, about seven miles away.

After ten years in general practice, I thought I could cope with most road conditions. That morning, my trip of fifteen miles needed all my experience and some luck. The sun shone in a cloudless sky but a bitingly north wind was blowing. I chose a route which, though less direct, took me chiefly along main roads which I expected had been treated with road salt.

Once I turned off London Road in Wheatley, the last mile and a half was hazardous. I knew the route well but the familiar features had largely been obliterated under snow, piled high in places forming deep drifts. The countryside around Oxford is predominately flat but that day, any slight incline became another potentially-insurmountable obstacle as my tyres struggled for grip.

I crept along at a funereal pace. Despite my caution, on several occasions, instead of negotiating a bend in the road, the car continued straight ahead, coming to rest on the opposite grass verge, often with a ditch beyond. A tractor had left its tracks on the access road to the farm and, following them, I slithered into the yard, relieved to be in one piece.

It was an understatement to say Robert was pleased to see me. He cut a familiar figure, quite tall and heavily built, wearing his dairyman's uniform of blue baseball cap, blue denim overalls and spattered wellies. Not normally prone to outward signs of emotion, now I had arrived, he was smiling broadly and whistling a nameless tune as he filled two buckets with warm water. I pulled on my wellies and waterproof gown, shaking shards of ice from the creases as I did so.

Edging past the stainless steel bulk tank, paddles churning, the chiller droning, we walked into a covered yard. Before me were nearly half the dairy herd, their heads through the barrier, pulling contentedly at the silage on offer in the feed trough, their breath vaporising in the cold air.

My patient was a well-grown Friesian heifer. She stood disconsolately in the corner of her pen, straining periodically but half-heartedly. She was clearly not comfortable but still bright and interested in my arrival.

Robert slipped a rope halter over her head and tied her loosely. She stood quietly whilst I washed my hands and arms. With lubricant liberally applied, I gently felt inside her womb. I could feel one of the calf's forelegs and, further inside, its muzzle. Advancing my hand forward, brushing the ear of the calf, I could feel the other foreleg against the calf's chest wall, extending forwards out of my reach.

This malpresentation had to be corrected before the calf could be delivered. The normal cone shape, formed when both forelegs and the forehead pass together along the birth canal, finally and fully dilate the muscles and supporting soft tissue during this late stage of labour.

I have been blessed with long arms and relatively small hands. At full stretch, I managed to gradually ease the foreleg towards me, whilst pushing the calf's head away from the neck of the womb. Eventually, I could place a calving rope around the wrist and pull the limb into the passage, my other hand covering the hoof. Once both forelegs were in the passage, with both hooves alongside each other, ropes attached, the head was guided back up towards me and a rope attached behind the ears, secured in the opened jaws of the mouth.

The heifer seemed to realise it was her turn now. A synchronised effort, with the patient straining and Robert and I pulling on the calving ropes, helped draw the calf out into the chilly morning. The sight of a live calf, in this case a valuable heifer calf, at the end of a calving procedure, is always a moment to savour; watching the mother licking her new-born is such a satisfying experience.

It makes an enormous difference when a vet is called in good time to a case; the chances of a successful intervention with a positive outcome are so much higher. Today, I had no time to stand and stare, my obligations lay elsewhere. After checking the heifer internally to ensure she had only been carrying a single calf and had sustained no internal damage, I washed myself down and hurried away to help Jimmy.

The journey of four miles to Cuddesdon involved leaving Wheatley village via Ladder Hill, which in these conditions was treacherous. I had a bit of luck. A farmer I knew came by in his four-wheel drive and recognising my car and appreciating my predicament, he towed me up the hill to the crossroads where my car was unhitched. With a friendly wave of thanks, we went our separate ways.

The snow was at its deepest on this higher section of exposed countryside where the lane led down to the village. I could hardly make out where the edges of the lane ended and the verges began. I found Jimmy's car slewed off the road and partially obscured in drifting snow. Collecting some equipment and drugs I might need, I followed Jimmy's footsteps in the snow towards the farmyard.

This patient was a large ten-year-old Friesian cow. Her latest heifer calf was lying in the straw looking hungry. The cow, with her substantial swollen uterus laid out behind her and inside out, was looking forlorn.

Brian, the herdsman, normally cheerful and upbeat, was looking worried. Jimmy had removed the remaining placenta and administered local anaesthetic solution as an epidural injection into the base of the cow's tail, to stop her straining against us. Jimmy and I huffed and puffed in unison but we could not push this unwieldy and slippery object back where it belonged.

We decided to lift the hindquarters of the cow; her internal abdominal organs would fall forward, allowing gravitational forces to assist us in our efforts. We were in an old barn whose wooden beams seemed none too sturdy. If we rigged up a block and tackle using a beam as an anchor point, the roof of the barn could come tumbling down on top of us all.

Brian went off to fetch the tractor which he manoeuvred expertly through the narrow gateway and into position. After ropes had been placed around our patient and attached to the bucket on the tractor, her hindquarters were gently raised. Our combined physical exertions were now more productive. The uterine wall is soft and friable with a consistency of dough and can be easily damaged if not handled gently. We each pushed evenly but firmly, returning the tissue sequentially back into the cow, whilst bearing the considerable weight of the organ.

Eventually, that critical point in the procedure was reached where we had replaced more tissue inside the cow than remained outside. At this stage, you can convince yourself that success will follow. Sure enough, the remainder returned quite easily from whence it came.

The cow was lowered onto some clean straw and we flushed the uterus with buckets of warm water using a funnel and a stomach tube. Stitches were placed across her vulva to retain the uterus in its correct position whilst it contracted over the next few days. We slapped the cow affectionately on her rump and with some encouragement, she got to her feet. She looked briefly over her shoulder at us, perhaps in thanks, before walking over to investigate her new addition.

Having washed ourselves down and made ourselves more presentable, Brian, his normal good humour now restored, gave us a lift on the farm tractor back to our respective cars, towing each of us back to the main road.

Reaching home, leaving my car at the bottom of our steeply-sloping drive, I had a shower and something to eat. How lucky I was to have Jimmy to call upon for support. A compassionate and dedicated man willing to turn out in blizzard conditions with no thought for his own safety, to go to the aid of an animal in difficulty. How much longer would I be able to call upon his services?

He was doing lighter duties now and I had taken on more of his sessions at the greyhound track. After finishing his round of visits and parked at the back of the practice, he would often fall asleep in his car. When we spotted this, I would creep up quietly to check that he was breathing and slip away so I didn't disturb his repose.

I worried about his personal safety and wondered how much longer he could or should continue to practice. I was at a loss to think what he might do with his time when he finally did retire completely. The practice and everything to do with it was his life. He was held in such high regard and with such deep affection, I did not want to be the person to tell him that his professional career was over. I took the coward's way out and did nothing, content he was out somewhere visiting his friends, the clients. He was an ambassador for the practice, much of his work being done gratis.

For many years, he had worked for the Oxford Animal Sanctuary, a charity based in Stadhampton, founded by Margaret Gray. They took in unwanted or homeless dogs and cats and more recently sheep, goats and ponies. He might spend a couple of hours there, though seldom was an invoice raised for this work. Consequently, when colleagues called to carry out work for the charity and raised an invoice for the time spent and for the drugs used, albeit at a discounted rate, it did cause adverse comment. One Sunday morning, I was at the practice seeing a couple of cases. I took a phone call from one of the many willing helpers, mostly young girls, who volunteered at the sanctuary in their spare time.

"I got a bitch on heat been got at by a dog."

Although it was Sunday, I suggested she brought the bitch down straight away to have a misalliance injection to prevent an unwanted pregnancy.

"I'm on my way. Can I bring a dog with a cut foot as well?"

Later, the front doorbell rang. On the doorstep was a young girl, sobbing.

"Can you come an' help. They're tied an' I can't get 'em apart."

I calmed her down. Nature had taken its course and we brought the animals into the practice. I gave the bitch her hormone treatment and cleansed the dog's paw, prescribing some antibiotic capsules for the wound in his pad.

I struggled to keep a straight face as she told me about her journey into Oxford. She had put both animals in the back of the estate car and closed the tailgate. The young driver, looking in her rear-view mirror, saw the dog doing what dogs do, reaching peak performance as they were negotiating the busy Headington roundabout.

There were several lanes of vehicles, their distracted drivers and startled passengers getting a close-up of the mating game. For the return journey, we put the bitch in the footwell of the front passenger seat, clipped to the seatbelt on a short lead, and the dog on his own in the boot of the estate car, attached securely by another lead.

As I started afternoon surgery in the run-up to Christmas, I noticed a couple in the waiting room without a pet. I called my early appointments through but became increasingly aware that the couple were still waiting patiently. Perhaps they had arrived without making an appointment.

I called them in and asked how I could help. This was an embarrassing moment for all concerned. The practice occupies a semi-detached building and next door is a branch of the Marriage Guidance Council (now Relate). They did say they were surprised so many families seeking counselling turned up for their sessions with their pets! I could only apologise for the misunderstanding and redirect them.

This year, the staff had voted for the Christmas party to be held at the practice, with each member receiving a financial bonus in lieu of the cost of a ritzy restaurant meal. It turned out to be a different but very enjoyable Christmas do, not least because everyone could relax and be themselves. When the time came to leave, some staff had close encounters with the bush at the bottom of the front steps on the way to their taxis. Oddly enough, they swore the bush had moved since their arrival.

It had been a year of steady progress and consolidation for the practice, with no major traumas or hiccups. I learnt more about business management and at home, about parenthood and thoroughly enjoyed these experiences.

Chapter 13

Heroes and Villains

The trope of not working with animals presents vets with a conundrum. It is occupying my mind as I write this.

I was on duty one weekend in January and had been busy all day. I had just sat down in the evening when the phone went. It was Simon who had a cow down in the field after an uncomplicated calving and she would not get up. Simon was a proficient herdsman, had great empathy with his cows and was adept at spotting changes in an animal's usual behaviour. I dragged myself away from the TV feeling miffed and drove out to the farm. I met Simon at the dairy, still in his working clothes.

We tramped off across the field. The stars glittered in the night sky, the grass scrunching beneath our feet as another frost set in. The cow was down in the darkest and lowest corner of the field near a hedge. She watched as two bobbing pools of light approached her out of the darkness. I was just able to detect the outline of her calf nearby when the cow decided she was none too keen on attention from these torchbearers. With an extra effort, she heaved her hindquarters up with her back legs, flipped her frontlegs under her with a characteristic forward lunge of her head, bellowed indignantly and walked off to stand guard between us and her offspring.

Simon grinned. "Well I'm blowed ... I'm sorry for calling you out."

We both laughed, enjoying the moment immensely; animals can make fools of us all. He picked up her calf, lodging it over his shoulders and walked back towards the calving boxes next to the dairy. Its mother dutifully followed at a respectful distance and soon both were safely in a frost-free pen with fresh bedding, food and water on tap. It was a much more hospitable location for the new mother and her baby to spend their first night together.

Six months later, I was on call again early on Thursday morning. The phone rang well before my bedside alarm. In his soft Irish brogue, Mr Carroll from Blackbird Leys told me he had a young pony mare which was foaling.

"She hasn't got on with it and is looking none too happy. Will you come?"

He gave me directions to a field in Nuneham Courtenay on the southern outskirts of Oxford. No traffic jams at this hour as I drove through Abingdon and out past the Science Centre at Culham. Notwithstanding the bright summer's morning, I wasn't feeling very optimistic about the outcome of this case. An uncomplicated equine labour usually lasts about a quarter of hour; much longer and the whole process can quickly go awry with unfortunate consequences. This pony was only three years old and too young, in my view, to be in foal.

Mr Carroll was an elderly man, short in stature, his complexion suggesting he had spent a great deal of time outdoors in all weathers. I remember quite clearly the gleam in his Irish eyes. I could see he was relieved I had come.

Freya, his chestnut pony mare, was standing some distance from her owner, looking uncomfortable with a hint of despair. There was a hoof protruding through the lips of her vulva. There was no running water supply here, so the owner filled a bucket from a yellow plastic jerrycan and slipped a head collar over Freya's head. Having washed and disinfected her perineum as best I could and smothered my arm in lubricant, I began to examine her.

As she strained half-heartedly, some rank brown fluid oozed past my arm. She had probably been trying to give birth for several hours; any foetal fluids had long since drained away and the lining of her uterus was now tacky. The foal's other foreleg, flexed at the shoulder, extended away alongside the body, the head deviated beneath the pelvic brim. Embryotomy was not feasible, as the uterine wall had contracted down around the dead foetus, leaving insufficient room in which to work safely. I thought it impossible to deliver this foal.

Standing in a slight hollow, I cleaned myself up and comforted the mare. The owner had taken the high ground, pacing back and forth along the top of a grassy ridge. Looking up, I gave him the news which I believe he already knew. He was unwilling to accept my advice that the kindest thing for the mare was to put her down. It was now after eight o' clock and the roads into Oxford and to the practice would be jammed with motorists on their daily commute. Whilst the Irishman considered his options, I phoned and asked my colleague Andrew to come to meet me there and bring the gun.

The owner continued his perpetual pacing, his silence emphasising his anxiety and agitation. I surmised the taking of a life under any circumstances may have been contrary to his religious principles. On the other hand, I was required to do all in my power to alleviate the suffering of animals in my care, using every possible means available. Suddenly, the owner stopped and turned to me.

"Isn't there *anything* else you can do? Anything at all?"

I chose my words with great care, explaining that doing nothing was not an option. The pony would die a protracted and painful death as the poison from her dead foal gradually circulated round her body. He hunched his shoulders further, refusing point blank to sign the consent form giving me permission to put his mare to sleep.

"Try something," he insisted. "You *have* to try something."

"The only procedure I could attempt is a caesarean section to deliver the foal through the flank of the pony," I said. "You can see that the pony has been weakened trying to give birth and from the infection building up in her uterus."

"Try," he said. "Just try."

Those were his last words on the matter. He resumed his pacing and his confrontation of his own moral dilemma.

At length, Andrew arrived with the gun. He was half way over the five-bar gate to the field when I announced, "We are going try a caesarean."

He jumped down from the gate and looked me in the eye, perhaps thinking I may have lost my presence of mind.

"Andy," he said quietly, "have you ever done this on a mare before?"

"No," I replied shortly, aggrieved at being questioned by my colleague.

"Has anyone done a caesarean on a mare in a field? There are no facilities or barn to provide shelter?"

"What else can we do? The owner refuses to give us permission to put his pony down and we can't just stand here and watch her die. By the time she has been taken to an equine hospital over thirty miles away, likely as not she would be too sick to withstand the surgery."

I could take matters into my own hands and put the horse down on humane grounds but I had never assumed that level of responsibility with the owner of the animal present. It would have to be a last resort.

"We have only one possible alternative to euthanasia and without the owner's permission, I think we have to try it, on the strict understanding if we think the mare is suffering, we must put her down without delay."

Rummaging in the backs of our respective cars, collecting surgical kits, drugs and equipment, the conversation between us grumbled on. Neither of us were happy with the position in which we found ourselves.

Andrew's customary smile returned when he realised it was my call. I am sure he was glad it was a decision which he did not have to make. His role would be to help me carry out the operation in the shortest time possible. As well as great care and attention, speed was vital if we were to have any chance of a successful outcome.

As the owner held a lead rope, attached to the head collar on the pony's head, I wondered what was he thinking now? Forcing myself to focus on the task in hand, I administered a small dose of sedative intravenously and a few minutes later, some local anaesthetic into her lumbar spine as an epidural nerve block. Briskly, we clipped her left flank, shaved the area, disinfected the skin, injected more local anaesthetic in a T pattern into the tissues of the body wall and completed our preparations. My mind was racing, trying to anticipate every eventuality and potential solution.

The pony stood quite still as I incised the skin and muscles of her left flank. Andrew quickly located the horn of the uterus containing the foal, raising it to a position outside our surgical site. The body of the foal could be seen in profile through the stretched uterine wall, now blotched and purplish in colour with an unhealthy sheen. The dead foal was delivered through a further incision in this discoloured muscular wall. Larger decomposing placental remnants were removed and four antibiotic oblets were inserted in the mucky depths of her uterus. I set about repairing my incision, dusting it with antibiotic powder before replacing it in her abdomen. The flank wound was sutured quickly in three layers using continuous catgut sutures in the muscle layers to save valuable time.

Thankfully, the mare seemed completely unconcerned throughout the procedure. I gave her an antibiotic injection, further powerful and sustained pain relief and some tetanus antitoxin. The owner removed the head collar and, pleased to be given something to do, went off in search of fresh drinking water for his pony.

The mare looked brighter already, despite the sedative drug still circulating in her bloodstream. Andrew and I cleared up an extraordinary amount of mess and debris that results from a rushed surgical operation in a field, then we leaned over the gate and watched.

She drank half a bucket of water and a few minutes later, had her head down and was grazing. I could not believe what I was seeing. It was simply incredible.

Throughout the day, we were furnished with regular telephoned updates from the owner. I visited the mare the following day. She had a slightly raised respiratory rate but her temperature was normal. She was eating, drinking and passing dung normally. The wound looked healthy with no sign of swelling or heat.

Ten days later, I removed her nylon skin sutures. The owner seemed delighted but graciously avoided saying, "Aren't you glad I told you to try something?"

I have never met another vet who has admitted attempting a caesarean section on a mare in a field. We were blessed with an amazing patient, an enormous slice of luck and an owner whose stubbornness was justified on the day.

Two years later almost to the day, I found myself standing in the same field, though my previous patient was nowhere to be seen. The subject of our attention this morning was a young bay pony stallion presented for routine castration.

Alasdair, my colleague on this occasion, would act as the anaesthetist whilst I fulfilled the role of surgeon. This time, Mr Carroll had signed a consent form giving us permission to administer an anaesthetic and perform the surgical procedure on his horse. We measured the girth of the patient using a waistband, which helpfully converted this value to the approximate weight of the horse. After a clinical examination, Alasdair gave the dose of sedative intravenously. When this had taken effect, he administered the anaesthetic and the animal lay down quietly on its side in the meadow.

I handed the owner a rope to hold which was attached to the left hind leg of the stallion; pulling on the rope drew the hindleg away, improving my sight of today's operational target. This area was scrubbed and disinfected and the surgery began. Having removed one testicle, it was obvious our patient was now only lightly anaesthetised and had a strong blink reflex. Alasdair gave a top-up dose of anaesthetic intravenously. Having removed the second testicle, I was removing my surgical instruments when Alasdair said tersely, "He hasn't taken a breath for 30 seconds. The heart rate is normal."

Alasdair injected a drug intravenously to stimulate breathing and delivered a running commentary on the heart rate, monitored via his stethoscope, whilst I pushed down sharply and rhythmically onto the animal's chest, using all my strength trying to induce a breath.

After four minutes, the stallion's heartbeat faded away and we watched helplessly as our patient died in front of us. It was an extremely demoralising experience, for myself as the senior vet in charge and for my young assistant, as well as an emotionally traumatic one for the owner.

Mr Carroll was now in high dudgeon. He would be seeking a post mortem which he would arrange to be carried out by another practice.

Two days later, I had a meeting with the owner to discuss the outcome of the case. In the end, a post mortem had not been carried out. Why hadn't I carried out a post mortem examination myself? I sympathised with the owner concerning his loss. I said the drugs used had been appropriate and the dosages which had been given were correct.

Despite having signed a consent form stating clearly that all anaesthetic and surgical procedures involve some risk, as is so often the case, Mr Carroll was convinced that the death of his horse was our fault.

He demanded to be recompensed for his loss. I provided him with the information he needed to make a claim against the practice and over the next few weeks, the bureaucratic wheels of the legal process turned slowly. Expert opinion was sought by our insurance company; this confirmed that the doses of drugs given had been calculated correctly and the drugs used were an appropriate combination.

A comment was made questioning whether it should be normal practice in the modern era to carry out routine surgical operations in a field situation. Expert opinion suggested that all such procedures should be carried out at an equine veterinary hospital. Where would that policy decision have left the owner's other horse, Freya, I wondered?

Hindsight is a wonderful thing. During my extramural training, I had seen many equine castrations carried out in field situations with some patients left lying *unattended* during their recovery. Field castrations under intravenous anaesthesia were common procedures, carried out most days, up and down the country, from early spring through to late autumn.

As a result of this accident, we reviewed and updated our practice protocols. Our equine clients were always offered the option of being referred to a veterinary hospital for all surgical procedures requiring general anaesthesia. A vast majority elected to have the surgery carried out in the field situation, both cost and convenience being major factors in their decision.

Alasdair and I were not held to have acted negligently, which was a relief for both of us. The length of time taken for the legal process caused a great deal of soul-searching and anguish. This was a lesson which underlined how quickly one can go from being the star of the show to becoming the villain of the piece. It is important to recall and enjoy the cases which bring unexpected success, whilst paying heed to the truism that you cannot satisfy all of the people all of the time.

Each vet's assessment of the risk posed to an animal by a certain medical treatment or surgical procedure against the potential benefit to that animal, will vary within broad limits.

I was asked to operate on a sixteen-year-old dachshund bitch with a solitary mammary tumour which had burst out through its skin covering. This client had not used our practice before but was the mother of one of our regulars. She had consulted several practices in Berkshire, close to where she lived, but all had refused to perform the surgery.

As well as her age, there were many factors to be considered. This tumour had been present for some time and was likely to have spread to other parts of her body, typically her lungs. I could not detect anything abnormal whilst auscultating her chest with my stethoscope. The dog had a heart murmur of moderate severity but this was not affecting her quality of life. This murmur added to my clinical suspicion she was not a good anaesthetic risk but I explained that if she died during the surgery, the outcome was no different to putting her to sleep.

We both agreed she could not continue her life with this lesion growing remorselessly and weeping constantly. Following treatment with a course of pre-operative antibiotics, she was anaesthetised and I took x-rays of her chest. These appeared normal for a bitch of her age and breed so she was taken to surgery, the mass removed and the wound repaired. The bitch made an uneventful recovery and lived her life without pain for many months afterwards. The owner naturally regarded my efforts as little short of heroic, which they most certainly were not. Neither were the other vets who were consulted wrong in the opinion which they gave.

This case serves to highlight that in many instances, there is no correct way to proceed. My role in this instance was that of an advocate for the animal, leading a detailed discussion of the pros and cons of one or more clinical courses of action. Where possible, after due consideration, I sought to carry out my client's wishes, provided I was sure beyond reasonable doubt that the welfare of their pet would not be compromised.

There will be many vets who have amongst their cases some they wish they had left untreated. I admit that I do but I am not blessed with the gift of hindsight. Henry Marsh in his book *Admissions* recounts that as a neurosurgeon, it took him three years to learn how to do an operation and 30 years to learn when not to do it.

Chapter 14

Tails of the Unexpected

When I learnt to drive in 1972, my instructor drummed into me that, as far as other road users are concerned, I should always expect the unexpected. It was good advice for my veterinary career as well as my driving.

Tony relished his Italian ancestry. A self-confessed coffee addict, he spoke with a distinct London accent and trained greyhounds which he raced at Oxford Stadium. After Easter, he asked me to visit a cow that wasn't eating. A cow? I didn't know he had a cow.

As I was getting dressed up, he explained he had been given this Jersey cow a few months previously. After the rough and tumble of Friesian cows with their larger and bulkier physique, handling this petite madame was a delight. More like a pet than a farm animal, her liquid brown eyes suggested she would submit to most things asked of her. It almost seemed a breach of trust on my part to fit a head collar to restrain her for my examination. She looked healthy, though she was not in calf as Tony had been told.

I walked down the sloping rough pasture to inspect her feed trough; it was overflowing with bread rolls. Tony drove to his London bakery each day in the early hours to make bread in the Italian style for his fellow countrymen in the capital. He brought back his surplus stock to mix with meat to feed to his greyhounds and now, to his cow. None of my lectures about animal nutrition had covered feeding baked loaves to ruminants. Initially, she ate some of the bread, perhaps to please Tony, but her enthusiasm waned and now the bread remained untouched. With my stethoscope, I could hear her rumen or forestomach was churning normally. Springtime in Oxfordshire produced sufficient new growth of grass in this field to satisfy this solitary cow's requirements.

I assured Tony that his new-found friend was not passing judgement on his baking prowess but had a supply of a more suitable diet in abundance in the meadow. I treated the cow for what I suspected might be ruminal acidosis, or bovine heartburn, brought on by an overly-rich diet. I had great difficulty in dragging myself away as the cow gently nuzzled the pockets of my farm coat expecting a treat. She followed behind us obediently, tail swishing, as we climbed the paddock to the top gate, apparently listening to our conversation.

Carrying out routine testing work on behalf of the Ministry of Agriculture was largely repetitive but provided some surprises to relieve the tedium.

I was working in a concrete yard beside a relatively new barn, testing a herd of beef cattle. Inside, the cattle were progressively channelled into a passage which narrowed so that having passed out through the gated entrance of the barn, the race along the outside of the barn wall leading to the crush was only wide enough for one animal. The wall of the barn formed one side of the race and a series of gates the other. Midway through the morning, without warning, the outer breeze block wall of the barn collapsed, falling into the barn.

Now there was nothing between the cattle and me. For an instant, the animals inside looked out, startled by the sunlight, whilst the few cattle in the race glimpsed their brethren, greater in number and higher than they were, elevated by the depth of accumulated soiled winter bedding. Then all hell broke loose. Reacting marginally more quickly than the animals, the farmhands inside the barn and myself on the outside beat a retreat. The herd instinct took over and the group of cattle charged back into the darker recesses of the barn bawling, tails in the air and kicking their back legs out behind them, a maelstrom of movement and mayhem. The excited beasts gradually settled, the handling arrangements were redesigned and rebuilt and the battle to complete the test re-commenced.

I conducted ministry work only on the farms of my own clients, so I was familiar with the handling facilities and the capabilities of each work force. The state of the cattle crushes employed varied greatly from brand new, innovatively-designed with labels still attached to those which, little used since my last visit, had languished in a corner of the field, exposed to the weather and rusting amongst the nettles. The operating mechanism of some had seized, only being coaxed back to life with copious amounts of oil and the skilled application of a sledgehammer. On several occasions, the weight of the first animal of the day entering the crush was too much for the rotten wooden floorboards which splintered asunder.

Most crushes were designed to accommodate cows but when it came to the bulls, it was a squeeze to fit them in. Often, they were simply too large, receiving their tuberculin injections with their forequarters in the crush and their hindquarters in the race. Some remained jammed in the race, restrained after a fashion by metal poles inserted side to side, in front and behind them. These bars often bent under the animal's weight and had to be held or better still, tied, to prevent them flying past my head when kicked or head-butted. Some resisted the race altogether and had to be trapped behind gates.

I was working in a vast new concrete complex with a race of six tubular metal gates per side, each tied to the next with orange baler twine, narrowing from the catchment pen, similarly constructed of gates, to the crush. I was wary of this crush because its wooden floor had been discarded but not replaced.

In normal circumstances, the weight of the animal standing on the floor of the crush added to its overall mass and stability but not on this occasion. I was testing young heifers for brucellosis, climbing in behind each animal to take blood samples from their tail vein. Towards the end of the group, when only the reticent and the rebellious remained, the tolerance of the current occupant of the crush snapped. Letting out a belligerent bellow and summoning all her strength, she began to drag the crush across the yard.

The combined bulk of the animals remaining in the makeshift catchment pen, caused these gates to part company with those forming the race. The gates of the race, still attached to the errant crush, as acolytes accompanying a cleric, careered crazily behind her. I do so wish I had been able to film this extraordinary pageant for posterity but sadly it is stored only as a memory in my mind.

I was called to the phone between consultations about a three-year-old bull that had suddenly become very lame. This was not such an unusual occurrence. Injuries were incurred when serving cows in the field, the heavy male 'slipping off' the back of the female, usually resulting in muscle strains, back injuries and the like. Bulls were also susceptible to infections or penetrations in their hooves in the same way as cows.

This bull was in a distant water meadow down by the river with no housing or handling facilities nearby. As a bare minimum, I needed to examine the animal closely, palpate the animal's affected limb with my hands, as well as to record the animal's temperature. Not many animals remain still when a thermometer is being inserted in their backside. The farmers recognised that when they called the vet out, time was money and with that in mind, I suggested that the bull should be moved slowly to the nearest barn where he could be contained in a pen and tied up, even if he could not be placed in a crush.

I visited this make-do-and-mend farm later that afternoon. Jumping into the elderly Land Rover, I held the door shut whilst being driven out to the barn where the animal had been housed. Unhappily, I could not help this magnificent male. Bizarrely, he had fractured a bone in his right front leg, the only time I came across such an injury in my career. There was no choice but to complete the official paperwork required to have the animal humanely slaughtered on the farm.

About six weeks later, a smartly dressed man from the ministry arrived at the practice to discuss my handling of this case. He was adamant I had been wrong to advise the animal should be moved to a barn with handling facilities. I was reprimanded for causing unnecessary suffering to this bull. I took his criticism on the chin since I did not want to end up in London, defending myself in front of a panel of the great and the good.

However, I thought I had been treated unfairly. Even though I had worked in the practice for more than five years, I was not familiar with the position of every field on every farm, let alone the detailed geospatial relationship between each field and the farm buildings. I would not intentionally have caused this or any animal to suffer unnecessary pain but equally, there is nothing more frustrating than arriving on a farm to find you cannot get near your patient. You are reduced to the role of onlooker, unable to help the animal or be of any practical use to the client. This encounter with the authorities was a chastening experience.

Back on Cyril Sellar's farm in Denton, where my dog Mostyn had disgraced himself, I was looking at a four-day old male Friesian calf standing dejectedly in the corner of its pen, a limp tail signalling his pain. He had broken one of his front legs. To Cyril, the farmer, the economic worth of the calf with four good legs at the time was about a pound per leg.

"What can we do?" he asked.

Buoyed by not being asked to put the poor creature down, I sent Cyril off to fetch a piece of plastic downpipe of the type used in modern guttering systems and a hacksaw. Cutting the pipe to the correct length for the calf's leg and then in half along its length, I created a simple bespoke splint. Covering the edges with protective sticky plaster, I wrapped wads of cotton wool around the injured leg as gently as possible, holding it in place with conforming bandage. The splint I had fashioned fitted comfortably enough and I secured it in place using rolls of broad sticky bandage. I left Cyril with a supply of injectable drugs for pain relief and asked him to keep the bedding in the pen scrupulously clean and dry.

As I drove away, I was full of respect for the farmer. Cyril had farmed using traditional methods for many years. He had no problem aligning his farming objectives with his personal values. From my point of view, I was in an enviable profession and in a position to offer a mix of mental and manual skills which could and should be applied in a socially acceptable way. I revisited the calf three weeks later to reapply the splint, using fresh dressings to allow for further growth of the limb.

I was on the farm again, just before Christmas, to attend a lame cow. I checked the calf, removed the splint and dressings from the limb, which had been supported for the last six weeks. The fracture had healed well. There was no pain when I felt around the fracture site and the calf seemed happy enough, stumping around the pen with a leg that must have felt strangely lightweight. I had arranged that the follow-up visits to the calf were done when I was passing by so that no visit fee was charged. I left with a freshly-pulled stalk of Brussels sprouts to grace our Christmas dinner; an ideal outcome for me, the farmer and especially for the calf.

It's difficult to retain a detached objectivity when treating an endearing pet of friends. I first met Barclay when visiting David and Louise at Hill Farm. Both fulfilled stratosphericallyimportant roles in London, to which they commuted daily. Their animals were left in the charge of the gardener and housekeeper. Passing by and calling in for a cup of tea as time permitted, I noticed an extra member regularly joined the household throng - a golden retriever.

He lived in the mansion opposite but obviously feeling he was not getting sufficient attention, he wandered up the long and winding drive to visit his new canine friends, Henry, Spangle and Flossie. Eventually, Barclay was spending more time at Hill Farm than in his own home and it was agreed that Barclay would be adopted into the Hill Farm menagerie. He was gentle, even-tempered and dignified, without a hint of assertiveness or aggression, happy to go with flow whilst enjoying as much fuss as possible. He craved human company as well as the companionship of other dogs. I would have happily taken him home to be a playmate for Mostyn but he had already found his ideal situation.

David phoned the practice in the early afternoon in the summer of '89. Barclay, having gained some weight, had tried to squeeze through a metal garden gate and had become stuck. I wasted no time driving out to Hill Farm and arrived to find he had been freed with a judicious attack on the gate with an angle grinder. The gate's construction was of squares of metalwork with iron spikes protruding part way into each square from its base.

Barclay had become impaled on one of these vicious spikes. He had a nasty stab wound close to his navel but otherwise seemed unfazed by his experience. His calm temperament meant he had not struggled, which had helped minimise the extent of his injuries. He came back to the surgery with me and was put on an intravenous saline drip to replace any fluids he may have lost. The practice was invariably busy during these summer months but I was not prepared to leave Barclay until later, despite the queue of clients waiting for me upstairs.

Abigail, my most experienced nurse, helped me anaesthetise Barclay and he settled well. What I wanted to do was to cleanse and repair his stab wound to his ventral abdomen, a relatively minor piece of surgery which could be completed quickly and was minimally invasive. However, at the back of my mind was advice given by Harold Pearson, my senior surgical tutor at the vet school in Bristol, who taught us that in such cases, we must check for internal damage to the abdominal organs.

Cyril's Farmyard 1988

Cyril Milking Parlour 1988

Abigail with Patient. 1986

Barclay

I knew I ought to conduct a thorough abdominal assessment but in Barclay's case, I would much rather disregard this advice and adopt my default position of doing as little as possible. I gritted my teeth and lengthened the wound in the ventral body wall. I checked each loop of bowel diligently for damage before gently deflecting it to check next the segment until eventually reaching the dorsal wall of the abdominal cavity. Phew! Everything appeared undamaged.

The cautiousness of a Capricorn in my character asserted itself, prompting me to ask Abigail to time five minutes on her watch before I could close the abdominal wound with a completely clear conscience. Nothing significant in choosing five minutes, except it seemed a reasonable length of time to wait. After four minutes and forty-five seconds, a spurt of blood shot upwards pulsing under pressure. This was my worst nightmare. Panicking, I placed my thumbs each side of the damaged blood vessel, exerting downward pressure to stem the flow of blood. Meanwhile, Abigail was calling for immediate assistance from colleagues.

What a relief to discuss the situation dispassionately with a colleague as cool and calm as Alistair. We had no choice but to attempt to repair the damaged walls of the aorta. This major blood vessel takes blood under pressure from the heart to the abdominal organs and hind quarters. During abdominal surgery, it can be seen pulsing synchronously with the heartbeats.

We could not ligate this major artery in the body effectively. Neither of us had attempted a repair of this nature before. If it failed, the life of this dog would be over. We did not have any of the sophisticated surgical devices now widely available to the vascular specialist medics. I had my thumbs, which continued to press and limit the bleeding, whilst Alistair swabbed and sutured the edges of the damaged arterial wall together. He completed this delicate surgery and we stood back to watch and wait.

We were well into the statutory five-minute period before blood squirted skywards again. Alistair repeated his surgical repair but the result was the same. The pressure of the blood pumping in the artery was so high, it was tearing the stitches apart. By now, the low-ceilinged operating theatre had become unbearably hot, augmented by the heat from the operating spotlights which were prickling the nape of my neck.

We changed over. Alistair's thumbs now limiting further haemorrhage whilst I tried to do my best-ever stitching. Desperation was setting in and I was trying to push the 'what if' scenario to the back of my mind when Abigail told me we had run out of sterile surgical swabs. The nurses were reduced to cutting off white swathes from the large roll of surgical gauze.

Barclay had now been asleep for two and a half hours. My back hurt, the lumbar muscles clamped in cramping spasms. My legs ached and I had a headache, exacerbated by the heat and the tension. Doubts dominated my thoughts. I was the most experienced vet in the practice and the responsibility for this dog's life rested with me. The staff, staying behind after home time, were each contributing to the collective will. Teamwork, tenacity and determination were needed more than ever. Barclay's mucosal colour was very pale now, his heart rate rising in response to his falling blood pressure. I tried a different suture pattern to try to spread the forces which were causing the suture material to pull through the vessel wall over a wider area.

I cannot remember how many attempts were made to stop the bleeding but believe me, when at the end of a further five-minute wait, no blood gushed forth, for a moment I felt euphoric. I supported my repair by anchoring normal healthy tissue, wrapping it around the weakened blood vessel. The abdominal wound was closed using many more stitches than usual, placed close together and using several layers of sutures to minimise the chance of any further seepage and loss of blood.

Barclay was returned to his kennel, laid on a heat pad and surrounded by plenty of warmed bedding. He had drip lines running into each foreleg to keep his blood volume above critical levels. He would not have looked out of place in the casualty ward of a TV hospital drama. Antibiotics were given directly into his bloodstream, together with powerful drugs designed to counteract the shock caused by the surgery and the amount of blood he had lost. We had done everything that we could to support our patient. At least he had a chance.

The operating theatre resembled a village butchery in the African bush and everyone looked shattered. The Cricketers Arms pub was only 100 yards from the practice. I sent my colleagues off to the pub with some practice cash to buy drinks and food. At this stage, the prevailing mood remained euphoric. A well-drilled team working to the limit of their skills had performed magnificently and I was proud of them. Later, they headed for home, whilst I settled down for an overnight vigil with my canine friend.

I phoned David to give him an update. I told him the next twelve hours were critical, adding that I didn't think Barclay could survive further surgery. I promised to ring if there was a change in the dog's condition overnight.

My wife exhorted me to come home but I could not leave this dog. He needed human company more than ever before. One of the reasons the bleeding had stopped was because his blood pressure had fallen so low. What would happen as the physiological factors within his body began to reverse this situation. Would the stitches hold? They were only as strong as the tissue in which I had placed them.

I sat with him, willing him to recover. He slept peacefully and, I suspect, so did I from time to time. I was an inadequate replacement for the machines used nowadays which blink and bleep, controlling drip rates, monitoring heart rate, respiratory patterns and the like. As the outside temperature dropped during the night, the creaking of the old building was interspersed with the distant sounds of the city, as revellers returned from summer balls to their digs to sleep off the night's excesses. A combination of tea and biscuits was all I had to keep me going through the small hours.

I treasured the look of glee on Abigail's face, when she came downstairs the following morning. Barclay was awake and lying on his side, his extremities warm, his tail banging enthusiastically on the kennel floor, pleased to see someone that wasn't me. The nurses were far more skilled than me in post-operative care. Content to leave him in their hands, I stayed just long enough to watch him eat some convalescent food with gusto. You can always win the affection of a retriever through his stomach.

He stayed with us for a few days; his bodily functions and his heavily-bandaged abdomen needed careful management. With the array of drips removed, he was able to enjoy his new-found freedom, walking unassisted into the garden to sniff the air. It wasn't home but home wasn't far off. By the time he was fit to go, the owners had installed a new wooden gate of a different design. He continued his recuperation with his friends and was spoilt rotten. It was only after I had taken his skin sutures out some ten days later that I completely relaxed and mentally ticked the box marked 'success'.

Reflecting on this outcome, I realised that many separate events and experiences in my earlier life had combined to mould my character, making me the vet I had become. To a greater or lesser extent, we are the product of our parents. My stubbornness I may have inherited from my mother. Perhaps persistent and passionate were qualities I could recognise in my persona. At any rate, I tried my best and set the tone by example, quietly influencing those around me. I think you need an idea of the limits of your capabilities but I had surprised even myself. Everyone played their part, setting aside the notion of normal working hours and were properly deserving of the description 'professionals'.

Barclay showed courage and stoicism beyond anything I had seen before. He was a model patient. Every time I met him, whether on social visits or for veterinary attention, I felt a thrill of pleasure at seeing him again.

Chapter 15

It Happened Today

The end of June 1989 marked the retirement of Jimmy Sheriffs after a career spanning sixty years. His contribution to the history of the practice was celebrated with another party in the garden at Iffley Road. His honesty and integrity were exceeded only by the considerate attention he gave to the animals under his care. Many of our farming clients turned up to thank him personally. Over a drink, they recalled stories of his life and experiences on their farms.

When Jimmy arrived in Oxfordshire in 1946, he stayed on a family farm in Great Haseley. The son of the family, then a young boy, came to the party and Mr Sheriffs, finding him at his shoulder, said, "I remember you when you were in short trousers."

It was a time for fond farewells, including an all-trophy greyhound race meeting held at Oxford Stadium featuring the JT Sheriffs Memorial Race with Jimmy presenting the trophy to the winning owner and trainer.

The practice, now trading as A. Bartholomew Veterinary Surgeons, was expanding steadily. I hoped it was a case of happy clients spreading good news about the practice. Word of mouth has always been my favoured method of advertising.

The expectations of our clients were the same then as they are today. High quality veterinary care, which is not necessarily synonymous with extremely expensive care. They value the services of a vet who is compassionate, inspires confidence and offers clear explanations. A strong commitment to animal welfare is essential. These have been my simple guiding principles.

Unexpected clinical cases as well as events outside the practice bubble kept cropping up.

Ev's remaining follicle factory functioned admirably and we were both overjoyed to find she was expecting our second child. I couldn't attend the ultrasound scan on this occasion either. We were grateful to Liz, my veterinary nurse *extraordinaire,* who offered her child-minding services for our daughter Anna during the flurry of hospital appointments which proved necessary.

Oxford, a city of about one hundred and fifty thousand souls, can prove to be a remarkably small world. I was sitting in a featureless waiting area of the maternity wing in the John Radcliffe hospital when my wife had been whisked off for a further assessment. As these experiences often are, it was late at night, the overhead lights had been dimmed, in contrast with the bright lights coming from the vending machine buzzing in the corner, dispensing such healthy food options as crisps and chocolate.

I was thinking about the events of the day when a couple came and sat beside me. I was recognised by the lady, who owned a cat called Madge. I was introduced to her Dutch partner. He worked on the oil rigs so his periods of leave were few and far between. I had last seen Madge as a patient about three months ago. She had suffered a haemorrhage into her left eye, causing an increase in the internal pressure of the fluid within the eye and a painful condition called glaucoma.

Specialist referral was not an option in this case so I had to advise that the eye be removed. It was an operation I hated doing. Performing this surgery often made me feel physically sick but it had to be done. Once the eye had been removed, an empty space remained within the bony eye socket. In surgical terms this is called dead space. I packed this space with an antibiotic-impregnated gauze dressing, folded into postage stamp-sized squares in the form of a concertina, the end of which protruded after the eyelids had been stitched together. The presence of the gauze filling this space minimised further haemorrhage and blood clots. A small amount of the gauze was withdrawn each day and trimmed off; this routine was repeated for about a week. The patient had to wear a plastic Elizabethan collar to prevent the dressing being hoicked out with an errant claw.

At a post-operative check-up, I recalled Madge's eyelids bulging, suggesting she had bled into her eye socket despite my best efforts. In previous cases, the blood clot had gradually been resorbed into the body with an acceptable cosmetic result in the end. Presumably because of the impending arrival of their first baby, I hadn't seen the cat recently. In the quiet of this darkened, purely functional medical space, perched on uncomfortable orange plastic chairs, an odour of antiseptics and surgical spirit in the air, Madge's owner was keen to update me on her cat's progress.

It seemed that Madge was really her partner's cat. Whenever he returned for a break, she would jump on the table to supervise his mealtimes. His favourite dish was scrambled eggs on toast which he liked to lace liberally with tomato ketchup. At home at the start of his paternity leave, Madge was stationed as usual as he consumed his preferred plateful. Madge sneezed. From her nose came a massive production of material which was indistinguishable in appearance from the food on his plate. The skin forming the covering of her eye socket had now completely inverted itself, forming a ghoulish fur-lined hollow on her face. Scrambled eggs have been off the menu since that day.

It seemed surreal in this impersonal environment, where feelings of anxiety and tension were never far away, to hear this case history recounted calmly and in such graphic detail by folk who were not in the least bit medically minded. Feeling jaded, I considered what I should say? Saved from saying anything, I was called to rejoin the medics and my exhausted wife.

On the day when two new rings were discovered encircling Neptune by Voyager 2, Rachael was born on Friday the eleventh of August 1989, a sister for Anna. Ev, now an experienced hand at this birthing business, had time for a wash and brush-up before breakfast was served. After making myself presentable and ringing friends and relatives with the good news, I hurried over to Marcham to tell Anna she had a sister.

Out on her motorbike, Abigail's luck finally ran out when a car collided with her on a roundabout south of Oxford. My esteemed head nurse sustained a badly-broken leg which required pinning. The only saving grace was I could visit her, a few floors below my wife and baby, during my trips to the hospital.

On Saturday afternoon, Ev and Rachael came home and I had the weekend to acquaint myself with my younger daughter. It was back to work on Monday though, starting with a session of timed trials at the greyhound track.

There had been a disappointing turnover of staff during the summer holiday season. Younger staff were always more likely to move on, to gain new experiences or to be nearer to boyfriends or girlfriends who lived further away. Members of my team were expected to work hard but not to work harder or for longer than me. I had to find time for interviews with applicants interested in replacing my departing colleagues. There was extra pressure on me to cover their duties at night, at weekends and at the racetrack. I had precious little time to spend with my newly-extended family.

Madge and I crossed swords again. She was presented losing weight, with a poor appetite and 'not herself'. She was certainly subdued and on examination I found one of her kidneys was massively enlarged and painful on the slightest pressure. After subjecting her to a series of tests, including blood samples and x-rays, it was clear this abnormal kidney would have to be removed.

A nephrectomy represents major surgery, with the associated pain and surgical shock both serious risk factors to consider, in addition to those from a routine laparotomy. An intravenous drip was set-up and Madge was anaesthetised and prepared for surgery. The kidney was easy to locate, being swollen and grossly haemorrhagic in appearance; it needed to be removed forthwith. This organ has a rich blood supply and the vessels which supply it must be ligated before they are sectioned. These ligatures must be applied close to the aorta which carries blood under pressure to the hind quarters of the cat.

My cautious instincts meant I applied two ligatures both to the artery and to the vein and having tied off the ureter, which drains urine to the bladder, the diseased kidney was removed. Madge would have to rely on her remaining kidney to filter all the waste products from her bloodstream. After the customary five-minute pause, with no untoward bleeding noted, I closed her abdominal wound in the normal way. She received pain relief and antibiotics and the drip remained in place to help keep her properly hydrated, assisting her solitary kidney as it took the strain. Considering what she had been through, I expected our patient to remain very flat, needing critical care for several days. Not a bit of it. She was lifting her head within half an hour and an hour later, she was registering her displeasure whenever the nurses went in to check on her progress. She was so difficult to nurse that in the end we had to give in to her tremendous strength of will and ask her owners to take her home and care for her there. What a cat!

In October, visiting a stable close to the spot where Matthew Arnold may have stood to admire Oxford's "dreaming spires", I could see as many tall cranes as church spires. I was there to castrate a five-year old chestnut Arab stallion called Suleiman.

It's possible he was named after Sultan Suleiman the Magnificent. He would have deserved the title. More than four hundred kilos of absolute magnificence. The castration operation carried out under general anaesthetic was uneventful but I was called back a few days later to look at his legs.

There is a complex system of drainage channels for the lymphatic fluid which bathes and nourishes the body's tissues. It is quite separate from the arterial and venous systems. Those of Suleiman, especially in his hindlegs, stood out under his fine skin like whipcords, tense, hot and painful to touch. His clinical signs were normal, the site of my surgery was healing nicely. I had not seen anything quite like it before.

Using first principles, I tried to fathom out an answer to this problem with objectivity and calmness. His temperature was normal and his wound was not infected. The owner and I discussed everything connected with horse since he was purchased several years previously. No unusual events in his history came to mind except vaccinations and routine worming.

Ah but wait. The owner recalled that the horse had developed a skin mass which my erstwhile partner, Russell Kyle, had diagnosed as an equine sarcoid. This lump was deemed unsuitable for sharp surgery so injections had been used to treat the lesion. At the practice, there were no record cards holding medical histories for our equine clients. Looking at the financial records, a drug, recorded as a vaccine, had been charged to the owner and its price didn't correspond with that of a routine vaccine. Used historically in human medicine to combat tuberculosis and leprosy, it looked as if Russell may have tried human BCG vaccine to treat this horse's sarcoid lesion.

I found a scientific paper, published in 1986, comparing results of treatment of sarcoid lesions using cryosurgery with those using BCG vaccine in thirty horses. An immunological reaction stimulated the animal's immune system to produce antibodies against certain proteins in the mass. I presumed that when I performed the castration surgery on Suleiman, which involved cutting and crushing body tissue, I had released similar proteins which re-sensitised his body to produce more antibodies in excessive amounts.

I treated Suleiman with anti-inflammatory drugs to dampen down his exaggerated inflammatory response. The owner hosed his legs with cold water several times a day and the condition subsided over the next few weeks. Nowadays, immunotherapy and gene therapy are at the forefront of the fight to treat some forms of cancer. In the 1980s, this technique was ahead of its time and typical of Russell to decide to give it a go.

On the ninth of November 1989, the Berlin Wall crumbled - with some encouragement – and took the illusory Iron Curtain with it. It was arguably the most significant event to have happened in my lifetime. Suddenly and dramatically, those living in the east of the city were at liberty to travel legitimately to West Berlin if they wished. I have read that these East German visitors were given one hundred Deutsche Marks to buy goods in the shops of West Berlin. The newsreel coverage showed their exhilaration at gaining this new-found freedom and, in many instances, their joy at being reunited with family members they had not seen for forty years. It served to emphasise how much I took for granted in my life, with only the vagaries of the M25 orbital motorway between me and a visit to my parents and my sister.

The personal pressure on my time increased still further in November. Russell Kyle, my former business partner, wrote offering me the chance to buy his share of the Wheatley surgery building together with the goodwill of his practice and his client list. It was conditional on the deal being completed by the end of the year.

I could not turn down this opportunity, despite the extra burden it would place on the finances of the practice and of my family. My wife said we should buy it, Jock Skinner my bank manager agreed and so did my solicitor. The deal was done in double-quick time, financed by increased borrowing at the bank, with the Wheatley building held by the bank as security.

I needed access to Russell's client list as quickly as possible so his clients could be informed of the changes. Especially important to me were the farmers who used to come to Iffley Road and who I wanted to regain as clients, uniting the practice once more. I visited them all to make sure they were happy to return to the Iffley Road fold. I was surprised to learn that a number had not realised they could stay at Iffley Road when the practice split in 1987. It gave me great pleasure to have them back and I vowed to do my utmost to keep them.

As we bid adieu to the 80s, I was deeper in debt but owned the whole of a commercial building, though it was mortgaged and I had to keep the bank onside. I could run consultations at Wheatley at times of my choosing though I needed to take care not to disrupt the routine to which the clients had become accustomed.

My challenge was to rearrange the rotas of the vets and the nurses so that Iffley Road, Wheatley Surgery and the greyhound track were properly staffed without reducing the amount of time off for each member of my tight little ship. I could not afford any more employees. The strain under which the team were working was highlighted when a staff member was off work for whatever reason. It was almost impossible to keep all the balls in the air.

Chapter 16

I Get Around

On the farm-animal side, the year started with a large tuberculin test at Hollands Farm in Great Milton. Two hundred and fifty cows, each with a mind of its own, had to be encouraged along a race and into the cattle crush. Groups of animals behave in much the same way as groups of people; about one third do what you ask willingly, one third reluctantly and one third are just bloody awkward.

The last were generally old hands and knew what was coming. Their ear marks had to be recorded, their skin clipped and its thickness measured. Injections of avian and bovine tuberculin, amounting to one tenth of a millilitre, were given in the side of their necks causing palpable blebs the size of a petit pois under the skin.

Starting at eight o'clock, we worked outside in the rain. By half past two, I was wet, filthy and frozen to the core. It was not an uplifting experience for me, the farmer, the farmhands or the herd. The cows often registered their displeasure by giving less milk in the afternoon following this government-approved indignity.

Three days later, I was back again, measuring any alterations in the skin thickness of each animal's neck. Understandably, the cows were even more reluctant to cooperate. Before I could depart, I had to take blood samples from the replacement heifers to be screened for brucellosis. The ages of these animals ranged from twelve to thirty months; they tended to be skittish and even more reticent about entering the crush. Pressure was mounting because on Fridays, I had to be at Wheatley surgery to begin consultations at half past twelve; there was no other vet free to do it. I was dependent on the efficiency of my helpers and the cooperation of animals. Not perfect for punctuality.

Tuberculosis and brucellosis are serious diseases which can infect both cattle and people. Jimmy contracted brucellosis early in his career and suffered symptoms periodically for the rest of his life. For tuberculosis tests, only vets who had been trained and licensed by the ministry were permitted to carry out this important but largely repetitive work. I used this time on the farm to have a wide-ranging chat about veterinary matters from the incidence of mastitis or lameness to the price of milk.

I drew up regularly outside the dairy of this farm for fertility checks and other clinical work. Later in the year, one particular visit had potential implications for the wider agricultural community in the area. I arrived to examine a cow which could not get up.

Out in the field, with her back legs splayed out behind her, she had adopted an unusual posture for a cow. Her heart rate and temperature were normal, her rumen was churning normally and she was heavy in calf. With a distinctly wild look in her eye, she exhibited extreme aggression when approached. Recognising this could be serious, I called the Ministry of Agriculture to discuss what could be my first case of BSE.

Bovine spongiform encephalopathy, dubbed mad cow disease, was an untreatable and ultimately fatal neurodegenerative condition, first recorded in Britain in 1988. It was a devastating disease which human beings could contract from eating meat products containing infected bovine material.

Prions were a new phenomenon; the presence of these malformed proteins caused disturbances in brain function, particularly affecting the perception of space. The disease could only be confirmed on post mortem specimens. The ministry required the brain tissue of all affected animals to be submitted for analysis in specialist laboratories. I had to remain on the farm, in temporary quarantine, to await another man from the ministry.

On arrival, this man seemed very young and rather unsure of himself. I noticed his pristine wellingtons as he unwrapped his waterproof coat from its brown paper packaging. He was sufficiently confident to assess this case from the other side of the field gate to our patient. He agreed the case warranted further investigation and asked me to shoot the animal. In this case, his authority exceeded my own, so I pointed out tactfully this wouldn't be appropriate. The animal would be shot in the head; his employers would require the brain tissue in an unscrambled state if my diagnosis was to be confirmed and compensation paid to my client.

The cow would have to be put down using intravenous drugs given into the jugular vein in the neck. This necessitated yours truly getting up close to the head and neck of this animal to locate this major vein and administer the drug successfully. To undertake this dangerous task with a disorientated, hostile animal seemed like madness to me. In her current mental state, she might maim me using her one remaining weapon, namely her head, weighing about thirty pounds. Surely such an exercise could only have been concocted by scientists and government mandarins who had seldom, if ever, been amongst a herd of cows.

Following a quick health and safety risk assessment, I concluded I would be much safer if I remained on the same side of the field gate as the ministry man. Not for the first time, I was facing a clinical dilemma. I began today's visit working for my client in a private capacity. As events unfolded, I had put my government hat on and assumed the responsibilities of an LVI. The ministry were now my bosses and calling the tune. I had a duty of care to end the suffering of this animal although my safety should rank of equal importance. Someone's safety had to be risked and that person was me.

Phlegmatic as ever, Robert as herdsman, managed to fit a rope halter on the beast for a second time, staying just out of range of her lunging head. Provided he was strong enough to keep her head relatively still, his skills with a lasso meant we had regained a degree of control of this situation. I put the cow to sleep with as much dignity as possible under the circumstances, ready to beat a rapid retreat at a moment's notice. I was supervised washing myself down using hot water, a parlour brush and ministry-approved disinfectant. My temporary quarantine duly lifted, I could leave the farm, my schedule of visits and consultations for the rest of the day now in complete disarray.

In the press, it was argued that previous governments' decisions to permit cattle to be fed processed feeds containing the remains of other cattle, albeit after heat treatment, enabled this disease to become established in the national herd and subsequently the source of human tragedy. Scientists and officials argued about the temperature to which such feeds should be subjected before they were considered safe and the energy costs of such treatment. Driving away from the farm, I was uneasy about the many budget meat pies I had consumed in my student days when money was tight and later at public gatherings, racetracks and such like. There but for the grace of God ...

Danger on a round of visits can be beautifully disguised. A long-standing client kept a herd of cattle and some brood Arab mares. She regularly sold Arab bloodstock to the Arabs as well as competing successfully at race meetings. In the hands of her experienced groom, these horses were well-behaved, gentle animals, easy on the eye and a pleasure to treat.

All that changed when she acquired a noble Arab stallion with attitude. He had a marked aversion to needles and the vets who came bearing them. It fell to me to vaccinate him on a regular basis. For safety's sake, he had to be placed in a covering stall. From a distance, you could hear his hooves crashing against the structure that held him, I hoped securely. Feeling like a criminal, I edged towards him keeping out of sight. Crouched with loaded syringe, I popped up beside his neck, jabbed him, and withdrew, as he kicked out with renewed vigour. He was led away before he could wreck everything in sight. We tried all sorts of strategies to calm him down with little success. Surprisingly, the administration of Herbal Rescue Remedy under his tongue a short time before my arrival did take the edge off his anxiety but after using this ruse several times, he chewed the glass pipette off the dropper, disdainfully spitting out the pieces in defiance of our attempts to subdue him. He was eventually sold, and when last I heard, he was being ridden out in Richmond Park, not apparently considered a danger to the local populace or those in prams.

Many people aspire to be their own boss. It does have some advantages; you suffer the consequences of your own decisions and cannot blame anyone else. I was beholden only to my wife, my bank manager and the Royal College of Veterinary Surgeons. But self-employment in a small business also has its drawbacks. There can be times when there is no-one else to call upon and the responsibility rests with you.

Successful Calving 1990

Porcine Packages

From a diary entry, I note I was off sick on a Thursday in March, expecting not to be fit to work for three or four days. On Friday, despite being under the weather, I had to attend a five-hour race meeting at the greyhound track, undertake evening surgery at Wheatley and be on duty overnight. This was not ideal for me, my clients or my patients but the practice had to be staffed at all times. I was more likely to make errors in diagnosis or in dispensing medicines in a befuddled state. I couldn't place a sign in the window stating, 'Back when I feel better.'

Offering a twenty-four-hour emergency service to our clients was mandatory and an onerous burden, interrupting precious hours of sleep as well as tying you to your home and landline.

At last, advances in technology offered an easing of these unwelcome restrictions. We purchased our first mobile telephone, a Motorola 8500x, referred to by my colleagues as the brick. It was bulky and heavy with poor battery life and indifferent reception in some locations. However, it did allow the duty vet the option to visit friends or go out for a meal locally. What luxury. Being on duty became more bearable, especially for my younger colleagues who revelled in their release. The search for a phone box to contact the practice or phone home after an emergency call became a thing of the past.

I had the Motorola with me at five o'clock on Saturday evening as I headed for Scholarswell Farm in Garsington to attend a sow which was farrowing. Tony and David ran a traditional mixed farm raising beef cattle, which were David's interest, and pigs, which were Tony's pride and joy. The two brothers, both past sixty, were there to greet me. David, the shorter of the two, uncomplicated, generally took the lead in dealing with the vet. Tony, disinclined to engage in small talk, still retained the physique of a prop forward.

My patient was lying on her side on the concrete floor of the farrowing crate. The sow had given birth to a solitary piglet which was nestling against her teats. The scene was illuminated by one low-wattage light bulb, encrusted in grime. A series of disconsolate grunts was all the sow had to say on the matter.

With the requisite bucket of warm water waiting, I washed and slathered my arms in lubricant. Laid out flat at full stretch, my cheek brushing the cold wet floor, the next piglet in line was tantalisingly just beyond my reach. I injected the sow with some *pituitary extract*, the hormone which should promote contractions of the uterine wall and bring the piglet within my grasp. Ten minutes later, I could touch and eventually deliver the second piglet alive. The conversational banter between the brothers, each pointing out the shortcomings of the other, became more spasmodic until it petered out altogether. I managed to fish out a third piglet but progress continued to be painfully slow.

I had been there for more than an hour and I was aware of the brothers fidgeting in the background. Finally, David broke the silence.

"Andrew, you see, we're in the darts team at the Red Lion and we've got a darts match about to start. We were wondering if you thought you could manage without us?"

"Of course," I replied, "You carry on. Just leave the back door of the farmhouse unlocked so I can get more water if I need it."

Delighted at being allowed out for their social highlight of the week, they made an incongruous pair, shuffling off in their mucky wellingtons, a light dusting of grain and pig feed forming highlights in their hair. They behaved like a couple of under-age teenagers caught trying to buy cigarettes.

This was a first for me. I had never before been left on my own to work on someone else's farm. In some ways, it was the highest accolade of trust.

The pattern of the evening had already been established. I would repeat the hormone injection, wait for twenty minutes, sitting on a straw bale, before having another grope in the depths of the womb of my patient. With luck, I would be able to deliver another piglet, sense that the head of the next was just out of reach and the video loop would be played again.

During this protracted parturition, I had plenty of time to take proper notice of my surroundings. The low roof was formed by corrugated panels supported by a series of rusty metal A-frames from which spiders' webs of varying vintage fluttered in draughts of stale air, festooned like expensive lacework created by a seamstress on some psychoactive substance. Dust from the pig food lent increased definition to the intricacies of their designs and adorned every surface of the farrowing house.

The soundtrack from the inmates consisted of discordant vocal passages, rising and falling as the squeals of one agitated piglet set all the mothers off, a dissonant grunting chorus which gradually subsided as they settled and sleep intervened once more.

That night, I had plenty of time to consider the special relationship between a farm vet, his client and his patients. Would I change places with the brothers tonight, chattering to others with a pint in the pub, in preference to ushering another small porcine package into this world? Of course not. This is what my lengthy veterinary training had prepared me to do. To be able to bring a newborn on to the stage and have a seat in the front row was an honour. It brought purpose to my professional life. Waiting for the next piglet to come within reach, I replenished my bucket of water, used the house facilities and phoned my wife.

"No, I don't know what time I'll be back. Could be after ten at his rate. Have your dinner. No, don't wait for me. I can't come home and come back later. I'll ring you as I leave. Have you had any more calls? No, good. See you later."

It was now past eight o' clock. I was pretty sure one horn of the sow's uterus was empty of piglets, but I could still feel at least one foetus evading my attention. My chest, shoulders and knees were sore from lying on the hard floor, a novel form of repetitive strain injury perhaps. I had to arch my aching back to maximise my reach whilst searching for the next in line.

Finally, the sequence was broken. Reaching inside the sow for the umpteenth time, I couldn't feel any more piglets. I gave a final hormone injection to be sure. Taking a moment to observe the results of our combined efforts, ten piglets were now fighting each other, scrabbling for the teats with the most milk. Their mother seemed peaceful and content, perhaps because this well-meaning soul had ceased to guddle about inside her. Each piglet settled on a teat and I left to the sounds of suckling and gurgling as they gorged on the colostrum now flowing in abundance.

It was after ten o'clock when I drove past the village pub at the top of Pettiwell. Judging by the general hubbub, a good time was being had by all. The darts match had finished and a singsong was getting under way.

A first for 1990 was assisting a red deer which was calving. A sheep farmer had invested in a breeding herd of more than a hundred red deer hinds and stags. A completely new handling system had to be installed, as well as miles of high and robust wire fences to prevent escape, since deer have a propensity to jump to considerable heights from a standing start. Red deer are not fully domesticated; they are fearful, can startle easily, kick ferociously and must be handled with care and patience.

My patient was held in a race so narrow that in theory, turning was impossible. She was coaxed into a crush of a different design to those used for cattle. This had solid wooden sides which narrowed towards its floor, forming a v shape. Once in the crush, a lever could make the floor of the crush fold away sideways from under the animal, which slipped down towards the base, becoming wedged with its feet raised above the barn floor. A rope was passed over the hind's neck from one side to the other to prevent escape by leaping and I could begin my examination. Two slim legs with small cloven hooves were protruding. I explored further along the internal passage, finding a calf which was very much alive and vigorous but whose head was deviated to the left and beneath its body.

In principle, the management of the case should have been straightforward. In the process of calving or lambing, I would push the body of the foetus towards the mother's head and having attached a rope to the calf's head, I would gradually draw it towards me and the open cervix. The difficulty in this case was caused by the length of the front legs of this deer calf. I would have to push the calf a long way forward to be able to manipulate the head successfully. I managed to loop a thin rope behind the delightfully-tactile ears of the calf, passing it between the lips of its mouth and pull it tight.

As I tried to push the body of the calf forwards away from the passage, the mother had quite enough of my attentions and was making renewed efforts to get away. Her legs kicked at fresh air where the floor of the crush used to be. Time was important in these cases; the calf had swallowed more foetal fluid than usual because of the lowered position of its head. I needed to deliver it quickly before it drowned. To gain extra leverage, I asked a farm hand to tug on a broom handle tied to the head rope, whilst I pushed the calf further away from me, using all my strength, my long arm fully extended.

My discomfort was balanced by the pleasure of feeling the head gradually ease towards me as it straightened, finally coming fully within my reach. Pulling the front legs back up into the passage and fully extending them relieved the logjam. I didn't have time to place ropes on the front legs as the hind decided the time had come to push. The farm hand and I caught the calf as it shot to freedom. After a quick check inside the hind to ensure no damage had been done, the operation of more levers moved the sides of the crush away, the hind dropped daintily onto the barn floor and skipped away at speed into a collecting pen beyond.

We placed her calf on the straw and retreated to a viewing area where we could watch her but she could not see us. She was too busy taking care of her calf to bother anyway and the calf was soon lifting its head in response to its mother's attention. The calf's initial breathing pattern had been rough, with sundry gurgles and coughing, but I had little doubt that nature and the passage of time would sort that out.

Back at headquarters, I had been offering advice and encouragement to my head nurse Abigail. Along with several other nurses, she had not received much in the way of useful careers advice. I'm not sure if anyone had ever really listened to her describing her dream.

She wanted to be a vet. We had wide-ranging discussions and walks by the river after work. I have found there is nothing like being near water and hearing the sound of it to clear the mind. Although I would be sad to lose her as a friend and colleague, I told her she should follow her heart's desire. She began by studying GCSE maths, taking evening classes in Oxford, and then studied three A level subjects part-time at a local college. Her working rota at the practice was adjusted to make these studies possible.

Her A level results were not quite enough to gain entry to the Royal Veterinary College in London but she left the practice in September 1990 to study for a degree in psychology at City University in East London. She hoped to gain entry to the vet course based on the results of her final undergraduate exams.

In the top flat at Iffley Road, we had a riotous party to wish her luck and say goodbye. I had depended on her, especially in the early months during the development of my practice. I was sorry that she was leaving but sure in my own mind that she had made the right decision to challenge herself to see if she could realise her ambition. During her university studies, she was a regular visitor to the practice, staying in touch throughout her course. As her confidence ebbed and flowed, we chatted on the phone and enjoyed more walks along the banks of the Thames.

Towards the end of 1990, Jimmy Sheriffs' wife Margaret and son William, who was over from Canada, asked to meet me for a chat. I was sorry to hear that Jimmy's health had deteriorated since his retirement. The family felt it was the right time to sell the Iffley Road property and they hoped to sell it to me. Such a purchase would stretch my financial resources to the limit but I simply had to grab this chance to secure the premises and the future of the practice. I found a building society willing to lend me most of the purchase price as a commercial mortgage and the transaction progressed in an amicable and dignified manner reaching a successful conclusion at the end of December.

As Big Ben's chimes at midnight signified the beginning of 1991, I became the proud owner of two commercial buildings and one private residence, all heavily mortgaged. On my salary which, for obvious reasons was the absolute minimum, I had two young children and a wife to feed and clothe. Absolutely no pressure at all as long as we continued to enjoy a reasonable rub of the green.

Chapter 17

Passing Ghosts

It takes time for historical associations with the names of local businesses and their reputations to fade from the collective memory. Arriving at Oxford railway station for a visit to help with childcare, my mother-in-law hailed a taxi and asked to be taken to 35 Iffley Road.

"Ah," said the driver, "Mr Heather's practice."

Mr Heather owned the practice when Jimmy Sheriffs arrived in 1946 and had been retired for decades.

Following his retirement, Jimmy's health deteriorated to such an extent that in January 1991, I visited him in a nursing home north of Banbury. He knew who I was and we had some confused conversation but he tired quickly and when I left, I looked back to see him cuddling a stuffed toy dog. As I drove away, I felt profoundly sad that Jimmy should be reduced to this, with only a soft toy for company.

Life in general practice can conjure up many contrasting yet linked scenarios. We began to see an elderly lady, probably in her eighties, who had given a home to a stray male cat. We neutered Bill, attended to his bad teeth, cleaned his ears, wormed him and treated him for his endemic fleas. Bill may well have suffered a severe attack of cat 'flu in his younger days, a viral condition which left a legacy of chronic sinusitis. During the autumn and often in the spring, this tended to flare up, causing him to sneeze, producing pus from both nostrils.

His new owner, who lived a few streets away from the practice in east Oxford, was a regular visitor. She knew her own mind and did not intend to let her 'young' vet put one over on her.

"I can't get him to take a tablet so I want him to have a pen'in 'jection"

She couldn't pronounce the name of the antibiotic but she knew it was white and insisted on checking the bottle and the contents of the syringe before I gave it to her cat. As Bill aged, he needed this injection repeated several times to completely clear his symptoms.

A keen young nurse, who was new to the practice, spent a while with her, trying to train her to give tablets. The nurse emerged from this consultation chastened, having learnt an important lesson. You need to pick your battles carefully.

With time, Bill's owner became more forgetful, even eccentric. One afternoon in high summer, she visited the practice with her pet. It was a hot day and she was too hot wearing her skirt. So she took it off and sat in the waiting room in her petticoat. Cathy warned me and I made sure a nurse was in the consulting room with me before I called her through. In a sense, as a vet, you are fighting a battle with time and it's a battle you are bound to lose. So it proved in this case.

Having performed the dreadful deed, the owner asked me, "When will you come to bury 'im? I can't dig an 'ole an there ain't no-one else."

There are times when you are compelled to recognise the logic of someone else's negotiating position and accept that you have been outmanoeuvred. On Saturday afternoon, after finishing at the surgery, I walked up Iffley Road armed with my old garden spade and fork hoping not to meet anyone who knew me.

I found her house and surveyed a back garden completely covered in mature couch grass. It was hard work to make any impression in the baked earth but I was honour-bound to keep my promise and I did. I went home with backache and any thoughts of elevating my standing in the local community well and truly squashed. Should I be more assertive in future?

Not long after being brought down to earth conducting burials, I was busy in the middle of Wednesday evening surgery. I had been treating a cavalier King Charles spaniel called Chalky belonging to Penny, who lived on the west side of the city. She rang to ask me to visit her dog, who had been suffering from heart trouble.

That day, his breathing sounded rough, though he was still eating and drinking normally. I had half a dozen clients to see so I agreed to come when I finished at Iffley Road. I left the practice about half past six and as I drove, I thought about Penny. She was a sophisticated lady in her sixties, well-known amongst the social elite for enriching the cultural life of the city and for her parties.

From the street, the front of her two-up-two-down Edwardian house looked unprepossessing. Inside, the building was spacious and tastefully furnished, with antique furniture, ceramics and pictures and a delightful back garden leading down to a stream. I had known her for several years as a client and had been invited to several soirees at her house, chatting to cultured, talented people whilst enjoying the best food and wine. As I turned carefully into the narrow street where she lived, she emerged from her front door carrying her dog on a cushion, her long dress billowing out behind her, reminiscent of a galleon in full sail.

"He started gasping. I think he's dead," she managed, before bursting into tears.

Leaving my car in the middle of the road, I had to confirm that death had occurred before anything else could be done. I did so, parked the car and entered the house. I was offered wine and nibbles at what had become a wake. A eulogy ensued, in which Chalky's exemplary attributes were listed and agreed upon.

After an appropriate interval, I prepared to depart and leave her to grieve. Would I help her bury Chalky in the garden? With some spotless garden tools, I dug a hole in a beautifully-tended flower bed, close to the stream and his favourite spot in the garden. He was laid to rest wrapped in the christening gown of her son; a moving experience and a scene which might have come from a play.

Driving home, I marvelled that you just never know what will happen next.

During the summer, a degree of civil disobedience came to areas of the city with the advent of joy-riding. An epidemic of car thefts took hold as disaffected youths turned some roads into impromptu race tracks. The stolen cars were systematically wrecked and left where they expired. One such raceway was in Blackbird Leys, close to Oxford's greyhound stadium.

My colleague Alasdair was on duty one evening and visited a farm off the eastern A40 to attend a cow which was calving. He dealt with the case using his calving aid, a mechanical ratcheted device which enabled the operator to winch out a trapped calf. The facilities on the farm were limited and he decided to wash himself and his kit when he got home.

It was half past ten at night and dark when he opted to take a short cut through Blackbird Leys to his house in Iffley. He was stopped by the police, who were there in numbers to clamp down on the illegal joy-riding activities. Alasdair had a torrid time explaining to the officers why he was there, smeared with cow muck and spattered with red stuff, especially when he was asked to open the boot and they discovered his heavily-soiled veterinary equipment. I had a telephone call from the officers and had to confirm he was a bona fide vet working for the practice and going about his legitimate business.

Vets Alasdair and Glen, nurses Karen and Jo, with Cathy and Hazel were a fantastic team who worked very well together and enjoyed having fun as a group in their spare time. Blessed with warm summer sunshine, we celebrated four years of positive practice development with a picnic in University Parks with punting, excellent food and a very relaxed and enjoyable Sunday afternoon.

A month later, Karen and Jo took the veterinary ambulance to collect an injured pet from Rose Hill. Twenty minutes later, they reappeared carrying a dog in a blanket. Sheba had been stabbed repeatedly. She was suffering and my colleagues were understandably and visibly upset.

In a reversal of roles, a policeman was in reception leaving his contact details; he asked for a report on the dog's injuries. The Barrett family owned Sheba, a German shepherd crossed with a whippet. She had recently given birth to four pups. What kind of person would inflict such injuries on a dog? Gary, Sandra and their fifteen-year-old daughter Kelly told Karen they wanted everything done for Sheba yet the cost of treatment was financially beyond them.

We were able to obtain some charitable funding as the family's circumstances meant they qualified for emergency assistance under the People's Dispensary for Sick Animals Pet Aid scheme. Hazel and Cathy sorted this out whilst we concentrated on preserving Sheba's life.

An intravenous drip was placed in her foreleg. An abdominal x-ray indicated the knife used to inflict the wound in her belly had probably penetrated her bowel. There were several, apparently less serious, wounds to her body, but they would have to wait. She was anaesthetised and the sundry stab wounds were clipped, cleansed and prepared for surgery.

After incising the skin and muscles comprising her body wall, I gently explored her abdomen. Miraculously, most of her internal organs had escaped injury, slipping to one side of the penetrating blade, though I could smell, and subsequently see, stomach contents which had seeped from a wound in that organ.

Struggling to prevent my anger getting the better of me, I had to remain objective and methodical in my approach. Karen was controlling the anaesthetic machine whilst Jo was scrubbed up and assisting me. We washed and wiped the wound in the stomach wall with warmed saline solution, drying it with swabs to remove as much contaminated material as possible. I used a double row of inverting resorbable sutures to repair the knife wound.

To flush away the free stomach fluids, we filled and drained the abdominal cavity repeatedly with saline. Without this intervention, these acidic secretions produced by the stomach lining, would trigger an acute painful inflammation involving the delicate membrane lining the abdominal cavity, resulting in death from peritonitis within a few hours.

Following further irrigation and cleansing, I reconstructed the entry stab wound in her side using several rows of sutures. Using a fresh set of instruments and drapes, I set about repairing a deep slash wound in Sheba's left thigh. Many important muscles had been cut. Jo swabbed away the constant ooze of blood, whilst I reattached each severed muscle belly to its mate. More than two hours later, all her wounds had been repaired, and we were able to place her in a cage on a heat pad and specialist absorbent bedding and her recovery began.

The Barrett family were busy at home with the important task of feeding Sheba's pups which, at five weeks old, were just about old enough to survive without their mum.

At the practice, media outlets including television crews and newspaper journalists had been alerted and were asking for interviews. A reward had been offered for information leading to the arrest of the perpetrator.

Interviewed in the back garden, it was my first experience of having microphones thrust in my direction and coping with the harsh glare of TV lights shining in my eyes. It wasn't easy to appear calm, coherent and in control. Is this how rabbits feel when caught in the headlights of my car? My wife recorded my appearance on the evening regional news bulletin. Four-year old Anna was very excited to see daddy on the telly.

Sheba responded well to our ministrations overnight. Although not willing to eat or drink, I felt she was strong enough to appear in front of the cameras. She was the real star of the show after all. She was very slight but had great spirit.

She was confused by the fuss and attention and just wanted was get back to her puppies. She went home later that day. Kelly's parents were very appreciative of the financial aid provided by the PDSA, whose funding helped pay for treatment. Sheba was registered on the Pet Aid scheme to help cover the cost of any future veterinary treatment which might be needed.

Encouraged by the progress which we had achieved, I felt confident to start planning improvements at Iffley Road. The cost meant only one floor at a time could be renovated. Even though the public seldom ventured down there, the basement was the first area to be addressed as it was in the worst condition. It suffered from damp and during a wet winter, water ran down the inside of some walls.

Measuring each room, I plotted and planned the work to be done. Using sheets of graph paper, I tried to visualise every detail, down to the position of the last electrical socket, to maximise the use of available space. I was impatient to update and re-equip the practice and recognised it was long overdue.

I had to bide my time until the potential expenditure on the project matched the profits being generated by the business. Although the improvements necessarily had to be staged, it offered a once-in-a lifetime opportunity to create an environment which was both functional and a pleasant place in which to work.

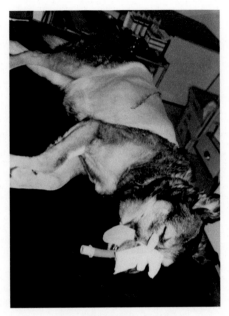

Top of my priority list was a cattery which was entirely separate from the kennels. I engaged an experienced builder to manage

Sheba. 'Knife Crime' 1991

the project. He advised that the basement walls and floor should be tanked to prevent further ingress of water. The practice had to continue during the works so we agreed the builders could have half of the basement to work on at a time whilst we had to cope with having the operating theatre, kennels and cattery temporarily crammed in the remaining half.

Health and safety was an increasingly important issue in veterinary practice, along with regulations concerning the use and storage of hazardous substances and the safe use of x-rays. I needed to know all the relevant legislation in detail and balance what I wanted to do with what was allowed.

It was a challenge to make a hundred-year-old building fit for a modern veterinary practice. Even the number of toilets was stipulated. I was keen to hear the thoughts of my colleagues and asked them to think about what changes they would make. We developed a wish list of equipment they felt we must have, together with a few pieces of kit they would enjoy.

Christmas came and went. It had been a good year for the practice, another year of consolidation but with exciting prospects for the future.

Chapter 18

So Far Away

The renovation of Iffley Road began in February 1992. Having waited impatiently for the builders to start, after the first few days of dust and disruption, I began counting the days until they were due to leave.

To their immense credit, we were never without water or electricity and if we required absolute quiet, for example, whilst we induced a nervous cat under anaesthetic, the silence reached monastic intensity.

The walls were stripped back to the Victorian brickwork and a new damp-proof course injected. The basement had to dry out before the tanking process could begin. New concrete floors would form the bottom of the tank. All the services including electrical wiring and plumbing were replaced and a new gas service with boiler and central heating was installed. I had a detailed schedule of what would be done and when to help my day-to-day planning of the veterinary workload. Unfortunately, this schedule omitted a traditional holiday break taken by the builders over Easter, which delayed final completion of the works.

Two incidents lodge in my memory, together with the immense skill of the tipper-truck drivers, reversing into the back garden without ever touching the gateposts.

Iffley Road Basement Kitchen 1990   Basement Renovations 1992

New Kennels 1992

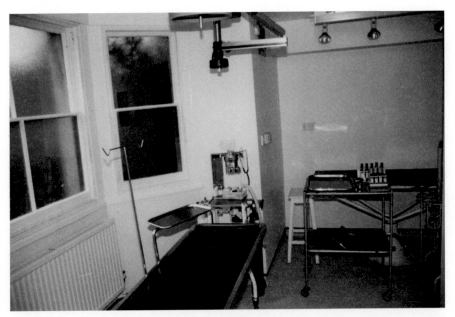

New Operating Theatre 1992

Prep Room 1992

Iffley Road is a semi-detached property with the Marriage Guidance Council, now Relate, occupying the building next door. The walls dividing the two properties are only a single brick thick.

Despite the builders taking great care, one brick in the dividing wall was dislodged. Very inconvenient and quickly rectified, it was an unexpected and amusing interlude.

I was consulting on a Saturday morning on the ground floor. Downstairs, the worst of the dusty work had been completed and the area was being tidied and swept in preparation for the tanking process starting after the weekend. There was only a single layer of floorboards and no plasterboard ceiling between the basement and the waiting room on the ground floor, where I was handing some treatment to a client. In the basement, the ample backside of the builder sweeping up 'touched' an original internal dividing brick wall in the kitchen and successfully demolished it in an instant. One moment, my client and I were talking face-to-face and the next she disappeared in a choking cloud of mortar and brick dust which rose up through the gaps in the floor.

High on our wish list were new cages for the kennels and cattery. I was chuffed to watch these tough plastic modular units being installed, each with their own integral heat mat incorporated within its floor. They were more comfortable for our patients, warm to the touch and cosy, as well as being easier to clean and disinfect. The cage doors shut silently.

In their own exclusive five-star accommodation, two walls separated the cattery from the kennels. The cats were calm when brought through to the prep room to be given their anaesthetics and needed lower drug dosages, meaning a safer procedure.

The building works with the upgrading of our equipment was expensive. In daily use for the last twenty-five years, the expense per annum equated to less than two thousand pounds. Exceptional value in my view.

In my life, highs have often been followed by lows, notably my O levels and my mother's illness, my initial clinical year and hospitalisation close to my twenty-first birthday.

This unwelcome cycle was repeated. Less than a month into these alterations, my father was diagnosed with lung cancer, which was deemed inoperable. I visited my parents frequently, spending as much time as possible at the family home in Essex. I brought mum and dad to Abingdon to stay with us and to see the transformation at Iffley Road. I fear dad was too ill to fully appreciate what he had helped me to achieve.

One May morning, bright and sunny, it was good to be out on a round of visits. I was on the way to see a mare called Leila who was having difficulty foaling. As I drove towards Wallingford, I mused that Leila was my mother-in-law's middle name. That must be a good omen.

The groom led me across the yard to my patient, in one of a series of spacious wooden stables of traditional design. Leila was standing with her head in the darkest corner, the embodiment of pain. What was that balloon-like structure protruding from her vulva? Having soaped and lubricated my arm, I investigated her birth canal and found her foal's forefeet had penetrated the upper wall of the mare's vagina and were now in her rectum.

The structure I had seen protruding behind her was her bladder rather than fluid-filled foetal membranes. My heart sank. I had to cut what little remained of the shelf of tissue which normally separated her vagina from her rectum. I attached ropes to the front feet of the foal and having cleansed and repelled the bladder, using moderate traction, a beautiful, delicate Arab foal was delivered on to the straw. The foal was alive, which was a minor miracle after a prolonged equine birth. But glistening loops of the mare's bowels followed the foal as the mare continued to strain.

The prognosis for the mare was hopeless. She would die from peritonitis, introduced through the inevitable tear in her abdominal wall through which her guts had passed. Horses are extremely susceptible to peritonitis with a very rapid onset. We had to put the mare to sleep before acute pain set in.

To maximise the chances of its survival, the foal had to suckle its mother's colostrum for nourishment and its antibodies, which provide specific disease protection. The colostrum did not amount to much and certainly not enough to secure the foal's future. These precious antibodies were also circulating in the mare's bloodstream. I suggested collecting a quantity of the mare's blood after she had died. Stored in a cool place, the blood would separate into the cellular component and the fluid component which was rich in these antibodies. We could administer this serum to the foal by mouth using a stomach tube.

It was a macabre and gory prospect but it could improve her foal's chances of survival.

Some clean bowls were sterilised with boiling water. Already, the mare was showing signs of increasing discomfort so it was a blessed release from the painful grip of colic as she was put to sleep. We harvested bowlfuls of blood drained from a vessel in her neck and carried them carefully to the cool cellar to separate.

A newborn foal can only absorb antibodies from its gut in the early hours of life and the sooner they are ingested, the greater the proportion which are absorbed. I gave this foal some of the separated serum by stomach tube. Further doses could be mixed with powdered mare's milk substitute, which would be used to feed her until she could suckle milk from a putative adoptive mother. The owner contacted an equine service which offered orphan foals the chance of being adopted by another mare. They put my client in touch with an owner whose mare had given birth to a stillborn foal the previous day. Quickly, arrangements were made to take our new-born foal to her new mother.

An uncomplicated foaling takes about fifteen minutes. It had taken me two and half hours to deal with this case. My schedule of visits had been decimated again.

The sixteenth of September 1992, Black Wednesday, is written large in the annals of the practice. I had a mortgage on my family home, on Wheatley Surgery and on Iffley Road, as well as the considerable expenditure of its recent renovation.

The day began normally, with a visit to Charlton-on-Otmoor to see a lame horse; a relatively straightforward case caused by poor shoeing. When I set out, bank interest rates stood at ten per cent. I was solvent but without much leeway. After the visit, I drove to Wheatley to begin my scheduled lunchtime surgery.

Hazel rang, "Have you heard? Interest rates have just been raised to twelve per cent!"

Ouch! I might just be able to cope with that level of financial pain in the short term. Later in the day, they were increased again to fifteen per cent because of a a run on the pound, whatever that meant. I started evening surgery and by the time I left Wheatley at half past eight, Prime Minister John Major and Chancellor Norman Lamont had taken the UK out of the exchange rate mechanism.

I drove home with a dreadful feeling in the pit of my stomach. Ev and I sat together on the sitting room floor, perhaps because we could not sink any lower. If interest rates remained at that level, we were bust. No doubt about it. The practice could not sustain monthly interest repayments on its various borrowings at that rate for any length of time. Our enterprise and our hard work would come to nothing. Had I taken financial risks which were unrealistic? What were the implications for our children?

The following day, I was booked to act as honorary vet at the Thame Agricultural Show. I didn't feel like going but having accepted their kind invitation, I had to attend. Ev and I went together. The atmosphere at the showground was glum, in marked contrast to the customary buzz of anticipation and excitement. Farmers I knew passed by with eyes averted and shoulders hunched as if the weight of the world was on their shoulders. Many farming families might be in a similar position to ourselves.

At eleven o'clock, an announcement came over the loudspeaker. A tinny, disembodied, expressionless voice informed the crowd that interest rates had been put back to ten percent, the same level as at the start of business the previous morning. I have never experienced such a collective lifting of spirits, even outpourings of joy. The hype preceding the appearance of bands at rock concerts couldn't match this. For the beer tent and the bars, business was suddenly very brisk. What a relief. We were able to fight another day.

I was called by St Francis Hospice early in the morning of the twenty-fourth of November. Dad was dying and I should come now. I had to negotiate the godforsaken M25 and he died fifteen minutes before I got there. I felt a shattering sense of grief coupled with remorse at not being at his side. My sister and I had our father's funeral to arrange but we also needed to discuss how our mother, whose balance was unreliable and whose mobility impaired, would cope living alone. Could she?

The weeks leading up to Christmas and the festival itself were particularly hard. Mum went to stay with my sister. Her wish was to stay in the family home. It was up to

Hilary and me, to her parishioner friends and her neighbours to try to make this happen. Such was mum's amazing willpower that she lived on her own for another thirteen years, with a little help from her friends.

I was trying to cope with intense anger and disappointment. I had looked forward to dad enjoying his grandchildren's childhood and the success of his son's veterinary practice, to which he had contributed in many ways. Activity at work in all its guises did not numb the pain. I suffered mood swings. Sunday, full of fun with my family, would be followed by another hectic week at work. If I had to put an animal to sleep, my miserable mood descended again and seem magnified. I'd had my fill of hospitals and hospices.

Perhaps a summer holiday with my family, away from the practice, would sort things out. In the event, my attitude did not improve. Something had to give, or rather, I needed to try something to reverse this unhealthy situation.

My wonderful clients came to my rescue. I learnt that John Havens, who lived around the corner from the Wheatley Surgery and was a regular visitor, took mixed ability groups to Nepal for adventure holidays. My interest was aroused. I had joined a new Rotary Club in Abingdon and invited him to speak to us.

My interest was piqued by his story, the slides and his enthusiasm. This kind of trip might offer me the chance to get my thoughts and emotions into proper perspective. I called on John several times for a chat. I was susceptible to back trouble, sometimes spending days lying flat, unable to function.

With perpetually dry and sore eyes, how could I cope with the heat, the dust and Nepal's notorious winds? John assured me he could handle any health problems that arose and let me into a secret. He had experience with the Special Operations Executive, which explained his self-confidence, his military bearing and his precise manner of speaking. Even his obligatory moustache.

Numbers were limited and the trip being organised to leave in October, less than four weeks away, was full. My wife is a great believer in fate so it was no surprise to her when John called to say that someone had dropped out of the forthcoming trip. Did I want to fill the vacancy?

Firstly, I had to organise veterinary cover. I rang Julie, a locum who had worked for the practice before. She was extremely competent, popular with the clients and free for the dates of the trip. My wife encouraged me to go.

The trip included three days' white-water rafting, camping under canvas on the shore overnight, two days in a jungle retreat, followed by a trek in the foothills of Annapurna with overnight camps. In places where our camps were struck, a medical clinic was offered to local villagers as recompense for the disruption our arrival caused.

Our group consisted of eight able-bodied and eight with physical or mental disabilities, together with a medical doctor and John. As I had missed a preparatory get-together weekend, I met my fellow travellers for the first time at Heathrow airport. It was a bonus to have listened to John's talk and be familiar with his modus operandi.

Teamwork was essential with each member helping the others according to their abilities. Our group included wheelchair users, so this adaptation started at the top of a flight of stairs in the concourse.

We landed in Kathmandu and were spoiled, staying in the comfortable Kathmandu Guest House. It retained an atmosphere of comfort and calm; hints of the Raj still lingered with bell boys and spotless marble floors. One of our number, James, was a victim of the Thalidomide tragedy of the Sixties and had stunted limbs.

At the gates of our guest house was a Nepalese mendicant with a similar affliction. He only had sections of inner tubing to protect his stumps and no specialist wheelchair to aid his mobility. My rehabilitation had already begun. The city was overcrowded and noisy, dirty and smelly, its chaos causing sensory overload to this tired traveller. A host of flashing neon signs advertised global brands of soft drinks to a populace that could not afford them.

After a day of talks familiarising us with what lay ahead, we went sightseeing. The following morning, we set off in two minibuses for the start of the river section of our trip. The vehicles and their extensive roof racks were packed with our personal baggage plus the food supplies and tents we would require along the way. I squeezed into a spare seat in the second bus.

After eight hours, we had left the town of Butval behind and were driving along a section of road raised above the surrounding fields. I had been studying the native zebu cattle with their huge horns; on the roadside verge, an eight-year-old boy was urging a bullock onwards, flicking its back with a stick.

Suddenly, the beast veered across the road, the boy behind it, right in front of the first minibus, which swerved off the road to avoid a fatal collision. I saw the minibus career down the bank, slithering to rest on its side. John, who was travelling in our bus, went to assess the situation with our driver. Taking control, he supervised the rapid evacuation of the group members from the vehicle. Most had escaped unharmed. Linda, the partner of James, may have fractured her wrist; Caz, our team doctor, whose face had been forced through a side window, suffered cuts to her face particularly her upper lip. John called me aside.

"Andy, you're the most medically qualified person in the group apart from Caz. I want you to go with Linda and Caz to a local hospital. The driver will act as your interpreter. You decide between you what should be done."

The luggage and equipment were unloaded from the undamaged minibus and left by the roadside, guarded by the remainder of our travelling band. With my overnight rucksack, we commandeered the bus, leaving the scene of the accident with Caz, Linda and James, their personal luggage and the medical box which we carried.

Great. I was on my way to another blessed hospital, the Lumbini Zonal hospital to be precise. We were treated with great care and attention by an Indian doctor who spoke excellent English. Linda's wrist was x-rayed and under sedation, was set in a plaster cast. Caz was the major casualty. She needed a general anaesthetic to repair her facial wounds to attain the best cosmetic result. She was offered transport to the international hospital in Kathmandu but we agreed her injuries should be treated immediately to minimise the risks of disfigurement.

Now came the greatest personal challenge in my life to date. Caz, an experienced doctor and member of many such trips around the world, would not let the local doctors touch her. After assurances that I would stay with her throughout and remain by her bedside until she woke up, she agreed to have the anaesthetic. However, she would only agree if I gave her the anaesthetic using products from our medical box.

So that is what I did. Summoning as much confidence as possible, I administered the ketamine injection successfully; the first and only time I have achieved venepuncture in a human being. The sight of a person falling unconscious as a result of my actions seemed horribly brutal and unsettled me more than I can say. As soon as I could, I stepped away, allowing the local medical team to take over. They were superb and the surgical skills shown by Dr Shrestha were outstanding.

Later, I was sitting in the dark by Caz's bedside in a communal ward with nine other patients. I don't think the patients or staff had seen a white man before close up in real life. I was a curiosity, suddenly aware of several faces peering around the door from the corridor, staring at me. Before long, the doorway was full of excited faces, chattering and giggling. The women came closer, holding their arms next to mine and rubbing my skin to see if the white colour would rub off.

I had plenty of time to appreciate the irony of my situation. I had taken a long-haul flight to south Asia, trying to clear my mind of all matters medical. Forty-eight hours later, I am sitting in the ward of a remote hospital, hour after hour, unable to speak a word of the native tongue with only the vaguest idea where I actually was.

I had come to Nepal to confront the causes of my anger and frustration and in the quiet of the Nepali night, this was as good a time as any to start. Of course, life is not like that. I felt very small and cast adrift. An angel brought me warm sweet cha at intervals as my vigil continued.

Ketamine is a neurolept-analgesic which disconnects the thinking part of the brain from the doing part. After midnight, Caz began to stir as those connections were reinstated. The utterances from the mouth of a colleague I had only met the previous day shall remain private. I was shocked by the personal and detailed nature of what she said during her recovery; her facial contortions suggested a painful jettisoning of surplus mental baggage during unimaginably bad dreams. It was like being in one half of a confessional cubicle with the sins of the penitent opposite getting ever more serious. As dawn broke, Caz regained full consciousness.

Behind the scenes, John had been working miracles and had managed to arrange for Caz to be flown back to Kathmandu by helicopter. Once the helicopter had lifted off mid-morning, the minibus driver and I thanked the staff and left with our depleted medical box and my overnight bag. Linda and James caught a regular flight back to Kathmandu before returning to Britain.

Our rendezvous with the rest of the group was at their overnight riverside camp at Samjighat after their first day on the river. We arrived at 4 am. My tent had been erected for me and I slept for a couple of hours before eating breakfast cooked on a campfire.

There is nothing I like more than messing about in boats. My first day on the river was heavenly and a perfect antidote to the turmoil of the previous two days. With Wang our river guide, the ultimate cool guy in his shades, and his crew, we rowed down the river in

Nepal Accident 1993

Evening Clinic. Nepal 1993

Morning Clinic. Nepal 1993

two inflatable boats. The scenery was stupendous, the river passing through deep wooded gorges with monkeys cavorting in the tree-tops and some marsh mugger crocodiles basking on the banks.

I had completely forgotten about the custom of running a clinic for the locals each evening. My excuse was my mental faculties had been addled through lack of sleep. It was dark and we had finished our meal when John took me aside again. Pointing to a group of villagers sitting patiently on the edge of the forest beyond the pools of light cast by our lanterns, he said, "Andy, as you are the most medically qualified person in the group ..."

Aarghh! I did not want to let these people down. Was it really that different treating a person rather than an animal? The animals cannot talk but here I would have the benefit of an interpreter. I wondered how the Royal College of Veterinary Surgeons might view my conduct. Surely, the humanitarian need was obvious and urgent. Besides, nobody would ever know ... would they?

I treated more than seventy Nepalis during the trip. Mostly outside in the dark, using head torches, I tried to treat conditions ranging from heart trouble to earache, a grossly-enlarged prostate gland to parasitic skin infestations. I erred very much on the side of caution, only prescribing for those diseases where I felt I could do no harm and might even do some good.

My memory of this medical interlude is haunted by Nandun, a fifteen-year-old girl. She had a suppurating sinus ten centimetres long in her anterior thigh. It had been present for two years; I could hardly believe it. The courage and fortitude shown in her eyes struck me forcefully when I met her. Two women from our group had some nursing experience. They spent a long time irrigating this lesion with cooled boiled water and antiseptic solutions. Once all the necrotic tissue had been cleared and cleansed, we dressed the lesion and she left with an extended course of antibiotic pills. At home, I would have carried out all sorts of tests and x-rayed her leg looking for sequestered or unhealthy bone, foreign bodies such as grass seeds, splinters and the like. I would like to know what happened to her but I did not receive any feedback from the doctors staffing future trips.

We visited a village where the major event in their year was felling a tree to fashion into a dugout. The locals were patient and friendly. With no electricity or pylons, no mobile phones or masts, no roads or vehicles, no aeroplanes overhead, they had a simple way of life unaffected by western ideals and ideas. At night, I lay looking at the stars, so bright with the absence of light pollution. I wondered whether the young people of the village would stay or leave to seek their fortune in the squalor of the cities.

With the river section of the trip completed, we were told to prepare for a hike through the jungle. It was approaching mid-day and very hot. We moved off and after less than a kilometre, walked unexpectedly into the luxurious Tiger Tops camp amidst the jungle of the Royal Bardia National Park. Oh joy! Spacious tents with proper beds and toilets. In the evening, I enjoyed the best curry I have eaten in beautiful surroundings with a wildlife soundtrack to match. At dawn the following morning, a memorable elephant safari began, swathes of wet savannah grass brushing against my legs. The closest we got to the Bengal tigers for which the reserve is famous was a footprint in the mud but we saw nature close-up and we saw it for real.

Our final few days were spent trekking in the foothills of Annapurna. I admired the ingenuity of small boys who appeared at this altitude of three thousand metres to offer 'cool' cans of fizzy drinks. The undoubted high spot was emerging from my tent before dawn, still groggy with sleep, to watch the sun rise over Annapurna and the majestic Himalaya mountain range. It was a scene of staggering beauty in the changing early morning light. This experience above all others soothed my soul and averted the gaze of the evil eye. But the presence of western litter scattered about on this landscape and in such quantities was an absolute disgrace.

What was the point of the trip? Self-indulgence? I would respond with one example. Mary was a secretary to a prominent cleric. She had been caught in the fire disaster at Kings Cross underground station. She suffered severe burns to her hands and arms and had been deeply affected by the trauma. Her injuries required extensive skin grafts involving both hands which she had to protect with gloves.

At the start of the trip, she cut a sad figure, lacking self-confidence; she didn't feel she was capable of doing much for herself, whether it was carrying her day pack or pitching her own tent each evening. She was listless, often walking far behind the main body of the group. One week later, she walked purposefully at the head of the group, dealing with her own tent herself, before helping others with theirs. What a fantastic, life-changing transformation. I realised how lucky I was to have witnessed her rebirth.

A final irony occurred towards the end of the trip. John's back started to cause him excruciating pain. I nursed *him* rather than the other way around, a reversal of the scenario we discussed in England. He could not bear to sit upright. During the journey back to Kathmandu, along terrible roads whose tarmac had frequently been washed away with landslides, he lay flat out at the back, on top of our luggage in a small gap beneath the roof of the bus.

It was good to be home but Anna, aged six, burst into tears when she saw my beard. I had to shave it off at once.

Chapter 19

Foolish Pride

At the beginning of 1995, I turned forty and celebrated with a meal at our favourite local gastropub. How had those years passed so quickly?

Such thoughts became more sharply focused when I heard that Jimmy Sheriffs had died peacefully in his sleep at the end of January. His funeral was attended by a great many friends and clients. Twelve years had passed since I had first met him and been so impressed by his character and charm.

Early in the year, a young Tonkinese kitten, beautifully marked with blue points, was brought to the practice. She was unable to urinate voluntarily. At first, she came each day, her bladder uncomfortably full. I could express the urine quite easily and hoped the problem might resolve as she grew and matured.

It was not ideal for a five-week-old kitten to have a prolonged stay at the practice so I took her home. By this time, Mostyn had moved upstairs to the great kennel in the sky and the tortoises were fast asleep in our shed so our house was an animal-free zone. With my wife holding her, I gently expressed Constant's bladder, typically twice a day. Anna and Rachael were thrilled to have a small kitten around as a source of special interest, especially her biological functions. We had a fireplace in the sitting room prepared with newspaper, kindling and small logs, ready to light should the temperature warrant it. One evening, the girls were in their pyjamas choosing their bedtime story when Rachael rushed into the kitchen in great excitement,

"Daddy, daddy, come quickly, the kitten's done a wee in the fire."

Never have I been so pleased to find wee in an inappropriate place in our house. The newspaper in the grate had clearly been christened. Alleluia. The litter trays, strategically placed around the house, were regularly replenished with plenty of shredded newspaper. Constant was praised whenever she used a tray and seemed finally to have accepted responsibility for her own bladder function. Repeated success, either in the litter tray or the fireplace, led to the fire being left unmade for a period.

I was pleased to return Constant to the company of her sister Pumpkin, her mother Truffle and her owner Julia, reasonably confident that normal urinary patterns would continue. She was eventually rehomed to a lovely lady in Kennington who became besotted with her. Constant was a regular visitor to the surgery and I took quiet satisfaction from seeing her on my appointments list until 2012.

I watched more cricket and played a few games for the local village side in Sunningwell. The appearance of my name in the batting order was initially sporadic but the games served to remind me how much I enjoyed playing, as well as how unfit I was. The opportunity of cricket nets on Sunday evenings was a welcome distraction in the post-Christmas period before the square could be mown and sightscreens moved into position at the start of another season.

My personal performances gradually improved, although form can be such a transient phenomenon. So many times, I looked forward to the next game only to be bowled by a shooter before I had scored a run.

Sunningwell were batting first in an away fixture at Deddington. We were making heavy weather of an early season pitch but I had struggled to forty-eight not out and was hoping to score my first fifty of the of the year. I noticed frantic gesticulations from the boundary. It could not have meant a declaration so it must have meant I was wanted on my mobile phone. My colleague Kirk, covering the weekend duties, was at the stables of

'Constant' the Kitten 1995

our breeder of Arab horses. He was examining a four-day old foal which had suddenly become very lame. Would I come and have a look? Of course. What else could I do but retire? Frustrated, I apologised to our skipper and left the match, still wearing my whites.

Our new x-ray machine, installed three years earlier during our upgrade, was portable. I suggested Kirk collected the machine from the surgery, together with all the cassettes pre-loaded with X-ray film, and met me at the stables. For much of the journey, I chuntered about being expected to be available even when I was off duty, barely able to suppress my annoyance.

When I arrived and saw that exquisite four-day old filly foal, I had a change of heart. So delicate, so perfectly proportioned, this beautiful animal was drop-dead gorgeous. She was holding her right foreleg off the ground. My fingers soon identified the first bone below her fetlock joint as being fractured. Presumably the mare had trodden on the foal's leg as she lay on the straw.

We took some x-ray views but had to return to the practice to develop them. They revealed a long oblique fracture which fortunately did not extend into the joint above or below the injury.

Back at the stables, we had an uncomfortable discussion about the foal's future. The injury had almost certainly put paid to any racing prospects she may have had. Most such injuries in horses result in them being put down because the sheer weight of the animal is too great for any man-made materials to support the fracture during healing. However, the foal in front of me weighed less than many large breeds of dog. I thought there was a chance of a successful outcome if we applied a supporting cast. Perhaps she would make a brood mare and produce future winners of her own. Besides, this foal was simply too stunning to lose at four days old.

I had plenty of helpers offering to restrain the foal and support its leg whilst I applied a great deal of soft padding and eventually a lightweight yet strong cast.

I left for home as dusk fell. I was relieved I didn't have to dispatch this elegant animal but I was also apprehensive. If my treatment strategy failed, the foal would have endured significant discomfort which could have been avoided.

I got hold of the captain of the cricket team in the pub. The match had been drawn, each side scoring 156 runs. The players all wanted to know about the foal. A toast to her future was drunk in a village pub, thirty miles away from her stables by more than twenty chaps who have never set eyes on her.

Whenever I was nearby, I dropped into the stables to check on the foal and the comfort of her cast. A fortnight later, the cast had to be changed because the length of the foal's limb was increasing rapidly and the presence of the cast should not limit that natural growth. I had used a modern synthetic casting tape composed of rigid fibreglass fabric impregnated with a polyurethane resin. Once it had set, I could stand on a cast just three layers thick and it would support my considerable weight.

Strong as it was, this presented its own difficulties when trying to remove it. Once the foal was sedated, I used an oscillating saw with a diamond-tipped circular blade to cut the cast, taking great care not to scuff the hoof. I applied a new cast over quantities of fresh soft padding.

After another fortnight, this cast was also removed and further x-rays taken. They showed that the fracture had healed but a very slight lateral angulation was evident on the films, although not with my naked eye. Half of the second cast was reapplied as a gutter splint, which offered some support as the bone gradually took more weight.

Six weeks after her injury, I was able to leave the filly's foreleg unsupported. As her weight increased, she developed a tendency to walk on the inner half of her hoof, but she was walking around and she was free of pain. The blacksmith made frequent visits to pare and rebalance her foot and later to fit and refit the foal's foot with a shoe incorporating an inner raise, aiming to correct any angulation of the lower limb during its growing phase. Six months after her injury, I was happy that the filly was sound. At two years old, as she approached physical maturity, she was sound at walk and trot, though with a slight nod of her head at a canter. She was never broken and never ridden but gave birth to her first foal in her fourth year. I never grew tired of leaning on the gate to her field, watching her graze, enjoying her very existence.

Every year, the practice was asked to provide veterinary cover for various local horse shows. These shows were as much part of the rural summer scene in Oxfordshire as cricket matches on the village green. Both of my daughters learned to ride and loved their visits to the stables, both to ride and to tend to the ponies. The time came, of course, when I was attending shows in which my children were competing in various classes. For Anna, Tonka could do no wrong, whilst Rachael, still quite small having just turned six, grew very fond of Weed. This sure-footed, slight bay pony used all her experience to keep Rachael safe, for which both her parents were truly grateful. I experienced an extra frisson of tension when I had to visit one or other of these favoured equines as an emergency.

I was at Wheatley surgery when we had a call to attend Weed, who was showing signs of colic. Horses are particularly susceptible to this clinical syndrome, causing abdominal pain, usually emanating from the animal's gut. So sensitive is it that the slightest perceived insult, such as eating frosted grass or mouldy fibrous hay, can set off a chain of events in which its displeasure can be registered by going slow or even downing tools altogether and going on strike. The accumulation of gas in the loops of bowel and the distention it causes triggers this painful condition. Some horses suffer repeated bouts whilst others never show symptoms. Weed was in her early thirties and had not shown signs of colic before. Driving up Ladder Hill, I turned right towards the stables in the shadow of the eighteenth-century windmill, which was undergoing extensive renovations.

Weed was looking bedraggled and extremely sorry for herself. She knew me well as a frequent visitor but today she didn't nuzzle me or give me any appreciable sign of welcome or recognition. Her mucosal colour and temperature were normal, though her pulse was higher than I would have liked. Placing my stethoscope on her abdomen, the normal bubbling and gurgling sounds heard from an active equine bowel were greatly diminished. The clinical signs being shown suggested an episode of spasmodic colic.

I gave her an injection intended to break up this spasm of her gut musculature and said I would call again after my late evening surgery. I preferred food and water to be withdrawn for an hour from these cases and I got unreasonably excited if some dung was passed. The owner rang later to say the pony was much brighter, had passed some moist dung, had drunk some water and was looking around for food.

This was very welcome news and it sounded as if Greedy Weedy was reverting to type. I said she could have a small net of sweet hay and as always, they should ring if they were at all concerned. Her condition settled as I expected which was good; I didn't want to be the one to give Rachael any bad news about her favourite horse.

In mid-summer, we received an enquiry from a TV production company responsible for the children's programme *Rosie and Jim*. They were planning to film an episode where the puppet characters paid a visit to the vets. Were we interested in being involved with this project? We were, both as a practice and as a family.

The storyline required a young girl to meet the puppets on their narrowboat, Ragdoll, on the banks of the River Thames. The scene then cut to a practice waiting room and then the consulting room as the child brought her pet, accompanied by the star puppets, to be examined and treated.

Rachael played the young girl and Snowy the rabbit was selected as a portable pet she could carry in its basket. The bankside scene was filmed by Donnington Bridge in the city. The scenes in the practice were filmed at Wheatley surgery. My Irish colleague Libby

Sheridan was rightly judged to be far more photogenic than me and won the audition for the part of the vet.

It was great fun watching filming and how the different sections of the production were linked to make the programme. For me, the highlight was the professionalism of the puppeteers. As they were rehearsing in the car park, a family with two children drew up. The puppeteers hid behind another vehicle and the puppets 'appeared' on the bonnet. The look of surprise and delight on the children's faces was priceless. They were transfixed. Later, the puppeteers had to crouch beneath the consulting room table for lengthy periods, a cramped position which I would have found taxing.

It was an interesting interlude in the history of the practice, preserved for posterity on YouTube, and an instructive insight into how to interact with children at a veterinary practice. I learnt a great deal and made a determined effort to actively involve young children whenever they visited the practice. At one point, I tried having a sweetie jar in each consulting room but the staff kept scoffing the contents.

In contrast to such frivolity, at the end of September, I was saddened by the death of my former head nurse Abigail Drake, a victim of breast cancer at the age of thirty-five. After she left the practice, (see Chapter 16), she gained her undergraduate degree in psychology from City University in London and was offered a place to study for a veterinary degree.

A small lump in her breast, present since her Oxford days, which she had been told was nothing to worry about, had become an aggressive malignant mass. She underwent surgery to remove the lesion but she was not fit enough to take up her place at vet school. It became clear that the disease had spread and the rate at which she declined was distressing.

I visited her regularly in Cromer. I walked and later wheeled her along the promenade at Cromer and at Sheringham. When I last saw her, a few days before she died, she had to fight for every breath despite oxygen therapy and just wanted the end to come. As vets, we would not have countenanced leaving an animal struggling as she was at the end of her life. She came so close to fulfilling her dream of studying to become a vet, only for that dream to be snatched away.

Always a mad keen motor cyclist, at her funeral at the crematorium in Oxford, her friends in the local chapter of Hells Angels escorted her coffin along the approach to the chapel. More than seventy machines moved slowly in formation, the defiant roar of their engines adding to the dignity of their salute to her, a sight and sound I will never forget. I inherited her Janis Joplin LPs, another sonic reminder of her short life and untimely death.

Attempting to turn a huge negative to a tiny positive, I began planning the overdue improvements to the ground floor of Iffley Road. This was the floor which the public used every day in considerable numbers. Significant logistical challenges presented themselves. How would we cope without the reception and waiting room for a period? How could builders and the pet-owning public safely mix on the same floor without coming to blows?

On this floor, I wanted to preserve the Victorian heritage at the front of the building in the waiting room and entrance hall. I located an original Victorian pattern wallpaper and a pale, patterned material of similar vintage for the curtains. The original Victorian doors were retained after the horrid hardboard panelling had been removed.

I wanted a more clinical feel to the rooms facing the garden, whilst gaining an extra (third) consulting room for the use of the nurses and a small-animal drug dispensary to save my ageing legs from running up and downstairs quite so often.

To make room for these changes, the office was moved upstairs to the first-floor flat. The central heating and hot water systems which had been installed in the basement were extended to the ground floor and the ugly inefficient storage heaters replaced by modern radiators with adjustable valves.

The builders arrived in April 1997 and were exceptional in working around us. Having created the third consulting room with new stud walls, that space was used as a temporary bijou waiting room, with reception in the tiny dispensary whilst the proper waiting area in the front room was renovated. Everything was proceeding exactly as I had envisaged.

St George's Day 1997 was an unforgettable day in my life, twenty-three years ago today as I write this piece. "In the moment" according to the photographer Henri Cartier-Bresson.

Starting work earlier than usual on the farm of a client, I gave two horses their booster vaccinations and examined a bullock with suspected wooden tongue.

The main purpose for my visit was to castrate Lehar, four hundred kilograms of amazing Arab stallion. Such was the experience of the farm staff in all matters equine, I was flying solo with no assistants from the practice. Following our tribulations detailed in Chapter 13, we had been castrating our horses in the standing position under sedation rather than lying on their side under general anaesthesia.

The Hungarian composer's namesake was given his doses of sedative and pain relief calculated by weight into his jugular vein. His taut muscular defiance was rapidly reduced to toddler-like compliance, head down and a leg at each corner. I also injected local anaesthetic directly into each testis, using a long, large-bore needle, on the basis that if he couldn't feel anything, it was safe to proceed. My instruments were beside me, neatly laid out on a sterile tray cloth on a bale of straw. I cleansed and scrubbed the area and was ready to start cutting. I incised the scrotum, the stallion lashed out and my world changed forever. His hoof missed my head, or you might have been saved from reading this and my wife might have been left a merry widow. However, his left hindleg did make forceful contact with mine, on which I was weight-bearing at the time.

Lying on the floor of the stable, I noticed my foot was at a funny angle. This was just before the pain set in. My instinct, ingrained since my childhood, was not to make a fuss. I had a heated discussion with Graham, the farm manager, about finishing the surgery standing on one leg and I remain obliged to him for winning that particular argument, at times physically restraining me until the ambulance arrived.

I felt remarkably detached from the events around me. I could hear the siren in the distance but I did not associate it with my dilemma. I do remember the medics using my sharp surgical scissors to cut my wellington boot into sections and remove it from my leg and their excruciating jokes which I endured on the journey to the John Radcliffe hospital. I remember lying in the casualty room. My wife eventually arrived and promptly fainted, successfully securing the attention of the medical staff for the next ten minutes.

Extended stays in hospital are invariably associated with pain, blinking red lights on bleeping machines, things that are just out of reach, clatter, harsh lighting and long hours of tedium for the patient and worse for their family. The doctors insisted they could not repair the fractured bones until the swelling subsided but did nothing to speed this process up.

Didn't they know I had a practice to run? I took matters into my own hands. An old-fashioned remedy for reducing swelling, particularly in horses, involves bathing the affected area with Epsom salts (Magnesium Sulphate) as hot and cold compresses. I asked Ev to bring some Epsom salts from the practice and a bowl and I bathed my own ankle twice a day on the ward. Word got round and hospital staff gathered at my bedside to observe this mysterious medieval ritual. The swelling did indeed begin to subside and the doctors got fed up with my asking when I could go home. I was booked a slot for surgery. The surgeons did a brilliant job of stabilising my ankle joint using screws on the inside and an orthopaedic plate and screws on the outside of my ankle. Despite chocolates and a card, I never properly thanked the medics for their efforts. Thank you.

The weekend of the bank holiday in early May was spent in bed, gazing through the window of the ward at the view of Marston and in the distance, the village of Beckley. Annoyed at missing the jazz festival I had been due to attend in Breda in the Netherlands, at least I could listen to some cricket commentary using my headphones. I looked forward to daily visits from my devoted wife, my sister and from some of the practice staff. Even some clients took the opportunity to come and assess the situation for themselves. And I must be one of the few bosses who have been handed a letter of resignation by a veterinary colleague whilst ensconced in a hospital bed.

I was asked what colour I wanted my plaster cast to be, as if I cared. A cast of many colours could have been considered a flippant riposte. All I wanted was to go home. I was useless using crutches, especially going downstairs, but eventually, the nursing staff could bear me no longer and I was sent home, being promised physiotherapy in due course.

The girls had been spared the trauma of hospital visits. At first, they thought it was great fun having daddy at home with his funny leg and shiny sticks but they soon lost interest when they realised that I couldn't chase them up the garden. Ev reminds me I was extremely difficult during my confinement. She decided some sea air might speed my recovery so we went to visit her parents in Ventnor on the Isle of Wight. Negotiating the steep slopes down to the sea front was extremely challenging but worth the effort to watch the girls playing on the beach.

My incapacity presented the practice with a nightmare scenario. The team rallied round splendidly, filling in for my consultations and duties until a reliable locum could be found. Before I could return to work, I had to change my current car with a manual gearbox for a similar model with an automatic gearbox.

Three months after my vae diei, I returned to work, chastened and on much-reduced power. I had been forced to accept that I was neither indestructible nor indispensable; the practice had managed perfectly well without me. It was another lesson for me to learn. My self-confidence had been dented and I was never as physically strong as before my accident.

My farming clients were kind enough to refrain from commenting on the difficulty I had climbing over five-bar gates and, where possible, they unlocked and opened them for me. My approach had to be reset from 'I can deal with anything that comes my way' to 'can I do it?'. Without exception, everyone who learnt of my misfortune took the side of the horse, particularly those who self-identify as male. What happened to my patient? He went to a veterinary hospital where he was castrated properly without further fuss.

Psychologically, it was important that, having metaphorically fallen off the bike, I got back on again as quickly as possible. In October, I castrated a Shetland pony in the standing position, using a similar drug mix as before but adjusted for weight. My greatest difficulty on this occasion was having to kneel so I could see what I was doing.

A couple of months later, a client brought her pet in for a booster vaccination. I thought she gave me a sideways look. "I was the nurse who sat with you when you came round from your anaesthetic. I could tell you a few things you said that night."

Hazel had been reminding me on a regular basis about her wish to transfer our trading accounts to a computer. Fearful of the technological future which seemed unavoidable, I gave in at the end of September, my willpower weakened by my recent injury. It seemed to take an age to transfer this data. Whenever I asked whether it could produce this or that figure or speed up the length of time it took to produce quarterly VAT and management accounts, the answer was always "no".

'The Hare is Running'

Chapter 20

Do It Again

During my enforced absence, colleagues at the practice were under considerable pressure. Well before I was fully fit to return to work at Iffley Road, one thing I could do whilst standing on one leg was supervise racing at the greyhound stadium. In my pomp, prior to each race, I walked the hundred metres from the vet's room to the steps leading up to the uncovered stand outside the paddock.

From this elevated vantage point, I kept my eye on the six dogs from the time they stepped on to the track for the parade until they returned panting to the paddock. Being unable to walk this walk, exceeding two kilometres per meeting, I watched the races on a TV monitor in the vet's room.

Hidden from public view in the paddock, this room was compact and described as pokey by some trainers and scruffy by others. I provided the consulting table, topped with a non-slip rubber mat, and a fridge in which vaccines were kept. Medicines and dressings were stored in recycled kitchen units with worktops above. There was a sink with cold running water and an electric wall-mounted heater which supplied hot water on a good day. A blue, plastic-covered, padded chair had been scrounged from somewhere. The TV monitor arrived after a great deal of nagging. I haggled with the management for months for a linoleum covering for the rough concrete floor.

Opened in March 1939, the stadium had a modern, though rather tawdry, main stand which was badly in need of a makeover. Elsewhere, the flaking paint on the chipboard fencing around the sand track and the moth-eaten state of the hare added to the down-at-heel atmosphere. After dark, the floodlights lent an air of respectability to the exciting evening programme, as the 'hare' started 'running', heralding another opportunity for punters to flash the cash.

My roots in east London served me well working in this slightly-seedy setting. The ambience, the hustle and indecorous language were reminiscent of the traders at the street market on Roman Road in Bow which I visited with my nan as a boy. I came to regard most trainers as likeable rogues rather than wideboys and a grudging tolerance, bordering on respect, grew between us.

Trying to stay ahead of the game, I clocked some of their stratagems and gathered, via mumbled quips, that I was beginning to get in their way. I took this as a compliment. I learnt to interpret body language and the messages picked up by eye contact, or lack of it.

Most of the time, I enjoyed the *craic*, the joshing and the jockeying for a notional advantage. They didn't know precisely what I did and didn't know; I played my part in this charade of bluff and double bluff with rising confidence. Each race meeting was another episode in the soap opera. If you had been away, it might take two or three meetings until you were fully conversant with the twists and turns of the current plot.

Greyhound racing could not take place without a vet being present. In 1986, no special training was required or offered. I learnt the basics from Jimmy Sheriffs but after that, I was reliant on my wits and my ability to play good cop and bad cop in the same production. I attended the meetings to safeguard the welfare of the greyhounds. When I felt the smudged line between the trainers' race craft and the potential risks to the dogs had been crossed, I became distinctly difficult company. I preferred to persuade and cajole rather than wield what pathetic authority was invested in me. After all, if the management didn't think I fitted in, they could summarily sack me and seek a more compliant replacement.

Early in my track career, I was examining a dog which had performed poorly, trying to ascertain if injury was the cause. It was a thankless task; most muscular and ligament injuries only become apparent when the dog has cooled down and often not until the following day.

The trainer looked down as I squatted beside his dog and said disdainfully, "You don't know what you're ******* talking about!"

That remark, and the venom with which it was delivered, together with my life experiences, made me more determined to learn as much as I could about the breed and the common racing injuries they suffered. I scrutinised my anatomy books again and attended a training course offered by an Irishman more experienced than me.

Every greyhound coming to the practice was palpated thoroughly until I could feel my way around the dogs with my eyes shut, confident in my knowledge of what was normal and laboriously learning about what was not. I had to master my subject if I was to hold my own in the daily disputes at the track. In every race, I noted the performance of each dog and the factors characterising its racing style.

Before long, after kennelling on race night, I could pick likely winners with a strike rate of seventy per cent. It is *verboten* for the track vet to place bets on dogs which race at that meeting. At the beginning of my tenure, I told the trainers that the day they saw me place a bet was the day they could no longer trust my judgement, since I would have a vested interest in the outcome of a race.

As always, there was one exception.

When a dog was winning, it was flavour of the month but if it was injured, in most cases, little effort was put into its treatment and rehabilitation. I hated this. As I grew in confidence, I operated on some of these injured dogs. The ultimate challenge was to operate with sufficient technical skill and a modicum of luck so that it led to a successful return to racing. My goal was to help them achieve a race time close to their best recent time before they incurred the injury.

A top-grade fawn dog with a formidable physique broke a bone in his right hock during a race. Not an uncommon injury, this type of fracture must be repaired with precise replacement of the fractured fragment if the dog is to return to the racetrack.

Applying casts to these injuries does not usually result in a fully-functioning hock joint. I repaired this fracture using a stainless-steel orthopaedic screw. The fracture healed well and the time came for the dog to run its timed trials to prove its fitness. His performances gradually improved and he returned to racing. I monitored his progress, wincing when he ran the bends or when another dog touched him, knocking him off his racing line.

He had completed four races, regained his racing fitness and on this particular Saturday night, he looked and felt ready to compete with a decent chance to win. Word had got out that I had repaired this fracture; kennel hands could be heard shouting across the paddock that the dog stood no chance of winning. They never come back after that sort of injury was the pronouncement of these self-appointed experts.

Based on my life history to date, you will gather this was a red rag to a bull. I took a friendly kennel hand, not connected with the dog, on one side and asked him to place my bet of ten pounds stake money with a trackside bookmaker at favourable odds. I assured him it was a one-off and that any proceeds would be donated to the Retired Greyhound Trust. Happily, the dog won and more importantly, came off the track without showing signs of soreness. The kennel hand collected the proceeds of the punt, handing me the cash in the paddock office in front of the dog's detractors.

The fastest, often the costliest and usually the sleekest stars of the meeting were lavishly cosseted before they appeared on the track. Afterwards, if the gamble had failed, depending on the trainer and the breeding of the dog, they might be washed down, dried and painstakingly anointed before being returned to a comfortable bed in their kennel. Alternatively, they could be chucked back in their kennel, with barely a nod to their cleanliness, their comfort or their welfare.

I noticed such behaviour, storing it away to be borne in mind next time a benefit of the doubt decision was required involving a greyhound in their care. I empathised with the lowly graders, the foot soldiers without whom any race card would appear threadbare. One such dog was Henry O.

At four years old, he was running in lower grade races, winding down his racing career before retirement. I was familiar with this recurring thread in the storyline. In the run-up to Christmas, on Saturday night with office parties in full swing over in the main stand, he was presented at kennelling and looked a different dog. Well groomed, coat shining, he was bright and alert, his muscles toned. I checked his ear marks to make sure it was the same dog.

The trainer came over to the paddock to check his dog during the early races, which was unprecedented in my experience. He was brought out of his kennel well before his race to be walked around the paddock. He was, in the local parlance, being warmed up. Great attention was paid to his pre-race preparation, including the comfort of his racing jacket and the proper fit of his muzzle. He was being treated like the favourite in the feature race on the card.

A final reassuring massage of his hindlegs as he entered his trap told me all I needed to know. This was a trophy race and he was a 'buzzer'. He won a close race in thrilling style by half a length and enjoyed all the trappings accorded to winners. The following Saturday, in a higher-graded race, he was unceremoniously bundled into his kennel with no comfortable soft bedding. This contrasted sharply with the treatment on his previous appearance.

I noticed that the trainer had two runners in the race. Henry O was lying on a cold concrete floor with no bedding before running in a race he must not win. I was incandescent. I had a quiet word with the kennel hand, letting him know I was abreast of the situation and giving him a chance to put matters right. As nothing changed, I rang the racing manager, high up with the gods in the pod above the main stand.

I was told this was a matter for the professional trainer and not the management of the track. I asked if I could put bedding in the kennel for the dog. I was informed that I could not unless the trainer gave permission and his representative was present. The connection was summarily broken. So, I was present to look after the welfare of the greyhounds but was powerless to intervene when it was compromised. I took the matter up with the regulator of greyhound racing in Great Britain but to no avail.

From time to time, some perceptive members of the public and owners frustrated with their dogs being out-graded or repeatedly given the wrong traps sidled up to me to ask why I continued to come. Surely my presence condoned this disreputable behaviour, which was masked by a veneer of respectability? My answer was that I was more proficient at spotting injuries and injured dogs than many track vets and therefore the greyhounds benefitted from my being there. Moreover, I was more likely to change the culture of poor working practices from within the organisation.

With that aim in mind, I joined the Society of Greyhound Veterinarians and later accepted an invitation to represent the society on the veterinary and scientific committee of the regulator of the sport at that time, the National Greyhound Racing Club. In this forum, we discussed a range of subjects which included a national initiative to record injuries sustained at meetings at every track. The intention was to develop a robust database from which policy decisions might be made, based on scientific data rather than myths and legends. We discussed how racetracks should be prepared before each meeting, the design of race traps and the frequency with which dogs should be allowed to race. The committee promoted best practice within the industry but the rate at which changes were implemented was dreadfully slow.

Nationally, I contributed to Lord Donoughue's Review of Greyhound Racing in 2007. His report called for far-reaching reforms to improve the welfare of racing greyhounds and led to the Welfare of Greyhounds Regulations introduced in 2010. In 2015, I appeared with others in front of a Parliamentary committee enquiring into greyhound welfare, the effectiveness of the current regulations and the efficacy or otherwise of self-regulation of the sport.

Advances in the welfare of the racing greyhounds at the racetrack, in their residential kennels and in their retirement must be properly funded. A mandatory levy of three per cent of all bets placed on horse racing is used to improve equine welfare and to fund research. Only half of one per cent of bets placed on greyhound racing may follow the same route. It is only a voluntary levy. Political will is required to change this iniquitous state of affairs and that has been sadly lacking in successive governments who only pay lip service to the welfare of racing greyhounds.

The annual Pall Mall competition was held at the Oxford track in March, with heats, semi-finals and the final, each run at approximately seven-day intervals. The final was the richest race of the racing calendar at Oxford, with prize money for the winning dog of five thousand pounds. For comparison, the BBC TV Greyhound Trophy was run at Oxford in 1995 with prize money to the winner of two and a half thousand pounds.

On such big race nights, the prize money and the run money for each dog in every race on the card was substantially increased. This attracted a bigger crowd, which helped to raise the level of expectation and excitement.

On one such night, I withdrew the favourite from one of the prestigious races on the card because I judged the dog to be lame. As I walked round the outer perimeter of the track towards the main stand, I was confronted by the enraged owner, threatening to exact all sorts of violent acts of retribution upon my person. A tall, dignified man, with long frizzy grey hair, worn denim jacket and jeans, quietly stepped between us and looking down on my accuser, asked calmly if there was a problem. Apparently, there wasn't. A misunderstanding had been defused in a moment.

My minder introduced himself as Paul and as we parted, he asked me to visit and vaccinate some greyhound pups he had bred "when it suited". I watched as the dogs in the race in question, including the reserve dog, went on parade. I sauntered round to watch the bets being laid with the trackside bookmakers. Seasoned gamblers liked to place their bets at the last possible moment, sometimes after the hare had started running. Punters who mistimed their dash with their cash to their chosen bookie could be left disappointed.

In June 2010, a runner in the final of the Pall Mall and a fast dog suffered a fracture of its hock. Emotions were running high in the vet's room. "He'll have to be put down," was oft repeated. At that stage, with a track record behind me, I was able to manipulate the bone back into place using only gentle finger pressure. I explained how the leg could be stabilised with a relatively simple surgical repair. To their credit, they listened to my advice and the leg was strapped with a support dressing. The dog went to Ireland for remedial treatment, subsequently returning to the track to win.

It was a conundrum trying to pitch the costs of patching up greyhounds at a level which the trainers regarded as economic. Owners were quite happy to spend five thousand pounds or more on the next big thing but never five hundred pounds on a proven dog which was injured. The expectations of some owners were simply unrealistic. Dogs which were 'owned by the kennel' were funded and fed from the run money supplemented by the odd successful stroke. Trainers were not allowed to bet on races in which they had dogs entered but this rule was conveniently and consistently overlooked. Should dogs owned by the kennel pick up an injury, they were laid off more in hope than expectation that one day they would miraculously regain fitness, return to racing and regain their winning ways.

Bitches were not allowed to race whilst they were in season. It was thought that they might have a disruptive effect on the male competitors in the race but opinions remain divided on this. Naturally, the use of any performance–enhancing drugs was banned, yet bitches could have their seasons suppressed, even though the drug commonly used improved the bulk and the strength of their muscles.

These injections were often requested after the bitch had raced on the night. This was far from ideal but was accepted practice. I always gave my injections in the muscle mass towards the back of the leg, though some of my colleagues preferred to use the muscle at the front of the hindlimb.

A black bitch received her injection from a colleague in the muscles at the front of her right hind leg one Saturday night after racing. She was presented to me, two days later, wobbly on both hind legs, her left hind leg being the weaker of the two. I suspected a haemorrhage into her lower spine, likely to have occurred after her race but the owner was adamant the problem was caused by the injection.

I treated her and asked to check her in three or four days. I didn't see her for five weeks. Some muscle groups in her left hind leg were now visibly wasted. The owner asked me to put her to sleep. I refused, fairly certain these changes were temporary and reversible. I believed she would recover the use of these muscles given time.

I suggested that ownership of the bitch be signed over to me. A few words on some headed notepaper, a squiggle of a pen and I was the proud owner of a racing bitch in her fourth year. The kennel fees were now down to me, though I never received an account from the trainer. When I neutered her, later in the year, the diameter of her left thigh was only two centimetres less than her right and she was sound. She was rehomed to Janet, a lovely owner who was thrilled with her new companion. On her retirement, this gentle dog frequently appeared on the stand of the Retired Greyhound Trust at local shows, sought out by her fan club, lapping up the attention of the passers-by and generating much needed publicity and donations for the charity.

I wondered whether betting was an inherited defect passed on in the genes. Family folklore says that my father's brother set out on Saturday morning to purchase a three-piece suite for his lounge. He returned without any furniture but with a third share in a racehorse called Hysopus. I remember watching her race on television as she won a maiden race at York. However, she did not set the racing world alight during her career.

Anna, my teenage daughter, came home from school with a ten-pound note. Each member of her class had been set a challenge of making this money grow using any means they deemed lawful. I hoped the idea behind the exercise was to test their entrepreneurial skills and ingenuity. My daughter passed the money and the responsibility to me, asking me to use it as stake money at the track. I passed the note to a trusted trainer.

"I don't need to know how you do it or when you do it but please would you double my stake money."

A fortnight later, he came to the vet's room and passed me more than twenty pounds. Tapping the side of his nose, and with a knowing smile, he left; no names, no pack drill. I would love to have seen the look on the teacher's face when she read Anna's slip of paper which detailed how the money had been grown? Betting on the dogs? St Helens and St Katharine's definitely was not that sort of school.

There can only be one winner. Many of the trainers, their owners and their connections suffer disappointment and sometimes heartache. What happens to the dogs when their racing careers are over? With no further financial return on their investment, many owners were not prepared to continue to pay the kennel fees needed to house and feed their dogs. There was pressure from the trainers who wanted the kennel space to bring on younger saplings.

Flo Partridge ran a kennel nearby, solely for retired greyhounds. It was not the smartest kennel nor a great money spinner but she was devoted to the dogs. For those lucky few, it was party time, with good food and daily exercise outside in fresh air, romping in her grass paddocks. Owners could come and walk their dogs at the weekends. For me, Flo was a star.

At the beginning of my career, the number of unwanted racers at Oxford being put to sleep when they were no longer fit to race was unacceptably high. This number fell dramatically and I see this as a notable success, achieved through persistent pressure and a sustained programme of re-education of owners and trainers, as well as the public. There are a few dogs who are temperamentally unsuited to rehoming but most greyhounds make excellent pets. One of the great pleasures of my working life has been to visit a house where a greyhound has been homed, to find a healthy and happy dog, possibly with a young child as a devoted companion and playmate.

When I started in 1986, race cards consisted of eight races on Tuesday and Thursday evenings and ten races on Saturdays, with intervals of twenty minutes between races. At this leisurely pace, it allowed time for kennel hands to wash away the sand thrown up from the racing surface before preparing their runner in the next race. At that time, I could reel off many of the regular runners, real characters, appearing on the card of Saturday night racing, Sandwinder and Rathkennan Red being two. Each race was an event, after which owners would congregate by the paddock gate to congratulate their dog on its efforts, adding a personal touch, symbolic of collective involvement.

Over time, more and more races have been squeezed in so that twelve races became the minimum on a race night, with fourteen on a Saturday night and even sixteen races on some special nights. With less than ten minutes before the next parade, there was only time for a perfunctory splash with some water and a quick rub with a towel before getting the next dog out.

The national bookmakers started televising meetings. BAGS (Bookmakers Afternoon Greyhound Services) broadcast these race meetings live to their betting shops via satellite, allowing free entry to the stadium for all. The first of these meetings took place at Oxford at the end of 1987. One meeting a week at Oxford became two, with more races to be graded and only so many fit dogs available to populate the six traps. In the run up to Christmas, it would not be unusual to stage more than seventy races per week, including two meetings on a Friday.

To prepare yourself mentally to face another night at the track on Friday evening, having spent more than five hours there earlier in the day, presented me with the personal challenge of maintaining the highest professional standards all the time. Understandably, it wasn't easy to be motivated, to get out of the chair and walk out again to watch the twentieth race of the day whilst retaining the same level of critical vigilance of ten to twelve hours previously.

Kennel hands who were probably up earlier than I was and would finish late at night earned barely minimum wages. I reminded myself how lucky I was but it was tough to continue to care about what was happening around me. In the Eighties, the trainers had time to prepare dogs properly between meetings but with the passage of time, each individual dog became less important; they were fed and watered often with only minimal exercise and training regimes. The time pressure placed on the trainers was immense; I watched grown young men quickly lose their youth and vitality, bowed under the weight of more and more dog racing.

And for what? From afar, the financial benefits gained for their extra effort seemed minimal. Kennel hands struggled to remember the names of the dog they were parading let alone what previous injuries the dog had suffered. It was no longer a game, no longer a sport, but a well-oiled commercial treadmill which provided an accessible and cheap medium for betting, from which it was extremely difficult to step away. Young fresh dogs quickly tired of the chase, becoming bored and simply followed the hindquarters of the dog in front.

On occasions when the hare failed during a race, the dogs would cross the finish line in similar times and order. BAGS racing took place when the track was frosted in January, when the more thoughtful kennel hands gave a tentative knock on my door to ask for hot water with which to wash the dogs down, and on hot balmy afternoons in July.

On a late afternoon in summer, the sun slowly sinking in a cloudless sky, a trainer was accosted by a disgruntled owner whose dog had under-performed in the last race. I overheard the explanation that was given.

"O'course, running up the back straight, he couldn't see 'cos he had the sun in 'is eyes."

It was difficult watching the desperation of reckless gamblers. I saw several instances where employees from the local car factory came to the track on Thursday evenings and left empty-handed, having gifted their wages to the trackside bookmakers. I wondered how that family would put food on the table in the coming week.

The bookies worked long hours, often having stood at a horse race meeting earlier in the day. I was fascinated by their quaint leather satchels or cases, their names emblazoned on the side. It was mostly a male preserve but the odd strident female voice could be heard shouting the odds. I have seen smug looks on some faces as they left after the last race in their expensive cars but also on rare occasions, I have seen a bookie broken during a race meeting and it was not a pretty sight. There cannot be many more stressful ways of earning a living.

I was due to undertake a sponsored swim, aiming to raise £680 to fund the hire of a specially-adapted barge for a week to give people with mobility problems, often wheelchair users, a day out on the Kennet and Avon canal. My sponsorship form had too many unfilled spaces and I was still about five hundred pounds short of my target. I explained to a friendly bookie what I was trying to do and why, leaving the form with him.

When I collected the form at the end of that evening's racing, the total amount pledged amounted to £680. Salt of the earth. I have never forgotten this generous gesture. These annual barge trips, held under my Rotary Club's banner, have continued for the last twenty-five years, with more than five thousand disabled, disadvantaged and elderly guests enjoying this scenic stretch of the canal near Great Bedwyn. Where would we have been without the Oxford bookies?

The track remained profitable but closed at the end of 2012. I miss the banter and the curious camaraderie which had evolved and of course, most of all, I miss the dogs. I continued to treat a number of greyhounds at the practice but I missed watching the dogs' speed, grace and agility as they raced.

But I welcomed having my Sunday afternoons to myself once more, to do as I pleased. It was a massive wrench driving away, leaving my children playing in the garden on another sunny Sunday. They have left now to live their own lives and I miss not having played a bigger part in much of their childhood. I don't miss the tinny loudspeaker, the banality of the oft-repeated announcements, the same Eighties music tracks playing unchanged, night after night throughout the year, until displaced by the customary Christmas ditties in early November beginning the run up to the festival.

I don't miss the razzamatazz which masked the tacky nature of the parades and the presentations of prizes on the podium, each one photographed 'for posterity'. Most of all, I don't miss being blasted by the pretentious first few bars of *Fanfare of the Common Man* played as the greyhounds stepped onto the track before every race I watched.

Chapter 21

Charity's Fine

No sooner had we purchased a computer and the requisite software to manage our accounts with suppliers than rumours began to circulate that most software programmes had an inherent flaw. When the new millennium arrived and the calendar clicked over to the year 2000, stored data could be lost. The company who supplied our machine assured us everything would be fine. Advertisements appeared in the veterinary and specialist press offering 'solutions to your data problems'. I fretted. Hazel ensured the practice reverted to its customary default position - heads in the sand and hope.

With the millennium looming, we backed up our data, each of us taking a selection of floppy discs home over new year. All we could do was hope that our first venture in computerisation would not be a flop on a par with the 'the river of fire' in London which was supposed to accompany Big Ben's chimes at midnight.

When we all assembled on the other side, I watched as Hazel fired up the object of my angst. I was relieved as various coloured charts and figures materialised on the screen, reassuring me that all had not been lost. The doom and gloom which had been circulating before the millennium was just ill-informed hype.

Charity begins at home. The practice offered discounts to deserving causes, both individually and collectively. Members of the public who rang about a dog or cat they had found, owner unknown, were asked to pay a notional sum confirming their commitment to the case. The practice covered the residual cost of the initial consultation and treatment. Hazel minded a war chest which could be raided if she or I approved. One such case was Jay, a brindled terrier cross brought to the practice on a Sunday afternoon having allegedly been found on the roadside, injured.

The family presenting the dog claimed to have no money for any treatment, despite arriving in an expensive car. It's difficult to avoid a *soupçon* of cynicism as you become experienced in the ways of our world. Might the dog have been the family's own pet which had been run over?

Jay was young and fit and I was unwilling to put him to sleep. The agreement reached was that if no owner came forward, the dog would be treated by the practice and rehomed. X-rays confirmed a fractured pelvis and a badly-fractured hind limb. The damaged limb was amputated and the dog showed great resilience in adapting to his new life on three legs. He had to be restricted to a cage for some time to limit his activity whilst the broken bones in his pelvis knitted together.

This dog had such an outgoing personality, he captivated those who met him. He received more than his fair share of attention from the nurses and on several weekends, I brought him home to my family, as we were still dogless at the time. He took part in whatever was going on, including being taken to riding lessons with the girls. He was homed to a family in time for Christmas. I have a photograph of him lying near their Christmas tree, amongst the presents and decorations. Such a satisfying result.

At about the same time, I met a small pup found apparently abandoned on a travellers' site. At first glance, he was an unprepossessing sight. We fed him, treated him for internal and external guests and loved him to bits. Gillian, now filling the role of head nurse, was a genuine, compassionate Irish girl and blessed with the gift of the gab. Even I found it difficult to say no to her.

Spotting a long-standing client in reception, she took Carrie downstairs and showed her the puppy. Henry was adopted instantly. Placed on the back seat of her new car whilst she paid her account, Henry passed the time chewing the luxuriously-upholstered leather seats. She didn't seem to mind. He was worshipped for the rest of his life and gave me pleasure whenever he appeared on my list of consultations.

All manner of wildlife from hedgehogs, foxes, deer and badgers to a host of wild birds were brought to our door by the great British public. First aid treatment was offered to all these creatures and in many cases, a great deal more. A result of our efforts were quite a few one-legged wild birds hopping about in Bagley woods and three-legged hedgehogs scuffling about in its hedgerows. My family has an unwanted three-legged tortoise amongst our crew of chelonian misfits, imaginatively dubbed Three Legs by my children.

A swan with a broken wing arrived in the back of a car. His was an old injury which had become badly infected. There was a risk of losing him under anaesthetic because of his debilitated state but something about the way he resisted all attempts to help him won me over.

The fracture could not be repaired so we amputated the wing. To reduce bodyweight to a minimum, the bones in a bird's wing are hollow. During such surgeries, this hollow space must be plugged to avoid air being drawn into the skeletal structure with a concomitant risk of infection. With the bone plugged, the wound was closed with very fine suture material using a buried suture pattern to minimise the chance of unwarranted attention from the patient.

The bird stayed with us during his convalescence, making a huge mess in his spacious kennel, with smell to match. Eventually, he had to take his chances and fend for himself. In most cases, I was not in favour of keeping previously-wild animals in captivity. My treatment regimes for these animals were based on assessing the chances of each patient surviving unaided in the wild after recovery. Hazel took him to an extensive lake near her home in Nuneham Courtenay. Following his release, he settled into his new life, happily paddling about, mostly in circles, and from afar he appeared to have adjusted well to his new earthbound existence.

Red kites became a protected species in the UK in 1989. Shortly after this change in legislation, a magnificent male lay injured beside the M40. He had a similar wing injury but his was very fresh, with the surrounding soft tissue still viable. I pinned this midshaft fracture, achieving good stability with minimal localised tissue damage.

He was collected by my friend John, a specialist in the care and rehabilitation of raptors. The wings of the patient were stitched together using fine sutures close to the base of the feather shafts, making flight impossible until the fracture had healed. The bird was housed in an small aviary and fed from behind a screen to minimise any habituation with humans.

Once the fracture had healed, the sutures securing the flight feathers were snipped and a long period of rehabilitation commenced. He progressed to more spacious aviaries where he could practise flying and strengthen the atrophied wing musculature. Almost a year after he was first presented, he was ready to be released.

At the bottom of the escarpment at Stokenchurch, in the company of John, Tracey from the RSPCA and the police's wildlife protection officer, I watched his official release. It was a gamble; you never quite know how these things will turn out. Would he take flight or would he fall to earth after flying a few yards?

Finally set free, I felt quite emotional as he flew across the hillside to perch on the top of a nearby tree, from which vantage point he performed his triangulation trickery. Suddenly, he was soaring in a wide arc, catching updrafts, before alighting again in a tree at the top of the ridge. Already, another kite appeared to check out the new kid on the block. I prayed my former patient would not be beaten up by a more dominant male. The release had proceeded perfectly. Daily food parcels were provided to support him until they remained untouched, suggesting he was sustaining himself using his own predatory skills.

I had just undressed and got into bed when the police control unit phoned to ask for help with an animal hit by a car outside the Nuffield hospital in Oxford. The flashing blue light of the ambulance guided me to the location, where not only was the dog injured but so was the owner. The owner left in style, courtesy of the ambulance service, but before their departure, the paramedics helped me get my patient into the back of my car using a blanket, clearly marked as the property of the NHS. This is a good example of cooperation in a public/private partnership capacity between two different elements of our undervalued emergency services. Happily, the dog's injuries were relatively superficial and he was transferred to a kennel, his keep subsidised by the police, to await the discharge of its owner.

The same control unit called early another morning. There was great agitation caused by a injured cow on the railway line near Bicester. They had contacted other local practices who had either been unwilling or unable to attend the incident.

When I got there, I sensed tension amongst the bystanders. The injured steer was lying across the railway track, blocking the London to Birmingham mainline. A massive diesel locomotive was pulling this service and the driver seemed impatient at having to wait.

By now, the farmer had arrived and we agreed that his animal was so badly injured that euthanasia was the best option. I loaded the gun and as I approached the beast, the diesel loco edged closer. Pressure, pressure. The incident wasn't even on my patch. Having cleared the line, there was much muttering into portable radios by important-looking fellows in fluorescent jackets. Finally, the signal turned green and the train was allowed to continue its journey. Not an auspicious start to what promised to be a very long day.

I have rescued animals from all sorts of fluid situations. The most aromatic was undoubtedly a cow which had somehow slithered into the farmer's own slurry pit; the most scenic was probably a young horse taking a plunge in the River Cherwell near the Northern Oxford bypass.

Rescued from R. Cherwell. 1996

evening in August. The fire officers, wearing thigh-length waders and waterproof suits, were in the river, threading straps around the horse's body. There was plenty of muscle available and no health and safety officer about as the horse was gently manhandled up the bank and onto the grass of the flood meadow.

After an inspection to check for obvious injuries, a firm slap on its back and a coordinated chorus of shouting persuaded the youngster to stand up. He walked round gingerly, apparently none the worse for his ordeal. And then, as often happens, the owner turned up at the end of the performance. She was a client of the practice and reassured that I had been there to check her animal. It was just as well I was on my best behaviour that evening as one of the fire crew turned out to be a friend of my next-door neighbour. In the days before social media, word still spread quickly.

As well as our own charitable efforts within the practice, we worked closely with other charities active in the local area. Developing a close relationship with RSPCA inspectors Doug and Tracey led to some absorbing experiences. This association made me fitter, bearing in mind the miles I walked in fruitless searches for injured swans along the river and injured deer "somewhere on Boars Hill".

Port Meadow was a popular venue for our joint exercises. The Freemen of Oxford and Commoners of Wolvercote were gifted by King Alfred this one hundred and twenty hectares, (approximately three hundred acres) of pasture next to the River Thames. Their collective right to graze their animals free of charge on this flood meadow was recorded in the Domesday Book of 1086 and has been exercised since that time.

A warden monitors the condition and welfare of the animals on the meadow. However, the care and attention paid to these animals by their owners was not always as it should have been. In some cases, it was a matter of out of sight, out of mind. I met inspector Doug on Port Meadow in January 2008. The meadow, serving its natural purpose, was almost completely flooded and the animals which remained were huddled precariously on some raised ground at the northern end above the encroaching water.

We went to check a group of animals on the opposite bank of the river, downstream from the abbey ruins at Godstow. We watched from afar in astonishment as a trailer drew up at Wolvercote and discharged yet another pony on to the flooded meadow opposite.

Scarcely believable. I learnt later that the pony was traced to owners in Slough. Friendly bombs and all that. Although hay was being provided daily, we decided all the animals should be moved off the meadow for their own safety. It was no small undertaking.

Occasionally, the health of a horse was a major cause for concern. Perhaps they were underweight, possibly because their teeth were in a poor state, or lame with their hooves overgrown and cracked. Patient detective work was sometimes required to trace the owners of these animals although all of them should have been registered with the authorities.

Cattle were required to have ear tags which identified them individually with their farm of origin. Since 2009, horses had to be microchipped, superceding the earlier reliance on freezebrands. Most owners followed these guidelines. In those cases where the ownership remained in doubt, the horses were moved to the RSPCA's Blackberry Farm to receive attention and often needed some sedation before their journey. There were no proper handling facilities available on the meadow and it was an overrated pastime trying to round up a recalcitrant patient with such an extensive area offering limitless opportunities to evade capture.

Most years, pet care could prove problematic in the summer. Some owners went on holiday leaving their pets or livestock without adequate provision of food, water, shelter or daily supervision. The owners of a rabbit on a housing estate in Oxford asked neighbours to look after their pet whilst they were away.

When the neighbours declined, the owners departed anyway, leaving the animal in the garden to forage for food amongst the herbaceous borders. The sympathetic neighbours, aware of the animal's predicament, provided food over the fence. These were hot days in August and eventually the RSPCA arranged a forced entry through a side gate to the garden. Finding that neither fresh water nor food nor shelter was available, the inspector took the rabbit to be cared for at Blackberry Farm.

During July in another hot spell, I was present with Doug and police officers when they forcibly entered the garden of a property in Botley. Here, we found three geese in the back garden. A fourth bird had succumbed, its partly-dismembered body lying under a hedge. No water, suitable food or fox-proof housing had been provided. The surviving birds were taken to the safe sanctuary of Blackberry Farm to be cared for until the owner returned and faced questions about their thoughtless actions.

On duty on Christmas day morning, I took a call from inspector Mike, on duty for the RSPCA. He was in Milton Keynes, having picked up a sick dog but couldn't find a local vet willing to look at the animal. An hour later, we met at the practice, enjoying freshly-baked home-made mince pies and tea together. The young dog, possibly a year old, was treated for a stomach upset and spent the rest of his Christmas as a guest at the RSPCA's table.

During the examination of this patient, a member of the public phoned to say they had come across an injured heron in Wallingford. Getting no answer from local practices, he asked if I would be prepared to look at the bird. Of course I would. It felt as if I was on call for much of the home counties as well as our clients during the festive period. When I qualified, I expected a varied caseload but this exceeded my expectations.

The practice worked closely with Cats Protection, a national charity with a strong local network of active voluteers which part-funded innumerable neutering operations as well as contributing to the costs of more complex surgery in cases of need.

The PDSA, another national charity, intoduced its Pet Aid scheme in Oxford in 1993. At the outset, a household which had fallen on hard times, living within certain defined postcodes, could pre-register their pet at a cost of three pounds so that if veterinary treatment were required, the cost would be covered by the charity. Hundreds of Oxford's pets have benefitted from this scheme since its inception, including Sheba (Chapter 17). It has proved its worth as a cost-efficient service in the city.

The Dogs' Trust, formerly the National Canine Defence League, started the Hope project in Oxford, which provided help with the cost of veterinary treatment for any dog whose owner was homeless. Free routine and preventative veterinary care were available under the scheme.

The animals must be microchipped and neutered during the first year of membership, procedures carried out at no cost to the owner. Additional treatments which may be needed were subsidised by agreement with the practice under the scheme.

In many cases, their dog is the one constant in the owner's life, offering them unconditional love and support and it was important that the animal did not suffer because of the difficult circumstances in which the owner found themselves. However, it was difficult to persuade some of these owners to have their animals neutered.

One fellow flatly refused to accept our advice. His bitch Dee had pups just before Christmas. Reports reached me he was telling anyone who cared to stop and listen that he knew best. He carried the puppies around the city centre in an old suitcase. His photograph on the front page of the local newspaper publicised his 'victory' more widely. Clients started leaving donations of dog food at reception. For years afterwards, I would be treating labrador-cross dogs and be told proudly that this is one of Dee's pups. It must have been a huge litter.

Two incidents are worthy of note. A chap, who had been living on the streets with his gorgeous red setter for company began his rehabilitation in Oxford living in a hostel, monitored by wardens. We saw him regularly with his dog when he called in for a chat. One day, he burst into the waiting room to tell us he had been offered a flat of his own. He was ecstatic.

I speyed a bitch under the terms of the Hope project in January. I discharged the bitch to the owner myself. It was very cold outside and I asked him how far he had to walk with the dog to his home. He said he was living in a tent on the west side of the city near the river. It was not fair on my patient to expect her to walk that distance in those temperatures so soon after undergoing abdominal surgery. I offered to drive him to somewhere close to his camp site if he was willing to wait about an hour until I finished at work.

He was very grateful for the lift and told me something during the trip which meant a great deal to me, "The word on the street is that you are a good guy. You will always help us if you can."

West Oxfordshire Animal Rescue was a small local charity run by a band of dedicated volunteers which offered immediate shelter to unwanted cats and funding for any veterinary treatment required. I gave talks to schoolchildren on their behalf on the subject of the care and feeding of common pets.

My own guinea pigs and tortoises were handed round and handled by the excited children. Who knows which of them might have been encouraged to be more responsible pet owners or to have their own pets after listening to these talks?

In the mid-1990s, the charity launched a daunting challenge to raise funds to build their own animal treatment centre close to the city. To help promote this initiative, I was the support act to a celebrity appearance by Robert Hardy at a local garden centre. He played Siegfried in the first TV adaptation of *All Creatures Great and Small.*

The actor certainly raised the profile of this ambitious charity with his presence and good humour. Later in the publicity drive, I had the great pleasure of meeting a boyhood hero of mine on the stage at the New Theatre in Oxford during rehearsals. Harry Secombe was self-deprecating but needed no encouragement to create mischief and mayhem. How I would have loved to have been at a recording of *The Goon Show* with Harry, Spike Milligan and Peter Sellers all trying to outdo each other.

We needed fresh blood to give the practice renewed impetus and life. Katharine Morrison took the first steps towards her professional career with a period of work experience with the practice in 1993. She gained further practical experience at Iffley Road during her undergraduate years at Bristol and late in the year 2000, she began her professional employment when she joined our team. Her long association with the practice gave her a head start; she knew exactly how the practice functioned and was working with people she knew and who were keen to encourage her.

Further veterinary assistance arrived in the personable form of Graham. A studious new graduate of immense ability from Cambridge, I got the distinct impression that he was interviewing me rather than the other way round.

The practice must have passed his test because he joined us and I was very pleased that he did. He helped to raise the standard both of our companion animal anaesthesia and our care of critically-sick patients. Not content with an easy life, he reported the staff's comments that our record-keeping was "so last century".

He tried to persuade me, his senior and twice his age, that it wasn't acceptable to rely on handwritten clinical records kept on six thousand eight-by-five inch cards. Some clients' records had become so thick, the restraining staples had given up the struggle to keep the cards together. These cards were easily mislaid. You couldn't look at the records of an Iffley Road client if they turned up at Wheatley and the handwriting of half the employees in the practice was illegible anyway.

A recent survey had suggested that young, tech-savvy employees should mentor their older, senior luddite managers. I agreed to fund the considerable cost of the investment in computerisation if he selected the necessary hardware and software and supervised its installation. He willingly assumed the role of digital supremo and managed the transition so skilfully it was as painless as possible.

For me, the greatest boon was the system's ability to print labels for the medicines I dispensed. This represented real progress. It was an overrated exercise trying to write the owner's name and address, the date, the pet's name and how to use the medicine on a small self-adhesive label. The result, although legal, was often smudged and sometimes unreadable.

Another notable advantage was the time saved in filling in insurance claim forms and attaching relevant detailed invoices. Inevitably, there were teething problems which at the time seemed interminable, especially when the computers at the branch surgery at Wheatley proved selective about if and when they would communicate with those at Iffley Road.

After a series of protracted upgrades over several years, we achieved our goal, able to look at appointments and the clinical history of a patient whether working at Iffley or Wheatley. The main limitation in my case was my unidigital typing. I had the impression many clients who watched me struggle felt the urge to push me aside and type for me. When I had a vet student in the room, I delegated the typing to them. After all, taking an adequate history and recording it was part and parcel of the training which the practice should provide.

Recently, I was reminded how quickly technology moves on. I asked a visiting student to enter a history and she reached forward and started to tap the screen. She assumed it was a touch screen and further claimed never to have used a keyboard. Really? Was she pulling my leg? Had I already assumed the mantle of the dinosaur I feared I would eventually become in the veterinary firmament? I could still take a better clinical history than she could but ...

Chapter 22

Changin' Times

The millennium celebrations were a distant memory as Graham wrestled with his modems and his modules, personal computer stations, thins and a boss who persistently failed to grasp the basics behind the developing digital age.

In the autumn of 2000, I was battling nationwide fuel shortages while trying to organise farm and horse visits. The practice had enjoyed a long association with Bryants garage in Wheatley and appreciated the fuel set aside for us. We were never in a position of having to refuse to visit an animal because of lack of fuel. No sooner had we surmounted that challenge than we suddenly found ourselves dealing with a farm animal epizootic.

I have been fortunate in my career never to have encountered a case of foot-and-mouth disease but in February 2001, this distressing disease was identified in a batch of pigs in Essex. It had last been seen in the UK in 1967 when the livestock trade was largely local.

By 2001, the trade was national and international, which facilitated its dissemination throughout Britain, causing a catastrophe for the livestock industry. This highly-infectious virus infects cattle, sheep, pigs and goats although it's not considered dangerous to humans. Be that as it may, I am grateful not to have had any contact with infected animals and thus avoided becoming instrumental in the wholesale destruction of livestock on affected farms and their neighbours.

My involvement with the government's response to this national emergency began with the immediate restrictions on the movement of all farm animals. With a bewildering array of licences at my disposal, my role as a local veterinary inspector acting on behalf of the ministry was to license the movement of livestock between different farms and in larger enterprises, movement between different parishes of the same holding.

With the coming of spring, many herds relied on hiring a bull to serve their cows. The movement of each of these individual animals had to be licensed. On the sixteenth of March, I signed my first of many movement licences.

On our clients' farms at the back end of the winter season, stocks of feed were running low. Using animal movement and local movement licences, batches of healthy animals could be moved to alternative sites and sources of food, including different fields. The total number of animals to be moved had to correspond exactly with the number on the paper licence. As I checked each animal for signs of disease, their individual ear tag number had to match that on the licence.

The drivers of the vehicles transporting these animals self-certified that their transport had been cleansed with a specified disinfectant at the recommended dilution. Similar regulations applied to the use of footbaths at the site and to the cleansing of the vet at the end of each visit.

Pressure on haulage contractors and the limited availability of suitable vehicles gave rise to many early starts and late finishes. Special occupational licences were required on some farms to designate specified points of arrival and departure for the animals. It was essential that these points, identified by grid references on Ordnance Survey maps, had solid surfaces of concrete or tarmac that could be cleansed and disinfected after the arrival or departure of each batch of animals.

Pressure on farm vets' time escalated, with the onus on me to plug the gaps in our limited manpower by working longer hours. Between mid-March and mid-May, I completed more than eighty licences, each free of errors or alterations. The Ministry of Agriculture had hitherto refused to recognise any document sent by fax. All certificates sent to practices and returned by them were sent using snail mail.

In a volte-face, fax machines suddenly became essential practice equipment. Our machine consumed reams of paper in printing official guidance notes, instructions to LVIs and the licences themselves, the paper spewing out over the floor of the office. Completed licences had to be returned to a central hub in Carlisle by fax within twenty-four hours for that specific movement to be deemed authorised and therefore legitimate. Our basic economy fax machine, previously undervalued, was now overworked with an insatiable appetite for paper.

Overnight I acquired an even more detailed knowledge of the geography of farms I had been visiting for years. Fields had specific names, the position of parish churches, even of specific gateways with lay-bys large enough to accommodate heavy goods vehicles, all became requisite knowledge. All this complicated and time-consuming extra work had to be fitted in with the normal practice caseload.

Greyhound racing was briefly suspended to minimise the spread of the disease via the movement of vehicles and personnel. Indeed, some greyhound kennels occupied redundant farm buildings and shared the same access roads. Lobbying from vested interests ensured that racing quickly restarted, with the provision of footbaths both outside and inside the paddock gates being considered a satisfactory nod in the direction of basic biosecurity measures.

A ban on the sale of livestock placed an enormous strain on the livelihoods of our local farming community. Understandably, levels of stress rose sharply, at times to intolerable levels. The ministry asked vets to be vigilant, encouraging us to report any farmer who seemed to be overwhelmed and could be contemplating suicide. This was not a guidance note I ever expected to receive from the Ministry of Agriculture when I was awarded local veterinary inspector status in Sussex back in 1979. It was an enormous extra responsibility. A greeting of "How are you? How are you getting on?" no longer seemed entirely appropriate.

The sight and smell of carcases burning on farm pyres throughout the land is something

I hope is never seen in Britain again. Official figures suggest six million animals were slaughtered, many of which were not infected with the disease. Britain was declared free of the disease in January 2002. What a time it was.

At this time, Graham, having single-handedly supervised the computerisation of the practice, was lured back to academia by the University of Cambridge. He had acquired an invaluable year's experience in general practice and the university's gain was our loss.

I recruited Cameron Forbes as his replacement. Cameron was keen to escape his current position and came with a wealth of experience, including farm work. It was getting more difficult to engage veterinary colleagues who were confident or even willing to do farm work. Some were happy with horses but were known to frown and fret when a farm call came their way. Cameron's integration into the practice team took some of that responsibility from my shoulders, which was a welcome release.

The emphasis of general practice workloads in and around Oxford had changed markedly in the preceding ten years or so. A neighbouring practice phoned to say they were giving up farm work and would we accept their farm clients who wanted to join the practice? I was happy to do this but it meant we were now the only practice undertaking farm work within a fifteen-mile radius of the city centre. The history of the practice as a traditional mixed practice with farm and horse work spanned the last hundred years and I wanted to preserve this heritage.

This shifting landscape included the small-animal practices in the city, which were gradually being acquired by national corporate veterinary enterprises. These businesses wielded much greater purchasing power than my small, privately- owned practice, as well as offering more varied employment prospects in the eyes of many, which exacerbated the difficulties I was having in recruiting committed staff who shared the ethos I was promoting in my practice.

Locum agencies were signing up more and more veterinary professionals, especially qualified veterinary nurses. The perceived freedom from any long-term commitment with the option of moving on to pastures new on a whim was being touted as a big bonus by the agencies. Combined with the additional levy of agency fees, this made the role of a small veterinary practice employer all the more exacting.

Many aspects of practice life had become more complex and bureaucratic, though not necessarily safer or more efficient. From my perspective as an employer, the balance had shifted from my choosing to be a responsible and supportive employer, encouraging the personal development of my staff, to a small business in danger of being submerged under a succession of changes in employment law, imposed to achieve similar goals. These edicts seemed more suited to large conglomerates than small practices.

From using common sense, based on the example I set for my staff, I needed to employ professional advisors to process the myriad of regulations emanating from a government which claimed to be committed to reducing red tape for small businesses. The evidence of their failed objectives was a lever arch file stuffed with policies and pertinent protocols to be referred to in the case of a dispute, with many sections to be read by each new member of staff at the start of their employment.

In the past, I had managed by consensus but this was set aside and replaced by rights, both real and perceived. The inclusive team ethic which I had striven to nourish and nurture was being eroded by government diktats and the latest 'guidance' from my veterinary professional bodies advising on to how best to negotiate this legislative minefield.

We had successfully trained veterinary nurses for many years, enjoying a hundred per cent pass rate. It was a simple, inexpensive training scheme with the first year based on a programme of lectures, in our case at the Berkshire College of Agriculture. In the second year, the emphasis switched from theoretical knowledge to gaining practical experience. As tasks were completed, they were signed off by a vet in the training practice in what was affectionately referred to as the 'little green book'. The final examination was a practical viva, dreaded by all our candidates.

However, this booklet no longer enjoyed universal popularity. The message from on high was that this uncomplicated and economical arrangement must be changed, though I never grasped the reasons why. My head nurse Gillian and I had to be 'trained' and certified as being competent to train nurses. Veterinary nursing training was now included under the National Vocational Qualifications umbrella (NVQs) and was delivered using a standardised approach. A similar model was used to train different categories of apprentices including hairdressers.

Gillian and I duly achieved our D32, D33 and D34 accreditation and were allowed to train nurses under the new system. Appointments had to made in advance with the trainee to discuss the task in hand, such as cleaning out an animal cage. After the trainee had completed the task being assessed, another session was required to discuss the trainee's experience gained by carrying out the task and to provide the opportunity for feedback. I acceded to the post of the practice's internal verifier.

Gillian and I were required to attend annual standardisation training days to ensure that teaching was delivered at similar standards countrywide. We had to appoint, and therefore pay for, an external verifier to monitor my performance, our in-house standards and to guide us in updating our training schedules. The introduction of regular practice inspections and assessments involved more comprehensive record-keeping and documentation as well as an increasing emphasis on health and safety. The burgeoning amount of paperwork required became ever more onerous, time-consuming and expensive.

The advantages of becoming a veterinary nursing training centre and retaining that accreditation became less obvious, with practice principals beginning to question what was in it for their businesses.

Such a question would never have been contemplated in earlier times. What used to be a rewarding task had become an expensive burden. From my standpoint, qualified and committed veterinary nurses remained an essential part of a modern veterinary practice team but even I questioned whether it was worth continuing trying to surf this ever-rising bureaucratic tide.

Nowadays, this training is delivered by clinical coaches, each with a maximum of two trainees under their tutelage. It might fall into the category of fake news but I have heard whispers that the little green book might make a comeback. I wish …

Some universities began to offer degree courses in veterinary nursing but an advance like this has to be accompanied by the establishment of a variety of rewarding career pathways which are open to graduates and with concomitant levels of remuneration. Far too many nurses have left the profession because they felt their contribution and skills were undervalued by the wider veterinary community.

When I started in 1977, a call from a farmer set in train a car journey, an examination of the patient, ideally a diagnosis, treatment and finally a basic invoice detailing a fee for each service and VAT. Now the mileage travelled on the journey has to be recorded as HMRC no longer trusted vets to provide an honest split between their business and private mileage in each tax year.

Once on the farm, it was considered best practice to record the ear tag number of every animal examined and treated together with the drugs used, the dose administered with the batch number and expiry date of each medicine. On my return to the practice, those details had to be transferred to the clinical and financial records of that client.

It was now taking longer to conduct my clerical responsibilities than my clinical duties. Prices had to rise to cover the extra time taken, which meant I was not flavour of the month with the farmers. This led to a fall in demand for visits and services, particularly for important preventative medicine programmes.

Calls to individual sick animals, so-called fire brigade work, usually ended up with the animal being sent for slaughter unless a simple fix could be guaranteed. A multicoloured triplicate form was required if the animal was less than thirty months old and being sent to slaughter for human consumption. If the animal was over thirty months old, a different form was used, as the carcase must not enter the human food chain but simply be incinerated.

All cattle now had individual passports which proved their existence and accompanied them throughout their life. These indispensable documents had to be cross-referenced during many of the form-filling exercises. I came across some absurd anomalies. Leaning over the fence one day, I commented on the presence in a group of Aberdeen Angus cattle of one impressive animal which stood head and shoulders above the others.

"Ahh, I haven't got a passport for Bruno. Officially, he has no passport and so doesn't exist, which means I cannot send him for slaughter."

From my point of view, the passage of twenty-five years since I qualified had seen the increasing importance of process which in turn has produced much more fuss but to less effect.

It's curious that whilst working on a farm, vets are held responsible for the safety of the farm staff who assist them. Consequently, I religiously pointed out rotting wooden fence posts at risk of collapse from the force of passing animals and dangerous faults with ageing crushes, including sheets of tin cladding adrift from their rivets or corroded metal structural supports which could fail completely.

Increased awareness of health and safety regulation in the practice was mirrored by a similar scenario on our clients' farms. Protocols were produced to ensure the safe handling of animals, including when milking cows, with additional protection offered to the staff carrying out these daily tasks. The incidence of leptospirosis achieved greater prominence, especially on dairy farms. This organism can infect cows, causing infertility, abortion and reduced milk production, but it is also a threat to human health, with potential for causing serious illness, leading to liver and kidney damage.

Farmers had to demonstrate how they were limiting this risk to their farm staff. In many cases this included an annual vaccination given to cows before they calved. Colourful graphic posters appeared in dairies, raising awareness of this and other serious disease risks. I enjoyed working with the farmers to reduce the disease risks to their stock and their staff.

The paperwork connected with the foot and mouth outbreak had been consigned to my cupboard when I visited Captain, the Welsh Black bull named in honour of Mr Sheriffs. The bull remained twenty-seven hundredweight of muscular masculinity but his exertions had taken their toll with the passage of fifteen years. His drive to succeed had been blunted by increasing stiffness but today he was much worse. I suspected he had 'slipped off' the back of a cow he was serving, causing his present injury. Reluctantly, his owner had decided to 'send him down the road' and my role was not to diagnose or to treat, as I had been trained to do, but simply to complete the forms required for his onward journey to the incinerator.

With more graduates from agricultural colleges securing posts on establishments in our patch, responsibility for castrating male calves on some farms had been taken back in house. A common technique employed was the application of rubber rings above the testes during the first week of life. These bands strangulated the blood supply to the testes, which consequently withered and died. Slightly older animals were castrated using Burdizzo emasculators, unwieldy powerful pincers which crushed the spermatic cords.

I was called to a farm in the spring by a farmer who noticed that some of his young replacement dairy heifers were showing signs of udder development even though they had not been running with a bull. Using rectal palpation, I diagnosed pregnancy in more than thirty animals. They were too young to be pregnant and too small to carry a calf to term and give birth successfully.

Each pregnant heifer was injected to induce abortion; it was an unappealing but safer option. As was customary on most farms, the young females had been running with some male animals previously castrated in house. My attention turned to this group of supposed steers to identify the culprit. Sure enough, one of the larger steers had three-quarters of his left testis and a quarter of his right testis remaining. Insufficient attention had been paid to carrying out the castration procedure properly; these remnants of vital testicular tissue were still able to fulfil the purpose for which they were biologically intended. I re-castrated this 'bull' under local anaesthesia using sharp surgery.

Earlier in my career, I have described my role as a farm vet surgically castrating groups of male calves at about six weeks of age. In scientific trials, this technique, which can only be carried out by vets, has been shown to cause the least setback in the growth rates of calves when done at this age. My post-millennial role had morphed into correcting the mistakes of less-qualified individuals. No wonder many new veterinary graduates were not inclined to undertake farm work.

Before I left this farm, I was taken to look at an older heifer that had recently given birth to her first calf. She had lost weight during the last fortnight and had developed a rasping cough. At the end of each breath, I could hear a soft grunt.

I suspected she could be suffering from lungworm, a parasitic disease affecting predominately young, growing cattle. Each spring in the 1980s, farmers would purchase oral vaccine to immunise their young stock before turn-out to prevent this disease. I hardly saw any cases of clinical disease during this period.

Post millennium, many farmers were cutting costs, including the cost of the vaccine.

Instead, they treated their young stock with drugs to kill lungworms and other internal worms which infest their animals. This represented an important trend away from preventative medicine to strategic symptomatic treatment. As a result, I encountered more clinical cases of lungworm as well as other parasitic diseases. Frequently, these patients were replacement heifers destined for the dairy herd, as in this case. Once they had suffered such a bout of illness, they rarely achieved a fully mature adult body weight or peak milk production.

More and more farms brought herd health medicines such as wormers and fly repellent treatments from agricultural merchants, which affected the profitability of veterinary farm practice still further.

More sheep farmers were bringing their ewes which were having difficulty lambing into the surgery, perhaps to save the cost of a visit fee. There were some definite benefits for me, including skilled help being at hand, but I wondered whether it was best for the ewes.

One such case arrived at Wheatley at the end of evening surgery. The farmer had driven his vehicle and trailer into the surgery car park, near the pavement. There was still an hour of daylight left as I pulled on my waterproofs and boots. My patient was suffering from a condition called ringwomb, in which the cervix does not properly dilate, blocking the passage for the lambs to be born.

I gave a drug to help relieve this constriction and then it was a question of using my fingers inside the animal to exert persistent pressure to manually open the cervix. As in this case, this can be a protracted process and the ewe took every opportunity to lodge her protests. By now, I could feel the lamb's hooves beyond the cervix and at length, managed to get ropes around each limb.

At this point, a police car on routine patrol passed by. The officer noticed signs of blood that had dribbled and collected in the gutter and his suspicions were aroused. Out of sight inside the trailer, the farmer was performing heroics, restraining the sheep by clamping his legs across her shoulders. Joy, my receptionist, who kept a few sheep of her own, was holding one lambing rope. After brief introductions and an inadequate explanation of the pantomime in progress, much to the officer's surprise, I handed him the other rope. My hand was still inside the sheep, aiding the full and final dilation of the cervix and making sure the tail was positioned correctly between the back legs to avoid any internal damage. With sustained pulling from Joy and the police officer and my internal handiwork, accompanied by much bawling from mum, the large singleton lamb was eventually delivered.

Profuse thanks were offered to the policeman, together with the opportunity to wash his hands. I promised faithfully to clean up the mess. As he left, he remarked, "Not much happens in Wheatley of an evening but this is certainly going in my report."

Always best to stay on the right side of the law if possible.

Lambings carried out in the back yard of Iffley Road were far less public. Lucy had come to spend a week of work experience with us and asked if she could carry on coming to help us out on Saturday mornings. She tidied up and cleaned cages without complaint so when a lambing arrived, I asked her to come and help me out. The sheer delight on her face as I handed her a live lamb to rub down with a towel remains a fond memory and sustained her enthusiasm in all things veterinary for weeks.

Chapter 23

Don't Be Afraid to Care

"Come to work in your helicopter, have you?"

"I beg your pardon?"

"You put the prices up so much, I thought you must be buyin' a helicopter."

"It would be nice. I'd miss the speed humps in Kennington and the queues of traffic coming into Oxford. Bit tight landing it in the back garden. Do you think they would let me use the running track over the road?"

It was Mr Collins who loved his bit of banter. He had been coming to the practice "since Mr Heather's time; he were a proper vet he were". Now, he had to put up with me. He often arrived without an appointment, clutching crumpled scraps of paper on which an unpronounceable name had been scrawled. This would be the latest thing to treat his racing pigeons, passed on by word of mouth and only to the chosen few.

His behaviour became erratic as he got older and recently, his wife had started to come with him, possibly to protect me from his excesses. But not today. It wasn't his pigeons this morning but one of his beloved lurchers. She had developed an ulcerated mammary tumour. As usual, he had delayed his visit; he knew that the mass must be removed.

"Keep the price down, remember, I'm a workin' man," he said in hushed tones, lest anyone else should overhear and get an equally good deal. In this instance, I booked his appointment for the surgery since I knew there was nothing he enjoyed more than aggravating the receptionists. I gave him a pre-operative sheet which among other things, reminded him to starve his dog before the anaesthetic. He left, delighted with his morning's entertainment.

It was one of those days. The next client was about to leave at the end of the consultation when she turned and said, "Mr Bartholomew, there's talk in the local shop on my estate about a puppy with a bad leg. What can I do about it?"

"Have you seen the puppy?"

"No but my friend has. She says it looks proper poorly."

I saw Sue at reception give her the telephone number of the RSPCA as I called in my next client. We were hearing about similar incidents far too often; the number increasing every year.

Later that day, driving back to the surgery, I was considering the day's events and trying to remember what still had to be done. The conversation about the puppy popped back into my head. Was our response appropriate? Would our client have the confidence to contact the charity herself? The practice was neither a social service nor a charity and was not responsible for safeguarding the welfare of every vulnerable animal in the city. As I reiterated these well-rehearsed arguments, I turned off the main road and drove through the housing estate at Rose Hill.

I slowed as I passed the address but I couldn't see much. Stopping further up the street, I wandered back to take a better look. I saw a tiny puppy, possibly three months old, tied to a metal pole which supported the porch, sitting in a sea of shattered glass. Dishevelled, head held slightly to one side in quizzical fashion, left front leg bent with only the toes resting on the ground, the pup seemed the embodiment of hopelessness. Surely this little creature deserved better than this? Returning to my car, I reminded myself I had no authority to act in such matters and spent a few minutes thinking things through.

The best remedy for anger is delay
Seneca

The following day, Inspector Doug Davidson from the RSPCA, the epitome of officialdom in his uniform, walked into reception with the puppy and one of the owners. I ushered them into the consulting room where the owner confirmed that Link, a German shepherd cross collie, was indeed about three months old. Her left forelimb was tender rather than painful on palpation, the forearm not straight and the paw turned outwards, barely touching the ground when she tried to walk.

I explained that I thought the pup had a problem with the growth of the bones in this leg. In time, this deformity would be likely to become more exaggerated. If a series of x-rays confirmed my suspicions, intricate surgery would be required to correct the defect. Amputation would be a much cheaper option but that seemed inappropriate in such a young animal, in my opinion.

The owner wanted the operation but said they could not pay for it. In any case, I doubted they could provide the necessary level of care. I suggested they signed an agreement transferring the ownership of the puppy to me. I would try to find funding to treat the puppy but only on condition I could rehome the puppy and they agreed not to keep any more animals. The owner admitted she had been 'given' the puppy by a friend but she was not willing to sign the puppy over to me.

It was a suitable moment for me to leave the inspector with the owner for what I thought might be a difficult conversation.

Next morning, a smiling inspector arrived with the puppy. He had reasoned at length with the owners and tried to emphasise that the puppy could not be left as it was. If they did nothing, the owners ran the risk of being prosecuted. Having arranged to revisit the property earlier that morning, he found the owners still in bed. Only when he began a formal summons charge sheet which would lead to a court appearance did the owners finally relent and hand the puppy over.

The poor little scrap was underweight, infested with fleas, likely to have a worm burden and desperately needed to be groomed. At least now we could start to improve matters. X-rays confirmed one of the bones in the forearm was developing normally but a growth plate in the other bone had closed prematurely, preventing further increase in its length. Precious time had been lost but with appropriate and prompt treatment, the puppy still had a reasonable chance of living an active life. The nurses in the practice loved this type of case and in no time the pup had been wormed, treated for fleas, groomed and fed with a special puppy food. There seemed hardly a moment when the puppy was not being cuddled and handed from one to another during break time.

The practice offered regular placements to vet students during their clinical studies at university, giving them a chance to gain practical experience under the same scheme I found so valuable during my undergraduate training. Blatantly calling in a favour, I rang one of our students from Cambridge vet school with a request she sought advice on this case from her lecturers.

Later, I was put through to Sorrel Langley-Hobbs, a specialist in orthopaedics. I photographed our x-ray films and sent them to her via my mobile phone. Quickly back in touch, she agreed with my diagnosis and discussed the complex corrective surgery which would be required. This procedure was outside my modest level of surgical expertise. As the case would provide useful teaching material, she agreed to undertake the surgery at a discounted rate whilst I undertook to raise the necessary funds.

My next free time was on Saturday, in a couple of days, and an appointment was made for me to drop the puppy off. I was sure this course of action was the best option for the dog. The alternative, which was for me to attempt an operation of which I had no experience, using inferior equipment, did not appeal.

Head nurse Gillian was responsible for coordinating the practice's relationship with our drug wholesalers and representatives of the major drug manufacturers who paid us regular visits to discuss new therapeutics and current offers on their products. By the end of the day, she had secured sponsorship from our principal drug wholesaler, three of the major drug companies we used and from the RSPCA. A hundred pounds remained to be covered.

Saturday found me and the little puppy on a hundred-mile trip to Cambridge vet school. Having silently wished her the best of luck, I left this diminutive diva in the care of Elizabeth and headed back to Oxford. Sorrel prepared to perform her magic just a week after the puppy's plight had first come to light.

Further x-rays of both her forelimbs and her hips were taken. These highlighted another problem of hip dysplasia - hip sockets which were too shallow to fully enclose the balls of each hip joint. As the puppy grew, more of her bodyweight than usual would have to be taken by her front legs.

A successful outcome to the proposed surgery was crucial to the puppy's future. The surgery involved cutting through both bones of her left forearm. The distal section of the radius was rotated and re-aligned with its upper portion to correct the limb deformity. Eight thin stainless-steel wires were placed across the bones, four above and four below the surgically-induced fractures, connected to and supported by an external stainless-steel fixator or scaffold. (See photograph page 255.). The left forelimb remained shorter than the right because of the growth defect and the delay in treatment. Seven days after surgery, Sorrel began to increase the overall length of the scaffold by one millimetre per day using an integrated adjustment mechanism.

On the pup's return to Oxford, these daily adjustments continued, slowly increasing the size of gap between the upper and lower sections of each bone which had been transected. Link stayed in the practice for two weeks during this critical stage of her treatment. X-rays were sent to Sorrel at weekly intervals, together with measurements of the length of each forelimb, so she could monitor the pup's progress. Once both forelimbs were of equal length, we ceased our twiddling and allowed the fractures to settle and heal.

The puppy reached a further milestone when she left the practice to go to her new home with Lorna, a client I had known for some time who had fallen in love with our waif. She named her Dora and for a brief period, she became a canine celebrity, appearing on local TV, radio and in the press. Her final appearance was on the breakfast show on BBC Radio Oxford just before Christmas as a 'good news' item.

Finally, permission came from Cambridge control centre to remove the fixator and the bone pins. Dora could use her leg, lighter now it was unencumbered by metalwork, normal in length, conformation and function and just in time for Christmas. It was the best present for her and for everyone who made this transformation possible. It was imperative that Dora continued to be confined in a cage, except when she was taken out on a lead for short periods of controlled exercise. No running and absolutely no joyful leaping was allowed. Anyone who has tried to control a five-month-old puppy will sympathise with this most difficult of regimes.

After Christmas, Dora came to stay with my family for a few days, forming an instant bond with Millie, our young border terrier bitch. Her short stay caused difficulties which I had not anticipated. My eldest daughter, hitherto ambivalent about the existence of dogs as they could not be ridden, spent most of the weekend with her arms wrapped around Dora's neck in a communion of mutual adoration. There were loud and prolonged protestations when the time came to hand her back to her new owner.

"Why can't we have her? Daddy you can't give her back."

Sustained sulking on a grand scale ensued.

Final x-rays were taken eight months after surgery when she was neutered. By now, she was a happy youngster with normal mobility and most importantly, despite all the veterinary interference, she had retained her wonderful sunny temperament. Every time she came to see me during her long life, she gave me a special welcome and sat down on my feet as if to convey her continued gratitude.

This is just one example of what cooperation between a vet school, a local veterinary practice and companies in the veterinary pharmaceutical sector with considerable help from the RSPCA can accomplish. It is the best possible antidote to the bad press which the profession often attracts.

Dora was awarded one final accolade. A Cambridge vet student, seeing practice with us, left her small-animal orthopaedic notes lying about. Who do you think was depicted on the front cover?

Surgical success cannot be guaranteed. Holsten was a well-bred yellow labrador. He was affectionate, calm, even-tempered and eager to please, many of the features which have made this breed so popular, but his luck had run out with his hips. He had dysplastic joints and his mobility was impaired to the extent that he had been referred by my colleague to a specialist for a hip replacement.

This operation involves inserting a stainless-steel prosthesis with the ball of the joint into the top of the shaft of his femur. The shallow bony socket in the pelvis is obliterated and replaced by a much deeper synthetic copy. Holsten underwent this surgery, which was a stunning success. When I saw him for his booster, his remodelled hindleg was well muscled, moving freely without pain. The owner was so impressed, he asked to be referred again to have the other hind leg fixed.

The same operation was carried out by the same surgeon but this time, the result was not what was hoped for. This second hip replacement never functioned well and remained persistently painful. After many trips back and forth, the difficult decision was made to remove the surgical implants. Holsten's body formed a 'false' joint where the natural joint used to be but daily therapy was necessary to limit his discomfort. The owner was heartbroken, partly because he felt he had inflicted the second operation on his dog. Nobody was at fault. The tendency nowadays is to blame someone, usually the veterinary surgeon. It is worth remembering that all operations come with a degree of risk.

I have made mistakes. Hanging in my office cupboard, I kept a collar and lead from a dog who died at my hands. Every time I donned my tunic, it reminded me to take extra care. There was an important balance to be struck between taking enough care and worrying about one's capabilities so much that medical or surgical competence was undermined.

Being the boss means you alone are your quality control. You don't answer to anyone or anything except your conscience and the disciplinary regulator. My colleagues, especially the nurses, had their way of making sure my feet stayed firmly on the ground. Any staff member who had concerns about how a case had been handled could always come for a confidential chat as my office door was invariably open.

Despite these checks and balances, there were times when I fell below the standards I had set myself. A tabby cat was brought to Wheatley with an injured foreleg. It had come second in an argument with a post office van, resulting in an extensive area of skin missing from below the elbow to above its paw, a so-called de-gloving injury.

This animal had no owners and lived a peripatetic lifestyle, calling at a cluster of households in the village for his meals and some fuss. Several families were willing to club together to fund the cat's treatment but costs were an issue. Referral was therefore not an option but as luck would have it, I had attended a recent lecture on the use of skin grafts and was keen to put my new-found knowledge to good use.

Having consulted my lecture notes to remind myself of the potential pitfalls, Gillian and I set about repairing the damaged limb. The plan was to take a piece of skin from the flank of the cat and suture it to the remaining living skin on the foreleg. The skin on the flank was clipped, shaved and cleansed, as was the remaining skin on the leg. A rectangular section of skin from the side of the cat was harvested and sutured in its new position on the leg. The defect on the cat's flank was closed using a special suture pattern, whilst the delicate repair on the leg was protected with a suitable dressing and bandage.

Our patient had to wear a plastic Elizabethan collar to prevent interference with its wounds or the bandage. The skin graft had to be kept moist for the best chance of thriving. Initially, the bandages and dressings were changed daily so the site could be irrigated with warmed saline. All went well and the cat went to one of his households to be cared for under house arrest.

The wound on the cat's flank healed nicely and ninety per cent of the transplanted skin remained vital, developing a healthy new blood supply. Doubts surfaced initially in my mind when I removed the sutures. Unfortunately, these doubts were confirmed when I checked the cat a month after his operation. There was no doubt about it. The new hair on the grafted skin was growing upwards, not downwards. I had warned the owners that the replacement fur would be likely to be longer than the normal fur on the leg.

How could I have put the skin graft on the leg *upside down*? I confessed my sin to the owners, who remained delighted with the surgical and the cosmetic result. To many untrained observers, one tabby cat looks much the same as another but *their* tabby was special and the only one in Stadhampton with the fur on its leg growing skywards. Apart from a slightly puzzled look when grooming, I don't think the cat was any the wiser.

Sometimes the outcome of cases can just be a matter of good fortune. There will be those who claim that you make your own luck. I believe it is true that paying attention to small details can seem to make a difference in some cases.

The condition of intussusception affects predominately young puppies and kittens. I met Molly one November when she was less than three months old. She arrived with her owners in an original Austin Mini, tiny in comparison to the SUVs and 4X4s in the car park. This golden retriever puppy seemed equally undersized, having already been operated on elsewhere twice before for the condition. On each occasion, the problem had rapidly recurred. The owners had heard wonderful things about me and wanted me to try to save their puppy.

I could feel a sausage-shaped swelling in the young puppy's abdomen. Whenever she ate solid food, she was sick and on the consulting table she looked miserably uncomfortable. Instinctively, I knew I would try to help her.

The challenge of using my experience to help animals like Molly was an important motivation for me during this later stage of my career. More difficult than the actual surgery was managing the expectations of the owners. Before they walked into my consulting room, their notion of my capabilities was unrealistic. For a pup who had already suffered intussusception several times in her short life, it was probable she would suffer a further episode however skilful the surgeon might be.

We agreed this would be the final attempt to achieve a surgical solution. We also discussed whether it was fair on the puppy to even try. But this honest, caring couple were not for turning. They agreed we could contact their previous practice for the puppy's history; indeed, Sue was on the phone as we completed the pre-operative paperwork.

Downstairs, the puppy was placed on an intravenous drip. Three quarters of an hour later, she was noticeably brighter. Having suffered two recent major interventions in her young life, she was not a great anaesthetic risk. She was given a reduced dose of pre-medication which included a drug to control her pain. We completed our preparations, perused the puppy's veterinary history and, as the operating table was free, it was time to get going.

Gillian was at the controls of the anaesthetic machine whilst Helen scrubbed up ready to help me get the surgery done as quickly as possible. Once inside her abdomen, the diagnosis was easily confirmed but the total length of bowel which had sleeved upon itself was disconcerting. The affected length of gut was a horrible puce colour because its blood supply had been strangulated; this entire length of affected gut would have to be removed.

Helen pinched the healthy gut at each end as I sectioned it. All that remained was to join the healthy ends of the gut together using very fine suture material inserted as small, simple, interrupted stitches. This was easier said than done but I was pleased with the surgical result. Blood could be seen coursing along the larger blood vessels supplying her bowel and there wasn't any leakage of fluids where the gut wall had been sutured together. Any such leakage would probably be fatal.

The whole length of bowel was repeatedly flushed with warm saline and then returned to the abdominal cavity. During a final extended inspection lasting my favoured five minutes, peristaltic waves, which normally travel continuously down a healthy gut, had resumed their rippling motion, indicative that nature was happy.

Current thinking suggests that a disruption in the synchronicity of these waves may be the underlying cause of intussusception. The wound in the abdominal muscle was closed, along with the skin. What the puppy needed now was a sizeable slice of luck.

Placed on a warm heat pad and fluffy bed, she recovered quickly. Receiving fluid and antibiotics via the drip, as well as incremental pain relief, she remained quiet but settled. Next day, she was brighter still and more importantly, she was hungry, happily scoffing the high-energy liquid food she was offered. The pup regained her strength quickly, eating everything in her dish with gusto, peeing and, more significantly, pooing at regular intervals. After three days, she was handed back to her ecstatic owners. I impressed upon them the importance of doing exactly what I asked, feeding measured amounts of special warmed food at specified intervals.

I emphasised I was unsure if the remaining length of gut was sufficient to digest and absorb enough nourishment from the food she ate. The puppy must be kept quiet and allowed to recuperate. Jumping or chasing after balls or toys was off the menu for the moment. Checked every day, and later, twice weekly, her recovery was as encouraging as it was rapid. I couldn't feel any swellings in her abdomen, she was bright and seemed comfortable, her puppyish zest returning with each passing day.

The introduction of solid food was negotiated without a hitch and after ten days, I took the skin sutures out from her abdominal wound. She had progressed much further than after her previous surgeries, which was excellent. Vigilance from the owners had to be maintained just at the time when they wanted to relax the high levels of supervision which I had stipulated. I warned them that in some cases, patients could develop cravings to eat abnormal material such as earth or coal. Faeces had to be passed at least once a day and the owners were encouraged to ring me about anything that was out of the ordinary.

As I have been writing these lines, I have been looking at a photograph of Molly included in a card I received that Christmas. She is four months old and looking angelic. As well as good fortune, success stemmed in part from handling the delicate gut tissue gently and from preserving the lumen of the gut during placement of the sutures to create a watertight repair. In many ways, Gillian had the most difficult task in keeping the puppy alive whilst I reorganised the internal plumbing. All members of the practice team had played an important part in Molly's recovery. Her name was another I looked forward to seeing on my appointments list for many years.

Dora 2002

Molly 2002

Chapter 24

What Is Life

My mother lived independently in the family home after the death of my father. I visited her once a month, usually on Saturdays, slotted in around the practice duty rota. My sister, living closer, worked nearby and was able to drop in more frequently for a chat. With the support of her neighbours, friends and members of the local church, mum continued to confound those who proclaimed she could not possibly live on her own. I kept in touch by phone and always spoke to her the day before my scheduled Saturday trips.

In June 2001, I rang to say I'd visit the following day. Arriving mid-morning, I was surprised to find the back door locked. I let myself in to find the house was empty, no notes left or any clue to her whereabouts. She hadn't walked outside without an arm to steady her for many years. I spoke to neighbours but no-one could shed any light on where she was.

You can imagine how I felt. When I'm stressed, I need tea. I made some and tried to think logically. I phoned my sister, who was as much in the dark as me; mum's doctor's surgery couldn't help either. I rang round local hospitals. Finally, I located her in Basildon hospital, ten miles away, where she had been admitted as an emergency during the night. I found her in a ward of elderly women. At home, she wore a pendant emergency button, which she must have pressed but she couldn't remember why. I guessed she must have had a fall but she would not admit to it. One of her legs was swollen and she was confused and very tired but comfortable.

She was transferred closer to home to Highwood hospital, the same hospital whose floors I cleaned for a summer job in the early Seventies. My sister and I had to counter the inevitable push from state professionals who advised mum would receive better care and be safer in a nursing home. Mum remained adamant she wanted to live in her own home and eventually that is where she returned, in hospital transport and with a care package in place. It was the beginning of an increasingly-difficult struggle as we supported her wish to live independently at home.

Her stays in hospital became more frequent and more protracted. In February 2005, she was not fit enough to return home. Entombed in Harold Wood hospital, her health and her strength steadily declined. I fought the M25 traffic to spend as much time as possible with her. On the night she died, I remember the tangle of Portex piping passing from patient to sundry containers, the rhythmic rippling of the waterbed, winking red lights flashing their mortal messages, the hiss of oxygen and the intermittent whirr of a syringe driver.

I recall the yellowish sheen of her skin with flushed red cheeks, clammy forehead, the wretched plastic oxygen mask, the look of incomprehension in her eyes and the weight she had lost. She was so very thin. When the coughing and gurgling coming from her chest became too much to bear, I sought refuge in the chapel. I was turfed out by hospital security. Retracing my steps, I passed a sign announcing 'Noah's Ark Children's Ward Welcomes You'.

I held mum's hand, trying to recall the many high points in the fifty years we had shared together. I was thankful for her company for the extra thirty-five years following her successful brain surgery.

At five in the morning, late in April, she sighed deeply and slipped away.

I was exhausted and overcome with loss and loneliness. I desperately needed extended time away from work to grieve but this was a luxury I could not afford. I had a practice to manage and insufficient staff to keep the many balls in the air for long without me. The lack of time for grief and reflection had a detrimental effect on me at the time and later as I grew weary of the veterinary practice scene.

After her death, I bought the bungalow adjoining the Wheatley surgery, which was perfect for staff accommodation. Its garage offered some useful extra space.

During my mother's declining years, my time and attention was divided between Oxford and Hutton, I still had to manage many important changes taking place at Iffley Road and in the wider veterinary field.

In 2005, the practice standards scheme was introduced by the Royal College of Veterinary Surgeons. I decided the practice should aim for accreditation. Much of the documentation required by a veterinary nursing training centre was also required for this new scheme. Initially, it was expensive to comply with all the regulations and subsequently, to maintain our compliance as the regulations became more complex and far-reaching, I found myself wearing numerous hats, including that of safety officer, fire officer and so on. For each hat, I had to produce and regularly review more and more local rules, producing paperwork which outlined how we would deal with every conceivable eventuality.

A positive benefit was the upgrading of our x-ray plates so that our radiographic images were more detailed. However, when I was advised that the textbooks in our practice library needed to be updated to the latest editions, I wondered if there really was much benefit to the practice. Eventually, accreditation was attained.

At our Wheatley surgery, the common drugs which we used daily were on shelves at chest height behind the consulting vet. During the first of our revalidation visits, we were told these drugs must be kept in a locked cupboard if they remained in the consulting room or in another room, out of sight of the client.

Niggled, I asked why. Apparently, it was to prevent a client looking at the name of a drug on the shelf and subsequently looking it up on the internet. The fact that this satisfactory arrangement had been the same for more than twenty years was of no consequence. We had to comply with advice which seemed to me to be farcical. I began to think I must get off this merry-go-round before my blood pressure reached dangerous levels. Most of the regular clients I asked didn't realise the practice was accredited or what accreditation meant for them, despite considerable efforts spent publicising the fact.

Social acceptance of risk has dwindled. In the new millennium, the practice spent considerable sums of money on protocols to ensure our clients and our employees were safe. As discernible progress has been made, the more intolerant the public and our regulator's view of any remaining risk has become. I wonder whether one more animal's illness has been cured as a direct result of these advances. Surely a more cost-effective model could have been devised, based on common sense and fair play?

It was clearly impossible to cater for every eventuality. Off duty one evening, I was enjoying a meal in a pub with two of my nursing colleagues and a client who was a local celebrity for her work with young people with life-limiting conditions.

The practice phoned. Towards the end of evening surgery, a rottweiler had been brought in to be put to sleep because of its indifferent temperament. The owners were shown into a consulting room to keep the dog away from other patients. The consent form requesting euthanasia had been signed when it struggled and broke its collar. The owner grabbed the dog around its neck whilst my colleague slipped out to get another collar and lead. When the vet returned, the owners had gone, leaving the dog unrestrained in the consulting room. Unsurprisingly, the dog was behaving aggressively towards anyone who opened the door of the room.

My appetite vanished like the dog's owners.

Disguising some sedative tablets in dog food was the logical first step. But when I arrived at the practice around ten o'clock, it was obvious our guest had no intention of eating any of it. We messed about trying to secure the dog with a dog catcher, basically an adjustable noose formed by a loop of rope at one end of a long pipe.

Someone was going to get hurt. Although he was frightened and agitated, the dog was only doing what he had been trained to do, which was guarding, in this case, our consulting room.

I telephoned the police to explain our predicament. We were put in touch with Ben, a marksman licensed by the police. He turned up at the practice at around one in the morning. I expected him to use a dose of tranquilliser fired from a dart gun so a lethal injection could be given after the dog was comatose.

But Ben decided to use a free bullet. Having assembled and loaded his firearm, I held the door slightly ajar. The dog threw its fifty-plus kilograms at the gap. There was a sharp report and that was that. Ben was professionalism personified and the accuracy of his single shot at a moving target was uncanny. A safe procedure had produced a painless demise for the dog and ended a stressful and potentially dangerous episode.

Ben's night-time call-out cost the practice a considerable sum but the safety of everyone involved was paramount.

When working in Sussex, I had to shoot an injured cow, which was temporarily housed in an old barn with thick stone walls, concrete floor and low slate roof. The noise of the explosion when the gun went off, echoing around the walls remained in my memory bank thirty years later and was triggered by the report from Ben's gun, amplified beneath the high ceilings of our Victorian house.

The inherent violence in shooting an animal is something I struggled with in my professional career. Further, it was one thing to end an animal's suffering in this way but quite another matter to shoot an animal such as a horse as a 'convenience' when the animal had outlived its usefulness. Whenever possible, I delegated the task to others who specialised in this field.

I had an unspoken regard for clients who chose an injectable, inherently more peaceful means of ending the life of a farm animal or horse. Mr and Mrs Gilbert were such a farming family in Sussex. They shared my philosophy and asked specifically for me to come to end the life of their long-lived and cherished cow at the grand age of twenty-two. She went to sleep quietly, with dignity and was buried in her favourite spot in their meadow. Silently, I saluted them.

In the consulting room, it was relatively straightforward to rationalise putting sick or aged animals to sleep in a calm and painless manner. In that instance, my role was to make the unbearable just a little more bearable. It surprised me how often a euthanasia consultation was followed by one for a puppy or kitten coming in for their first vaccination.

More problematic for me were requests to put young and fit animals to sleep. I recall being asked to put a medium-sized fawn dog to sleep at the young age of four. When

I asked why, the client told me they had redecorated their living room and bought new furniture and the dog no longer matched the colour scheme. I persuaded the owners to take the dog to an animal charity; they claimed not to have considered this alternative.

Over the years, it was disheartening how many clients tried to have a fit pet put to sleep rather than paying boarding fees while they were away on holiday. This became so commonplace, especially in the days leading up to a bank holiday weekend, that the practice team referred all such enquiries to a vet to be discussed by telephone first.

Most clients were only too happy to discuss alternatives to euthanasia for their pet. A great many animals were rehomed through the contacts of the practice with our clients and their network of family and friends. If that approach failed, there remained the option of our staff. I have admitted homing my fair share of waifs and strays, as our collection of tortoises and guinea pigs which were acquired over the years will testify.

Gizmo, a four-year-old guinea pig, was brought in for euthanasia. He was struggling to pass his faeces properly, which caused his hindquarters to become soiled. This was a common and by no means insurmountable problem but his owners were not interested in being shown how to manage it. I asked if I could take him home to live with us. The owners were delighted. We performed the daily interventions necessary to express his poo and he lived for a further five years, representing more than half of his lifespan. What a tragedy it would have been if his life had been cut short at the age of four. As is often the case, he was one of the most vibrant characters amongst the host of pigs who joined our menagerie.

Most distressing were consultations during which the unsuspected presence of a terminal and often painful condition was discovered. Following advice that euthanasia was the best option, a few clients would snatch their pet from the consulting table and storm out of the practice. This was a case of blaming the messenger. The interests of the pet should come first - it is surely part of being a responsible pet owner.

With our years of experience, Gillian and I were pleased to take every opportunity to help and guide young people considering careers in the veterinary field. Youngsters who aspired to become veterinary nurses or veterinary surgeons came to the practice for work experience, Gillian having organised the placements with their schools.

Whenever possible, I tried to involve them directly in a surgical operation. Whilst they had blood on their hands, I asked them what they found stressful in their young lives. Often, it was maths homework, the behaviour of a sibling or pressure from a parent.

Then they were asked to consider what aspects of day-to-day work in a veterinary practice they might find stressful. Working under time pressure or within financial constraints, trying to satisfy unrealistic expectations of some clients and limited leisure time are reasons frequently cited by those who have called time prematurely on their professional careers. The unpredictable, varied nature of the caseload has proved stressful to many whilst to others, it is an exciting aspect of the job.

As you get older, perspectives change and that which used to be exciting can in later life prove stressful. When I was asked what I found stressful about the job, I offered this example. I was neutering a bitch on the day the Queen Mother, then in her nineties, was undergoing a hip replacement. I gave thanks I was not one of the orthopaedic surgeons, anaesthetists or nurses involved in carrying out that complex surgical procedure, especially with the world's press camped outside the hospital. In my view, that would have been properly stressful.

I was invited to give practice interviews to pupils in my daughters' secondary school who wanted to study veterinary science at university. I subsequently found myself doing the real thing for the Royal Veterinary College in London.

Invariably, the young applicants were inspiring individuals and many had enjoyed a much wider experience of life, including foreign travel, than I had at their age. I recall one particularly impressive young lady. When I asked her about her future veterinary career, she had planned it already. She wanted to work in the important field of veterinary ethics. I cannot remember another candidate who professed an interest in this undervalued but absorbing field or who had gained such a broad veterinary knowledge at such a young age.

Veterinary ethics - the moral principles upon which the practice of veterinary medicine and surgery are based - is fundamental to the approach each vet takes to their professional duties. After so many years in practice, I thought my ethical reference points were well-established and clear-cut until I was challenged by circumstance.

During evening surgery, a new client arrived bringing a dog for his booster vaccination. Lionel, a male Lhasa Apso, was eleven years old and had a wonderful trusting nature but he had no eyes. Only two skin-covered fur-lined sockets remained. The clients said each eye had been surgically removed when they became painful and diseased, one eye being affected about two years after the other.

I completed my health check and gave the vaccination but later I found myself dwelling on the condition of this courageous little dog. It had really unsettled me. It seemed abhorrent that a dog should have no eyes, especially as a direct result of veterinary intervention. I have treated a number of dogs with two eyes, both of which had become sightless, but I had never been in the position of having to decide what to do if a patient had only one remaining eye, which subsequently became painful. If removal of the eye was the only treatment option, could I or would I have removed it? I suspect I may have referred the case to a specialist and delegated the responsibility to another.

A few months later, I was called to visit this client's home to treat their horse. It was a sunny summer evening and as I got out of the car, Lionel emerged from the open front door and walked down the long curving drive to greet me. He walked in the centre of the drive down its entire length of about three hundred yards without straying anywhere near the herbaceous borders. As I drank a cup of tea in the kitchen, I watched the dog navigate obstacles, mostly baby toys, on the floor without any collisions and play vigorously with a younger dog. The scenario was incredible but the question of what was right and what was wrong in this dog's case remained unanswered. The mind of this vet was even more muddled.

Not long afterwards, I visited an elderly man at his home in a downstairs flat near the surgery. Wherever possible, I tried to take a nurse with me and Gillian accompanied me on this call. The flat was very sparsely furnished and badly needed a spring clean. The dog was suffering from a localised area of sore skin, which we bathed and treated with a topical treatment. Whilst we were chatting before taking our leave, the gentleman took a handful of cornflakes from its packet and put them in the dog's bowl. His pet ate them gleefully. The old chap followed this by taking a handful of dog mixer biscuit and eating them himself.

Gillian and I discussed it in the car. The owner was clearly confused. In broad terms, the cornflakes probably would not harm his pet and the dog biscuits were probably produced to the same standards of hygiene as human food, though the question of nutritional value to each respective consumer on this occasion was a matter of debate.

We concluded that neither the dog nor the owner was likely to be harmed by the mix-up. If we reported the incident to the authorities, in all probability, the owner would be removed from his flat, placed in a care home and separated from his beloved pet. In my view, this would have been a most unsatisfactory outcome and rightly or wrongly, I decided to do nothing and silently wished my client well.

Chapter 25

Out of Time

In December 2007, I was looking at another greyhound with a fractured hock. I had taken countless radiographs of such damaged joints before, producing detailed diagnostic images under light sedation. The dog, perfectly calm and relaxed, was muzzled and laying on its side. I pressed the button exposing the film and obtaining the first view of the joint. My nurse helped me move the dog before taking a different angled view of the joint.

Without warning, the dog ripped the muzzle off and bit deeply into my right hand and then my left forearm for good measure. Very shortly afterwards, he was lying settled and sleepy once more. It was a disconnected panic attack. They are said to be rare but for me, it was a major moment in my career because I was angry with the dog. Until now, I found contentment in the company of the animals under my care and although I had been hurt badly, I never previously blamed the animal. Having bathed and dressed my wounds, the greyhound was given a full anaesthetic and I completed my radiographic investigation.

I ruminated about this incident for a long time. The notion that I may not want to continue in veterinary practice for ever came as a shock. Suddenly, old certainties seemed less certain. The root cause may well have been the lack of time for me to grieve properly following the death of my mother.

Evidently, I was not the man I was before my contretemps with the stallion. I was not as strong or as fit in my fifties as I had been in my forties and my energy levels had dropped. Setbacks which I had previously dealt with easily now tripped me up. I dwelt on the mundane; a resignation letter from a staff member wishing to move on and its implications for locum cover suddenly presented problems which seemed insurmountable. I needed help and sought it from within the practice and my colleagues.

Katharine and Cameron had expressed an interest in becoming partners and I didn't want to sell the business to a corporate veterinary enterprise. In my view, one's professional identity could be subsumed and clinical standards lowered. When I qualified, ownership of practices was restricted to vets and the majority worked in practices which they owned. This seemed to me to be a better system. Following protracted negotiations, our business partnership began in 2010. Once a blueprint for the future of the practice had been mapped out, I was able to focus on my work, harmony restored once more between my objectives for the practice and my personal values.

The chance to share managerial and recruitment responsibilities represented a real breakthrough and I found little difficulty in accepting their ideas. Eventually I became an anachronistic hindrance so in 2014, I withdrew from the partnership, leaving the practice, now called Iffley Vets, in their hands. Mr Sheriffs had been happy to pass his practice on to me and now the time felt right for me to do likewise, as graciously as possible and with the minimum of fuss.

Working part time gave me time and space to consider my future and reflect on what had passed. Some difficult questions occupied my thoughts.

What type of boss had I striven to be? When I set out, my guiding principle was that everyone working in the practice should be equal and an integral part of the decision-making process. I have been fortunate to work with talented and committed colleagues who have helped me more than they will ever know by their commitment to the cause. Thanks to you all for the memories and for the fun we enjoyed together.

I do regret that, from the moment I slid into the boss's chair, I could play only a minor part in the daily banter of practice life, particularly that which goes on behind the boss's back. I encouraged new projects they wanted to pursue. I lost count of the number of nurses who came to the practice anxious to start puppy and kitten clinics and remain disappointed that such projects were never fully realised during my tenure. I recognise I must shoulder some of the blame.

I employed members of staff who had suffered unpleasant experiences in other practices, often because of subjugation or bullying. They joined the practice mentally crushed and it gave me great pleasure to watch them flourish, building their confidence within a settled, supportive and positive practice team. Many were able to relaunch careers which they feared had be lost to them.

What kind of boss had I turned out to be? I think that question is best answered by other members of the clan.

If I were setting out on my career now, fifty years later, would I still choose veterinary science? Probably no. Some comment on my vision of the future of the profession must be linked to that answer. Besides, what on earth I might do instead is a question that defeats me.

My first hurdle would be acceptance for the veterinary science course. I doubt whether I have the academic ability to achieve today's entrance requirements. I wonder how many students, who would make excellent and committed vets, are not given the chance to achieve their goal because of these exacting standards. Is this the best way to select potential veterinary students?

The psychometric element of today's selection process would probably rule me out on the grounds of aptitude and mental dexterity. Without due time to marshal one's thoughts, my capacity to answer such questions as 'What is the value of the human-animal bond' and 'Discuss the role of zoos in the 21st century' in a measured, coherent manner might be found lacking.

My second major hurdle would be financing my studies and my student life. When I went to Bristol, I received a grant from Essex County Council. I appreciated this financial assistance and without it, I doubt I could have considered a university education. I think the cost to the state of educating me to veterinary degree level in the 1970s was upwards of £20,000. During my working life of 40 years, I have more than replenished the state's coffers with prompt payment of my due taxes. The system in place at the time worked well for me. Nowadays, I could not countenance accruing a massive student debt during the five-year course of study. Debt does not sit comfortably with my inherent caution and my upbringing.

Veterinary education has undergone a transformation. The number of students enrolled on these courses has increased exponentially. I was in a cohort of thirty-three students; now the number of students in a year group can be in the hundreds. I was expected to know everything about veterinary science but that is no longer possible. Specialisation in either small animal medicine or surgery, production farm animal medicine or in matters equine, is becoming more widespread and may well become the norm.

Therefore, few graduates qualifying now will have the option of following the career path which I chose as an all-rounder. Some may think that is a good thing but I question that view. Recently at a friend's practice in Wales, a locum arrived to undertake small animal work. After completing Monday morning's consultations, the vet was asked to perform some neutering operations.

"Oh, I don't do any operations. It's too stressful."

The final consideration would be changes in the veterinary climate. The profession used to be a vocation, characterised by thoroughness and decency, where a detailed examination of the animal was paramount. Nowadays, unnecessary investigations and overtreatment have become a scourge.

In my view, there is still a place for clinical intuition based on experience but I fear the profession has been drawn into a culture of ticking boxes and hitting financial targets and this challenges its legitimacy. Today, the overriding requirement is to provide evidence to prove the diagnosis; without it, your efforts are deemed worthless.

One example among many was an elderly dog which was presented to me for marked weight loss. On abdominal palpation, I could feel a grossly misshapen and enlarged liver. I suspected I was palpating a liver tumour. I offered an exploratory operation to confirm my clinical suspicion but I advised euthanasia as the most appropriate option.

When my first dog Mostyn showed similar symptoms, I could feel his abdominal swelling, which was a liver tumour. A blood sample supported my suspicion and I put him to sleep when his lesion became painful. No reason then to put him through additional investigations to confirm what I could feel perfectly well with my hands.

My clients took their beloved pet away. I heard from their daughter that another practice had taken blood samples, then x-rays, then images of the abdomen using ultrasound and finally carried out an exploratory operation which confirmed the presence of a liver tumour before putting the dog to sleep. To me, that level of investigation was excessive and not cost-effective for the owner.

It is important to recognise the need to cater for different levels of veterinary care according to the client's wishes, coupled with what they are willing or able to pay.

Today's veterinary landscape, promoted on websites, in tweets, blogs and theatres as well as innumerable TV programmes, is unrecognisable from the one in which I set out in the Seventies. For me, making animals better was a serious business. It most certainly was not showbusiness, with some veterinary surgeons granted star status. Nor did I see myself promoting the practice or myself as a brand.

I did not embrace logos and mission statements. I have ignored the opportunities offered by the proliferation of social media. I hear there are one or two unpleasant posts about me in the ether, posted I presume by paid-up members of the vengeful online hordes. I prefer not to know what unfounded unattributed comments have been written about me.

Modern jargon used nowadays also grates, with consultations termed 'episodes of care' and outcome measures now all-important. Vets wearing stethoscopes slung nonchalantly around their necks as a badge of authority does nothing to enhance the public's image of the profession in my eyes.

The topic of virtual consultations was being widely discussed when I set out to write this account but overnight, lockdown measures following the coronavirus pandemic have resulted in them becoming routine.

For me, the prospect of a detailed hands-on examination no longer being regarded as the norm is an alarming prospect. Looking at my patient, touching and feeling the animal and looking into its eyes were a critical part of my examination technique. So much important information which I required for the highly-nuanced art of diagnosis could so easily be missed if the hands-on examination were to be set aside.

Diagnostic skills could be reduced to interpreting various computer algorithms, which, as we have seen lately, can be flawed. Will the latest healthcare applications on a smart phone become a must-have therapeutic monitoring tool? If this is what the future holds, with artificial intelligence increasingly taking centre stage, could vets be threatened with imminent obsolescence?

In my early childhood, there was no telephone or television in the house, nor car in the garage. The arrival of the internet has been both a blessing and a curse for the practising vet. Increasingly, clients coming to consult me have already decided on the diagnosis of their pet's illness following a quick trawl of non-peer-reviewed posts and anecdotal information on the web. They seek only confirmation that they were right.

For a long time, I believed the public would realise not all statements on the internet are true. Exasperated, I bought a new mug for my tea, placed on a shelf above my computer. On it was the inscription 'Please DO NOT Confuse Your Google Search with MY Veterinary Degree'.

I am sure new graduates are aware of a recent survey which found that one in five vets regret their career choice, with one in ten vets expecting to leave the profession completely. The single aspect cited as being disliked most was the clients. I find that both astonishing and depressing. Were they given incorrect careers advice at an earlier stage? Is this another effect of the high academic entrance requirements needed to study at vet school? My career would have been nothing without the animals which were my patients and their owners who asked me to treat them, adding much-needed colour, variety and vitality to my working life.

I envy the current crop of graduates their youthful enthusiasm, energy and the wonderful opportunities open to them but they are joining the veterinary workforce during uncertain times. And yet, this is such an exciting time to be in practice.

There is so much science still waiting to be discovered.

Don DeLillo (Libra), Viking Press

Be assured, the results of such research do trickle down to the practitioner in due course.

Stress is a major factor cited by those leaving the profession. The importance of mindfulness and well-being, under the umbrella term of mental health, has been recognised, appearing in the list of topics taught and webinars delivered and is gaining importance each year. The support services available to the new graduate are evolving and are under constant review by our regulator, our professional bodies and our universities.

Top of a recent list of monthly veterinary webinar subjects being offered was meditation, placed above another on 'the approach to common first-opinion clinical cases'.

It has been suggested that the loss of young vets can be reduced by retaining senior clinicians, not necessarily practice principals, who can offer reassurance to less-experienced colleagues. I had acquired a great deal of experience which I did not want to be suddenly lost; indeed, it was one reason I wished to withdraw in a measured fashion from the life of the practice.

One of my most stressful experiences in practice was being reported to the Royal College by a client with a grievance. I was summoned to London to explain my actions. During my tenure as sole principal, I was able to resolve almost all complaints amicably with a meeting at the practice but one is powerless to do so should the client choose to write directly to the college in the first instance. I was one of approximately one thousand vets a year about whom complaints are made to the college.

In the autumn of 2005, I sat in the college foyer on my only visit, talking to my legal advisor. I was waiting to be interviewed by the preliminary investigation committee, consisting of my elders and betters, about my alleged refusal to attend a dog, belonging to a notional client, which had an epileptic fit overnight.

I had seen the client with their dog once under the PDSA Pet Aid scheme because their pet had suffered a fit. The owner had been asked to return for further assessment a week later. They did not return and we heard nothing further until I received their call, four months later, at 4.45am on the morning in question. By the time they were speaking to me on the phone, the fit had passed and the dog was reportedly calm and settled. I advised the client that the PDSA did not pay for the cost of house visits and suggested they bring their dog to the surgery when it opened in less than three hours. The dog died unexpectedly an hour later and a letter of complaint sent to the college.

My legal advisor, who was very experienced in such investigations, accompanied me to provide both specialist support and advice during my initiation in these formal proceedings. I thought I could use the time to discuss an impossible situation I had found myself in the previous evening. I was keen to get his advice about what action I should have taken.

I explained I was in the middle of a fully-booked evening surgery at Wheatley. My colleague Joy was performing reception duties in her customary efficient manner. She received a phone call at about half past six from one of our clients. She had a friend's St Bernard bitch staying with her, which had been mated by her own stud dog and was due to whelp in a week or so.

She feared the bitch might be suffering from gastric dilatation, which occurs when the stomach swells with gas. This was a genuine emergency which needed to be dealt with immediately. She rang to warn us she was bringing the dog down straight away. Joy relayed this message to me at the end of my current consultation, by which time the bitch was *en route*.

Clients who had arrived for their booked appointments were told of the situation and were happy to rebook and head home. On arrival, the bitch was already struggling to breathe because of the pressure exerted by the gas-filled stomach on her diaphragm. I used a hypodermic needle to relieve some of the pressure but produced only a minimal improvement. I could not pass a stomach tube to release the gas, probably because the stomach had twisted - so-called gastric torsion. The bitch needed an immediate anaesthetic but I did not have either a skilled veterinary nurse available or the facilities needed to keep a bitch of this size and weight asleep.

I advised the client to drive on to Iffley Road where I would ensure there was a vet and nurse ready and waiting. The client refused. She maintained the bitch would die during the fifteen-minute journey.

"In that case, I will put the bitch to sleep."

The client refused to give me permission. During these tense discussions, the bitch's condition was deteriorating in front of us. Finally, it was agreed I would administer a reduced dose of an injection normally used for euthanasia and with the bitch asleep, I would attempt to deliver the puppies by caesarean section, before finally putting the dam to sleep.

This injectable solution was not sterile but was the only available product at Wheatley. I calculated a much-reduced dose, dredged up from previous experience with a variant of the drug I had used much earlier in my career. I gave the patient her anaesthetic; at least she was no longer suffering pain. Surgical sterility was abandoned in the interests of speed. I clipped the fur and with only a cursory scrub of my hands and her skin, I quickly opened her abdomen and her uterus and began passing live puppies to Joy and to my client, whose job it was to revive the sleepy creatures. Fluid had to be cleared from their mouth and noses and their chests rubbed vigorously with towels to stimulate their breathing.

At this point, my client changed her mind, insisting I must save the dam. I released the gas from the stomach by making a stab incision in its muscular wall. This small wound was easily closed and the displaced stomach untwisted, correcting its three-hundred-and-sixty-degree torsion. Such a manipulation represented a tremendous shock for the patient. She sighed deeply and her breathing ceased. There was nothing else I could do. I closed the wound in her uterus and in her abdominal wall. As she left, the owner was clearly unhappy with the outcome, despite having five live puppies, each with a fighting chance of survival.

It had been a thankless task. Joy and I began to clear up, cleaning the surfaces, mopping the floor and discussing the case as we did so. I was sickened at what had taken place. A situation had developed which was certainly not of my making and outside my control. What else could I or should I have done? This ranked amongst the worst experiences in my veterinary career. When I got home, my wife thought I had seen a ghost as I sat and agonised over what had taken place.

My legal supporter, his complexion now a whiter shade of pale, offered little if any advice.

Eventually, it was my turn to be questioned by the disciplinary panel. I told the committee that mine was the only practice in the city which still saw animals belonging to our clients, twenty-four hours a day, seven days a week. As was becoming increasingly common, the other local practices referred their out-of-hours cases to another practice, in this instance to Woodstock, some ten miles away.

With reference to the complaint made against me, my inquisitors accepted my account of events. They were interested in whether my practice would continue to see cases for the PDSA and other charities, and whether I would continue to offer a twenty-four hour on-call service to our clients. I assured them that was my intention.

During the prolonged period in which the client's complaint was investigated, my mood had been adversely affected, an undercurrent of uncertainty producing an unwelcome, predominately negative mindset.

For some years, I had been giving lectures on greyhound racing and its common injuries to students studying on the McTimoney chiropractic courses. These lectures took place either in Abingdon or on the Moreton Morrell campus of the University of Warwick. Sometimes I took a greyhound along for the students to gain some much-needed hands-on experience in canine palpation.

In 2009, I was delighted to be invited by the clinical club at Bristol Vet School to give a lecture to the students on a similar subject. I drove into the campus at Langford and heard the familiar tune of *All Things Bright and Beautiful* ringing out from the squat clock tower. After more than thirty years, the cracked sound of these bells engendered all sorts of memories. I reflected how proud my parents would have been at this turn of events. It was a humbling experience, walking on to the lecture theatre stage to talk to these young people who would play an important part in the future of the profession. The students were very receptive and asked many searching questions.

The informal chat over the ubiquitous student hall meal of chilli con carne was a relaxed affair. A few months later, I hosted some of the students at the Oxford racetrack to watch greyhound racing on Saturday night. No lecture can replace the thrill of the live experience and I have a suspicion that one or two successful bets were laid that night, boosting the kitty of the Langford students' common room.

Delivering the lecture in Bristol completed the tortuous circuitous pathway representing my professional life. It has been said we will be known by what we do. I hope that my consultations offered more than just my expertise and that Mr B was part of the spirit of the place (genius loci?) during my tenure at 35 Iffley Road, as Jimmy Sheriffs was before me. I may be remembered by some as the corn king, dealing with a succession of those painful lesions seen in footpads, especially those of whippets and greyhounds.

Early in 2018, when I told Cameron and Katherine of my intention to retire, I thanked them for giving me the opportunity of winding down slowly. I had reached a stage where the prospect of retirement beckoned attractively. I would not find myself hiding behind protocols and edicts or living with the constant fear of sanctions from my professional regulator. I was weary and my mind was jaded.

After an extended period of rest and recreation, my desire to write about what had happened proved irresistible. I wanted this exercise to help place events in some sort of order and in their proper perspective. I could consider some in greater depth, not having the time to do so when they took place.

This book is the result of those recollections and musings. Its contents just some of my yesterdays, a collage of fragments of my life, preserving a story which might otherwise be lost. Some ordinary experiences of life in general practice, extraordinary only in so far that they happened to me.

Diary entry for Thursday 29ᵗʰ March 2018. 5.50pm. Dog scooting on bottom

For my nurse, it was nearly home time.

For me, a dream which had started with a week's work experience in a practice in Shenfield, Essex in 1969 and a rabbit with a broken leg, was ending in Wheatley, Oxfordshire, with one more dog with impacted anal glands. This dog, however, marked the end of my professional journey and I would go no further. All that remains are these memories.

I was adored once too.

Sir Andrew Aguecheek, Twelfth Night, William Shakespeare

Thank You

Preface

Times are Bad. Children no longer obey their parents, and everyone is writing a book.
Marcus Tullius Cicero

"to taste life twice, in the moment and in retrospection."
Anaïs Nin

Chapter 13

Henry Marsh recounts that as a neurosurgeon,
"it takes three years to learn how to do an operation, but 30 years to learn when not
do one."
Admissions   Henry Marsh   Orion Books

Chapter 23

The best remedy for anger is delay.
Seneca

Chapter 25

There is so much science still waiting to be discovered.
Libra   Don DeLillo   Viking Press

Sir Andrew Aguecheek 'I was adored once too.'
Twelfth Night.   W. Shakespeare

Images

Page 188. *Nepal Accident 1993*. Photo reproduced courtesy of Martin Wood.

Page 255. *Dora 2002*. Picture reproduced courtesy of the Oxford Mail published by Newsquest Media Group..

Page 267. Kipper Williams cartoon reproduced courtesy of Kipper Williams and the veterinary journal 'In Practice'.

Thanks to Peter Dann for his diligence in digitising a number of elderly and tired photographic prints, negatives, and slides.

Thanks to Robert Bullard for his guidance and counsel in writing and producing a manuscript suitable for publication.

Please note: some names, characters, animals and places have been amended to protect those who may prefer to retain anonymity.

Astoria Publishing Ltd have been in business for over 20 years and we specialise in publishing certain types of books, namely veterinary, food and sport.

The veterinary profession in particular, has a reservoir of interesting stories.

It was calculated several years ago, that during the lifetime of an average veterinary surgeon, they would meet 14,000 different people with their pets This has given rise to an increasing number of them, wanting to tell their own riveting tale.

Astoria are an outlet for that creativity.